*A*FALCONGUIDE®

TALLGRASS PRAIRIE
WILDFLOWERS

A Field Guide to

Common Wildflowers and Plants of the Pr~

SECOND E

TEXT BY DOU~ ~ADD
PHOTOS BY FRANK OBERLE
AND OTHERS

FALCON®

GUILFORD, CONNECTICUT
HELENA, MONTANA

AN IMPRINT OF THE GLOBE PEQUOT PRESS

A FALCON GUIDE ®

Text design: Nancy Freeborn
Text production and layout: Sue Cary
Illustrations: DD Dowden

Library of Congress Cataloging-in-Publication Data is available.
ISBN 0-7627-3744-1

Manufactured in China
Second Edition/First Printing

" . . . I started with surprise and delight. I was in the midst of a prairie! A world of grass and flowers stretched around me, rising and falling in gentle undulations, as if an enchanter had struck the ocean swell, and it was at rest forever. . . . You will scarcely credit the profusion of flowers upon these prairies. We passed whole acres of blossoms all bearing one hue, as purple, perhaps, or masses of yellow or rose; and then again a carpet of every color intermixed, or narrow bands, as if a rainbow had fallen upon the verdant slopes. When the sun flooded this Mosaic floor with light, and the summer breeze stirred among their leaves the iridescent glow was beautiful and wondrous beyond anything I had ever conceived . . . "
—Eliza Steele, near Joliet, Illinois, in 1840
from *Summer Journey in the West*

FRANK OBERLE

CONTENTS

AUTHOR'S ACKNOWLEDGMENTS

Many people have contributed to this project, only a fraction of whom can be acknowledged here. For their time, effort, and expertise, I extend special thanks to Valerie Baten, Blane Heumann, Jeff Knoop, Mike Nolan and Nathan Taylor of The Nature Conservancy; Bob Tatina of Dakota Wesleyan University; John Taft of the Illinois Natural History Survey; Mary Kay Solecki of the Illinois Nature Preserves Commission; Mike Homoya of the Indiana Department of Natural Resources; Bill McKnight of the Indiana Academy of Science; Marc Evans of the Kentucky Nature Preserves Commission; and Don Kurz of the Missouri Department of Conservation. George Yatskievych of the Missouri Botanical Garden has helped in many ways since the beginning of this project. I am also grateful for the use of the herbarium and library facilities at the Morton Arboretum and the Missouri Botanical Garden, and for the helpfulness of their staffs.

Gerould Wilhelm and Floyd Swink of the Morton Arboretum patiently provided detailed manuscript review, technical input, and a wealth of advice based on decades of field experience with tallgrass prairies and their flora. Megan Hiller of Falcon Press has been a patient, helpful, and open-minded editor.

Any major undertaking benefits from a supportive and understanding family, but in my case, being married to another botanist also allowed me to inflict many requests for editing and review upon my spouse, Deborah Bowen Ladd. I am deeply grateful for her assistance and encouragement, and for the support she and our daughter Melica provided throughout the process. In many respects, this book is the fruit of early efforts by my mother, Yvette Bienvenu Ladd, who shared her love of wildflowers with me and taught me at an early age the common wildflowers of New England.

Many people throughout the tallgrass region have inspired the concept and content of a book such as this. We owe an immense debt of gratitude to them for their largely unsung efforts at understanding and instilling an appreciation for our prairies, and for their tireless work to insure the stewardship of remaining prairies. It is to them that this book is dedicated.

Doug Ladd

Author's note: Several other people generously provided expertise or assistance for this revised second edition, including Pete Bauman, Anton Benson, Kathy Duttenhefner, Thomas Meyer, Scott Moats, Brian Obermeyer, John Shuey, Eric Ulaszek, Brian Winter, and Steve Richter.

PHOTOGRAPHER'S ACKNOWLEDGMENTS

FRANK OBERLE

The idea for this field guide came upon me while I was photographing for *Tallgrass Prairie*. It was a hot, muggy, July morning at Niawathe Prairie in southwest Missouri. I was standing in a sea of wildflowers reflecting all the colors in a rainbow. I was forced to carry a total of no less than six books for plant identification purposes. The weight was burdensome, and plant identification was bewildering. There should be an easier way. I proposed the idea for a field guide to tallgrass prairie wildflowers to The Nature Conservancy and received overwhelming support and encouragement.

Many thanks to Chris Cauble at Falcon Press for recognizing the need for a thorough, user-friendly field guide specifically for the tallgrass prairie region. To editor Megan Hiller, you did a stellar job.

A heartfelt thanks to my mentor, John Madson, prairie writer extraordinaire, for his wonderful writings. They were the fuel for my passion to succeed with this project.

I traveled throughout the tallgrass region photographing close-ups of plants. I could not have achieved this without the scouts who helped me locate the many species. I thank Wayne Ostlie, The Nature Conservancy Regional Office; John Challey, Fargo, North Dakota Conservancy; the Missouri and Iowa Conservancys; Alan Wade, Prairie Moon Nursery; Neil Diboll, Prairie Nursery; and Merv Wallace, Missouri Wildflowers Nursery. Don Kurz and Tom Toney from the Missouri Department of Conservation deserve a special thanks for their invaluable time and information.

To say this project came with ease would be a misstatement. Some of the plants bloomed late, some early, and some not at all. While I needed to be ubiquitous, I had to settle for the greatest number of possibilities at a general location. My lovely wife Judy and daughter Heidi get crowned with sainthood for enduring all my absences and for their assistance with this project. They share my love for the prairie.

Frank Oberle

FRANK OBERLE

INTRODUCTION

TALLGRASS PRAIRIES

Little remains of the tallgrass prairies that blanketed millions of acres of America's heartland just 170 years ago. These prairies were the lushest expressions of a vast grassland complex that ranged from the Gulf of Mexico north into Canada. They extended from the flanks of the Rocky Mountains east through Illinois, and even occurred in scattered locations between there and the Atlantic Ocean.

Here were seas of grass sometimes taller than a horse and rider, carpets of wildflowers presenting a stunning spectrum of colors, and black, loamy soil that seemed endless. Bordered on the west by the shorter, mixed-grass prairies adapted to lower rainfall, and mingling with deciduous woodlands in the east, tallgrass prairies were dominant facets of the midwestern landscape prior to European settlement.

Tallgrass prairies are characterized by an abundance of grasses that typically grow three or more feet tall, including Big and Little Bluestem grasses, Gama Grass, Indian Grass, Switch Grass, and Prairie Cord Grass. Shorter grasses and sedges are common, as are a rich assortment of flowering plants. Elk, bison, and wolves once roamed parts of this landscape, along with innumerable birds and a myriad of other creatures, from butterflies to badgers.

There is no single model of a tallgrass prairie but rather an endlessly variable, dynamic tapestry of plants and animals that for thousands of years have been responding to and in turn influencing their landscape and each other. Prairies occur in subtly changing forms and patterns, from the lush black-soil prairies of Ohio, with their abundant rainfall, to the sandy western outposts of tallgrass prairie among the dry, mixed-grass prairies of the Great Plains. Variations in rainfall, climate, soil, and terrain produce an infinite spectrum of conditions.

Prairies range from parched, rocky hilltops with plants stubbornly clinging to a few inches of shallow soil to lush, grassy wetlands with standing water and many feet of black muck. Prairies occur on leached sand flats, deep rich loams, accumulations of glacial till, and thin soils over expanses of bedrock that have never been scoured by glaciers. Not all prairies in the tallgrass region are uniformly dominated by tall grasses. In sterile or rocky sites, the vegetation may be sparse and low.

TALLGRASS PRAIRIES

Approximate Presettlement Range of Tallgrass Prairies in the Midwest

Green indicates areas where a majority of the landscape was composed of prairies and related communities. Tan characterizes areas with scattered, smaller prairies, extensive savannas, and open oak woodlands mixed with other vegetation types. Prairies also occurred in scattered locations to the east. Other tallgrass prairies occurred as far south as the Gulf of Mexico.

Although prairies are typically thought to be treeless, they display close biological relationships with open woodland communities, often called savannas. Prior to European settlement these woodlands occupied large areas of the Midwest. It would have been hard to clearly separate prairies with a few scattered oaks from open oak woodlands with prairie grasses underneath. There was a continuous variation from treeless grassland to grassland with a few scattered trees to rather dense woodlands with abundant grasses, sedges, and wildflowers. This subtle dynamic was the tallgrass prairie landscape of the Midwest.

Wet Prairie

FRANK OBERLE

Today, tallgrass prairies cannot be viewed as elements isolated from their surroundings. It is more realistic to consider much of the Midwestern United States, and large parts of the southern states, to be part of a prairie biome—an integrated landscape where the prairie suffuses all aspects of the natural world. Within this region, even woodlands and wetlands reflect the influences of tallgrass prairies.

Attempts to classify prairies into discrete types can be frustrating. The problem is intensified because little is known about the composition and dynamics of presettlement tallgrass prairies. A few broad classes of tallgrass prairie are described below.

Wet Prairies are found in sites with saturated soils through much of the growing season. Wet prairies range from areas with mineralized groundwater seepage, such as prairie fens, to alluvial expanses along major rivers. There is often abundant standing water. Soils range from leached sand and gravel to organic peat and muck. Typical wet prairie plants include Blue Flag, Common Ironweed, False Aster, Prairie Cord Grass, Swamp Milkweed, and various sedges.

Mesic Prairie

Mesic Prairies occur on sites that are relatively well drained, but have high moisture available through most of the growing season. This results from a combination of factors, including rainfall, location in the landscape, and soil depth and type. Mesic prairies are the prairies most apt to be described as lush or luxuriant. They are among the most threatened of our prairies, because most of them were converted for agricultural use in the last century, and only small remnants remain. High-quality mesic prairies also contain some of our most diverse prairie wildflower displays. A few of the hundreds of typical wildflowers in mesic prairies include Big Bluestem, Lead Plant, Prairie Blazing Star, Purple Prairie Clover, Rattlesnake Master, Showy Goldenrod, and Switch Grass.

Dry Prairies occur on slopes and well-drained uplands, and once occupied vast areas, especially in the southern and western portions of the tallgrass region. These prairies are often interspersed with areas of mesic prairie in valleys and swales. Dry prairies range from very dry to somewhat moist—with the moister ones sometimes called "dry-mesic prairies." Most dry prairies have an abundance of Little Bluestem. Other typical dry prairie plants include Side-Oats Grama, Bird's Foot Violet, Blue Sage, Sky Blue Aster, Heath Aster, Pale Purple

Dry Prairie

Coneflower, Prairie Larkspur, and Round-Headed Bush Clover.

Hill Prairies are a special variant of dry prairie. These prairies occur at the tops of hills, bluffs, and ridges, and are often on steep slopes. Hill prairies are excessively drained, with immediate absorption or drainage of rainfall, and often have droughty growing conditions. Hill prairies range from prairies in calcium-rich glacial gravels to knife-edged ridges of windblown glacial soil, called loess, to steep slopes above rocky bluffs and cliffs. Many hill prairies have exposed rock, and the rock's characteristics strongly influence the prairie vegetation. Some typical plants found on hill prairies include Aromatic Aster, Prairie Dandelion, Pasque Flower, Prairie Smoke, and Side-Oats Grama.

FRANK OBERLE

Hill Prairie

Sand Prairies occur in areas of extensive sand deposits. These prairies range from wet depressions along the Great Lakes to dry hills in the Great Plains. Although sand prairies are diverse, some common characteristics of their sites are reflected in their flora. Sand areas are usually excessively drained and leached, resulting in nutrient-poor soils with little organic matter and an unstable, shifting substrate presenting special challenges to

JOHN TAFT

Sand Prairie

Savanna

plant growth. Some typical sand prairie plants include Little Bluestem, Prickly Pear, Sand Milkweed, Sessile-Leaved Tick Trefoil, Silky Prairie Clover, and Wild Lupine.

Savannas in the tallgrass region, are communities with scattered trees and a well-developed ground cover of grasses and wildflowers. Typical savanna trees include Bur and Black Oaks in the northern regions, and Black and Post Oaks in the southern regions. Most of the few surviving savannas have strong prairie affinities in their flora, including species such as Downy Blue Gentian, Flax-Leaved Aster, Goat's Rue, Hoary Puccoon, Little Bluestem, Rattlesnake Master, Royal Catchfly, Shooting Star, and Sky Blue Aster.

History of Tallgrass Prairies

Evidence indicates that our tallgrass prairies expanded greatly beginning about 8,000 years ago as the last glaciers retreated from the Midwest. From that time until about 3,000 years ago, the region's climate was hotter and drier than at present, favoring grassland development as woodlands retreated. Many factors, including soil type and moisture capacity, rainfall, evaporation rate, and summer droughts, play roles in determining the location and extent of tallgrass prairies.

Prairie development also reflects the relationship between plant life and grazing animals. Many prairie plants have adapted to grazing, by developing growth-producing tissues located near the base of the plant or the ability to branch near the base. The origins of tall-grass prairies and the roles of climate, grazing animals, and human activity are still not completely understood.

Humans have been a part of the prairie environment since before the last glaciers retreated from the Midwest. Prairies and their associated communities were home and hunting grounds to Native Americans for thousands of years prior to European settlement. These early inhabitants of the prairie biome depended on the land for their survival and managed it according to their needs and abilities.

One powerful management force available to Native Americans was fire. Deliberately set fires, along with the occasional lightning fire or escaped campfire, were major forces in shaping prairie vegetation. Landscape fires were used to facilitate travel and hunting, to stimulate new growth for game, to reduce fuel loads near habitations, as acts of warfare, and for a variety of other purposes. Numerous studies and accounts confirm the presence of frequent dormant-season fires in the Midwest, and the important role of fire in Native

FRANK OBERLE

Prairie Fire

American culture. The patterns and processes that existed on the prairies for thousands of years resulted in the selection of organisms that are superbly adapted to life under a specific range of conditions. Fire was a major component of these patterns, and many prairie plants and animals are ultimately dependent on periodic fire.

Most tallgrass prairie has been obliterated. Millions of acres have been destroyed through conversion to agriculture, intensive grazing, or development. Large areas of former prairie that have not been overtly destroyed have been degraded through fire suppression, drainage, or other alterations jeopardizing their survival.

What were once extensive tallgrass prairies with regular dormant-season fires, abundant bison, elk, and deer, and intact water cycles are now largely reduced to small, isolated fragments. These often have no mechanisms for periodic fire or healthy water cycles, and either no large mammals or too many cows. The water once held by deep prairie sods and gradually released through the season now races off the surfaces of lawns and fields, scouring the land as it runs into ditches and drainage tiles, and it is no longer available during dry periods. Remaining prairie fragments are often isolated in a developed landscape that no longer allows normal plant and animal migrations to recolonize sites where organisms have vanished. In the face of these changes, our rich mix of native prairie species is being replaced with sterile, brushy thickets and disturbance-adapted Old World weeds.

Successful prairie conservation requires protecting prairies throughout their range on multiple interconnected scales ranging from small prairie remnants to entire prairie landscapes. This will ensure that populations of plants and animals can be maintained along with the essential natural processes they depend on. Accomplishing this will require people participating in direct management, stewardship and restoration of our remaining prairies, just as human involvement was essential in the pre-European prairie landscape. North American tallgrass prairie is a manifestly human-influenced system and must continue to connect human beings with nature in order to survive.

Nowhere on the planet was there a grassland complex like the Midwestern tallgrass prairie. Examples of its richness, diversity, and scenery must be maintained here, or they will be forever lost. With them will go an irreplaceable facet of the American landscape.

Tallgrass Prairies Today

Many public prairies are open to visitation, and a directory listing some examples across the tallgrass region is included in this guide. Our few remaining prairies require care and respect. Many prairies are small, with correspondingly small populations of plants and animals. Visitors to prairies should never dig or collect plants, or otherwise damage the area. This book is designed to facilitate identifications without having to damage plants, and purposely avoids using features that require digging or collecting. Plants are best appreciated, viewed, and photographed in their living environments. When visiting privately owned prairies, be sure to get permission before entering and leave a good impression, offering words of encouragement for the landowner's prairie stewardship efforts.

Prairies are spectacular places throughout the year. They are, however, harsh environments. Prairie explorers should be prepared for the worst the season has to offer—frigid winds in winter, soaking rains and deep mud in spring, and unrelenting sun, ticks, and chiggers in summer.

A number of groups such as The Nature Conservancy are working to conserve and manage prairies to ensure their survival for future generations. Recent interest in and concern about our prairie heritage is a first step toward developing a greater understanding, and it is hoped this book will help readers along that path.

PRAIRIE PLANTINGS AND PRAIRIE RESTORATION

Appreciation for our nearly vanished tallgrass prairies has increased in recent years, along with interest in restoring prairies and landscaping with prairie plants. Prairie wildflowers provide many benefits in horticultural, utilitarian, and restoration applications in the tallgrass region.

Prairie plants can be used as garden ornamentals, for erosion control, to restore prairie vegetation in degraded sites, and to create attractive, low maintenance landscapes in industrial, roadside, and residential settings.

Tallgrass prairie wildflowers provide multiple benefits for conservation and society, including:

- reduced need for site maintenance and watering
- generally no need for fertilizer and pesticides
- increased erosion control and water table recharge
- Wildlife habitat enhancement
- enhanced visual appeal
- creating a unique local identity linking natural and cultural heritage

In the tallgrass region, use of native prairie plants can also yield increased visual displays, since prairie species are perfectly adapted to local conditions and climate, and flower profusely even in what are considered to be "bad" years for garden plants.

When using prairie wildflowers, including native prairie grasses, in planting and restoration projects, a series of factors must be considered. These factors are outlined below; the references listed at the end of the book provide more information.

Site selection: Whether for a small prairie garden or a thousand acre prairie restoration, the site must be suitable for tallgrass prairie plants. This means full or nearly full sun, no frequent intervals of standing surface waters, and soil types capable of supporting tallgrass natural communities. While native woodland and savanna plants are suitable for shaded sites, tallgrass prairie species generally require full sun. Even a few hours of daily shade can significantly reduce vigor, flower production, and survival.

Plant materials: For any project involving prairie plants, one of the first steps is to determine the appropriate species for the area and site conditions. The resulting list of potential plants will be product of the local flora (what tallgrass prairie plants grow—or once grew—around here?) and site characteristics (what prairie plants are characteristic of this specific habitat?). Several of the references at the end of this book provide helpful information, including plant lists. It is also useful to consult with local experts, and to explore similar soil and site conditions in the area, where the remnant native vegetation can provide clues about the local flora.

Much has been written about the genetic origins of plant materials used in native plantings and prairie restorations, and much remains to be learned. As a practical guide, the more similar the source of the plant material is to the project site, in terms of both geography and site conditions, the better the chances for success. In other words, closer is better, but except in cases of plantings adjacent to native prairies, practicality should also be a consideration.

Prairie plantings can be established from seeds, bare root plants, and potted plants. Seeds have a lower probability of per-plant survival, but are far less expensive and labor intensive to install, making them the only practical choice for all but the smallest areas or highest budgets. A seeded planting can later be enhanced with additional plants of species that are difficult to establish from seed. Seeds of tallgrass prairie plants can be obtained from commercial vendors, by hand collecting with permission from private lands, and by raising prairie plants in a garden or nursery bed and harvesting their seeds. Plants may be purchased from nurseries or raised from seed and transplanted. Prairie plants should not be dug in the wild, except for approved salvage in rare cases of areas slated for immediate destruction. Ensure that commercially purchased seeds are accurately labeled and are not contaminated with seeds of invasive weeds or inappropriate species.

It is usually best to avoid improved strains or cultivars, which can reduce the success of other species in a planting. These strains are usually identified with names such as "Blackwell Switch Grass." Vendors who specialize exclusively in native plants and seeds are generally better versed in local conditions, and are more likely to offer a diversity of locally adapted seeds with appropriate expertise and instructions.

A key to long term success is to maximize the diversity of the seed or plant mix, always adding a few species considered to prefer conditions both slightly wetter and slightly drier than those of the site. This accommodates site variability and miktaken impressions about site conditions, and provides increased native diversity as the planting becomes established and itself starts to influence site conditions.

Site preparation: Each site has a unique combination of habitat, current status, land use history, and desired outcomes. However, a few common rules apply to all sites: 1) insufficient site preparation can doom a project or create years of expensive remedial work; 2) site preparation should be designed to minimize competition from invasive weeds; 3) site preparation should create optimum conditions for germination and/or establishment of desired plant materials; 4) site preparation activities should minimize soil disturbance and compaction as much as possible. Site preparation can be as simple as preparing a garden bed to receive plants, or spraying a former crop field to control annual weeds. Preparation can also be a long, complex task involving treatments to control problem exotic species, recover degraded soils, and restore site hydrology. Depending on site conditions and other factors, an area may be sprayed, disked, tilled, mowed, and/or rolled as part of site preparation work.

Installation: Techniques for installing plants or seeds are diverse. For seed plantings, this can range from hand sowing to machine broadcasting or no-till drilling. Key goals for seed planting are to ensure good seed-to-soil contact and prevent overly deep plantings which reduce germination. Since many prairie seeds require a period of cold after their first contact with soil moisture, season and timing are important. Another goal with either seed or plant installation is to minimize soil disturbance which stimulates weed germination. Fertilizers generally should not be used with prairie plants.

When using seed mixes to establish diverse prairie vegetation, there is often a tendency to use too much native grass seed, which can create competition problems for other prairie wildflowers. It is often best to use a reduced seeding rate and opt for greater overall diversity. Sometimes a short-lived native grass, such as Canada Wild Rye or Broom Sedge, is included as nurse crop to provide quick erosion control and fuel for the first burns. These species will decrease in time, allowing other plants to become established. Again diversity of native plants is one of the most important factors for long term success and sustainability – even more than overall quantities of seeds and plants.

Site Management: There is a common misconception that most of the work associated with a prairie project consists of site preparation and planting. Post-planting management is perhaps the most important factor for a successful prairie restoration. Prairie plantings are much like raising children – the process begins with birth or planting, but must be followed by years of patience, intensive work and attention to ensure success! First year management should include regular mowing to prevent weeds from smothering prairie seedlings. Aggressive weeds should be controlled before they have an opportunity spread. Fire is essential for all projects except intensively cultivated garden plantings. Seeded plantings should be burned during the first dormant season that they have sufficient fuel. This is generally in the second year, but can sometimes be in the third or rarely the first year. Burns should occur annually during the establishment process – typically the first 5-10 years, and at regular intervals thereafter. Fire is a complex, potentially dangerous process, so burn activities should only be undertaken with proper planning, training, equipment and experience.

Site Enhancement: To achieve diverse prairie stands, additional seeds and/or plants can be installed for several years after the initial planting. Many sensitive prairie species will not establish themselves in new plantings, and may take years to appear after they have been seeded. Some are best installed after a native plant cover has been established. Sometimes, additional site treatments, such as close mowing or light disking, are needed to allow enhancement seedings to be successful. In larger projects, consideration should be given to restoring other essential parts of tallgrass prairies, such as pollinators.

Monitoring and Documentation: Prairie restoration and cultivation of many prairie plants is a new field. Every project provides lessons that can advance our overall knowledge. It is important that records be kept to assess progress, direct management actions, and to help others learn. This may be as simple as a list of plant materials installed and annual lists of species present, along with a few annual photographs. Notes on abundance and other factors, and accounts of management can provide valuable records useful far beyond an individual project.

Tallgrass prairies are incredibly diverse systems. Although no restoration or planting has attained the diversity or functional complexity of a native prairie, projects at all scales can provide enduring benefits, and contribute towards the conservation and understanding of a nearly vanished phase of the North American landscape.

USING THIS GUIDE

This guide differs from conventional wildflower guides in two respects. First, instead of being a guide to the wildflowers of a particular region, it is a guide to the common wildflowers of a general habitat type, across a vast area. Second, although this is a guide to the common and characteristic wildflowers of tallgrass prairies, tallgrass prairies themselves are now so rare that almost none of their flora is common. The user will pass many old fields, overgrown woodlots, and weedy roadsides before being rewarded with a prairie.

Many of these non-prairie habitats will have their own mix of wildflowers, including native plants and species introduced from other parts of the world. While they are often attractive, open, and grassy, most of the meadows and fields in the modern landscape are not prairies. On the other hand, if you locate an area with a dozen or more of the plants shown in this guide, you probably have an area with remnant prairie character. Such areas are usually worthy of attention and management to insure their continued existence.

Anyone with an interest in America's rich prairie heritage can use this guide as a tool for understanding the unique tapestry of plants in our remaining prairies. The book is designed to be used without any specialized knowledge, and technical terms have been eliminated, with a few necessary exceptions. There are more than nine hundred species of native flowering plants in Midwestern tallgrass prairies. This guide covers the more common and characteristic plants of tallgrass prairies from northeastern Oklahoma north into Canada and eastward through Ohio. This area is referred to as the "tallgrass region" throughout the book.

Included here are photographs and descriptions of more than 300 tallgrass prairie plants, including a few examples of very rare plants that epitomize the tallgrass prairie. A few weedy native plants that are regularly found in degraded prairies are included here as well, since they are a part of the modern prairie landscape. Plants are grouped according to flower color and divided into the following categories: blue and purple; pink; red and orange; yellow; white; green; and grasses, sedges, and rushes. A section at the end of the book features some of the most common and aggressive exotic weeds in tallgrass prairies.

Flower color is a convenient means of quickly grouping plants, but a word of caution is needed. Wildflowers, like all living things, are variable: no two individuals are exactly alike. This results from a combination of heredity (what were the parents like?) and environment (what are the conditions where it grows?). Just as there may be blond, black-, and red-haired people, a single species of plant may have a range of flower colors. Most plants with pink flowers, for instance, also have white-flowered forms. A second problem with grouping plants by color is the difficulty in determining the line between colors, such as between blue and purple. Some plants have multicolored flowers. In this guide, the plant is grouped under the color that is most prominent in the flowers.

The best way to identify a prairie wildflower using this book is to go to the color section in this guide that matches the plant in question. Within each color grouping, plants are arranged alphabetically by family, and alphabetically by scientific name within each family. By scanning the selections, users will quickly locate the plant they are attempting to identify, or a close relative. This arrangement also provides a quick means of determining whether close relatives of the plant also occur in prairies.

To further aid the user in plant identification, we have included information in this book about the flowering season for each plant, such as early spring or midsummer. The large geographic span of the tallgrass region and year-to-year variations in weather patterns make this information only approximate, and flowers will not always bloom in the time frame described in this book. A quick glance at this information will also provide users with tips on the best times to visit the tallgrass region to see its diverse species in their natural habitat.

A written entry accompanies each plant photograph, and includes the common and scientific names of the plant. Most prairie plants have several common names, and a common name used in one region may apply elsewhere to a totally unrelated plant. The common names used in this book are selected to be the most appropriate through the tallgrass region. In some instances, additional common names are given in the **Comments** section of each entry.

Because of the confusion surrounding common names, the scientific name of the plant is also provided. These names, rendered in Latin, are a more stable and universal means of referring to a particular plant; the same scientific name can be used worldwide. The scientific name consists of two words. The first word, the genus, is the name of a group of plants with similar general characteristics—such as milkweeds, which are in the genus *Asclepias.* Sometimes the scientific and common names for a genus coincide, such as the genus *Aster.*

The second part of the scientific name is the **specific epithet,** which identifies the particular species of plant. Thus, there are many species of milkweeds in the genus *Asclepias,* but *Asclepias tuberosa* can only refer to the beautiful orange-flowered Butterfly Milkweed. Besides being consistent, scientific names show relationships by identifying species in the same genus. Most of the scientific names used in this book are from a standard checklist of North American flora compiled by John Kartesz in 1999. For convenience, some commonly used older scientific names are also cross-referenced in the index.

In a few cases, the scientific name for a plant will have a third part, preceded by the word **variety** or **subspecies.** These are plants that differ slightly but consistently from other plants of the same species, and often have distinct ranges.

Plants are grouped into **families** according to similarities in their structure and biology. The scientific name of a plant family always ends with the suffix "aceae", such as Asteraceae for the aster family. With surprisingly little experience, many common plant families can be identified at first sight. Most people are already familiar with the unmistakable flowers of the bean family (Fabaceae), including peas, beans, sweet peas, lupines, and locust flowers. Being able to determine the family of an unknown plant helps in field identification.

The main part of each entry contains a **Description** of the plant. This description starts with general characteristics and identifying features. Growth form, leaves, flowers, and sometimes fruits are described. For many features such as plant height, leaf size, and flower dimensions, an approximate size or range of typical sizes is given in inches or feet. Unless otherwise stated, leaf measurements are for the leafy part of the plant and do not include the leaf stalk. The size ranges given are for typical plants. No size measurements are absolute, and diligent searching will reveal the odd, stunted individual or over-fertilized giant, but the measurements provided here will apply to most of the plants encountered in prairie habitats.

When identifying plants in the field, it helps to take a minute to study the plant, noting its general growth form, leaves, flowers, and any other distinguishing features. Look around for other plants of the same species—maybe you will see better-developed or more fully blooming individuals. A small magnifying glass or hand lens with about 10X magnification helps in seeing telltale hairs and flower parts.

The descriptions and photographs in this book are intended to be used together to identify a plant. There may be occasions when a plant does not exactly match an entry but is clearly a close relative. In many cases this will be because the plant in question is of a different species but the same genus as the plant in the photograph. Sometimes the **Comments** section mentions related species and how to identify them.

Although this guide keeps technical terms to a minimum, users will find knowledge of a few special terms is necessary. These terms, easy to learn and useful for all plant identifications, are discussed below. A complete list of terms is included in the glossary at the back of this book.

Most prairie plants are **perennial,** that is, parts of the plant live anywhere from a few years to more than a century. Familiar examples of perennial plants include tulips, raspberries, and oak trees. Perennial plants can be divided into two types: **woody plants** such as trees and shrubs, and **herbaceous** plants that die back to ground level each year, with only the underground parts overwintering. Most prairie plants are herbaceous perennials, and only a small percentage of prairie flora is composed of woody plants. In addition to perennials, herbaceous plants may be classified as **annuals,** which germinate, flower, produce seeds, and die within a year, or **biennials,** which take two years to produce seeds before dying.

It is often easy to determine whether a plant is perennial, since parts of the previous year's growth may be visible. Perennial plants generally have well-developed underground parts, such as bulbs or large tuberous roots, while annual plants typically have a small system of fibrous roots. Plants discussed in this book are perennial unless stated otherwise, and all plants in the book are herbaceous unless they are specifically listed as woody.

Each plant description provides the diagnostic features needed for identification, including discussion of overall appearance, leaves, and flowers. Sometimes features such as fragrant leaves or colored or milky sap will be mentioned. These can be determined by gently squeezing and then smelling a leaf and by slightly tearing the tip of a leaf and noting the sap color. Some plants have **winged** parts; these are thin strips of tissue attached edgewise along a stem, branch, or other part.

Another feature often useful in plant identification is the presence of hairs on leaves, stems, or flower parts. Some plants are always hairless, some are always hairy, and some species range from hairless to hairy. The size, abundance, and type of hairs are often useful for identification purposes. In this guide, the discussion for each plant includes whether the plant is hairy or smooth if this is a useful feature for identification. If the hairiness is not mentioned it means that the plant can be smooth or hairy, or that the hairs are small, sparse, and easily overlooked.

Leaves are important identifying features of wildflowers. To describe small differences precisely, botanists use dozens of technical terms for the shapes, textures, surfaces, margins, parts, and attachments of leaves. This book avoids such terms. Leaf shapes are described using common language, such as "long and narrow" or "broadly oval."

Important leaf features to note include arrangement of the leaves on the stem (**opposite** each other, **alternating** along the stem, or **whorled**—several leaves at one point), and the leaf tip (pointed or blunt), leaf base (tapering, rounded, heart-shaped, or clasping the stem), leaf edges (smooth, toothed, wavy, or lobed), leaf texture (thick, leathery, waxy, thin, or brittle), and whether the leaves are on stalks or stalkless. Many plants produce

basal leaves; these leaves originate directly from the underground parts of the plant and are not attached to the stems. Sometimes the shape of the basal leaves may differ from the stem leaves, or the basal leaves may have different stalks.

A distinction crucial to plant identification is **simple** leaves versus **compound** leaves. Simple leaves have a single leaflike blade above each bud. This blade may be lobed or unlobed, but is clearly a single leaf. Compound leaves are divided into two or more distinct segments called **leaflets,** with each segment often looking like a separate leaf. The only sure way to tell a compound leaf is to look for buds. If there are several leaflike segments above a single bud, then you are dealing with a compound leaf. This can be tricky, but is important to master since many plant groups can be quickly determined by this feature. Leaflets of compound leaves can be arranged featherlike along a stalklike axis, or originate from a common point like the fingers on a hand, or even be doubly or triply compound, with each segment divided once or twice again into further series of leaflike segments. In all cases, however, the leaflets of compound leaves are arranged in the same plane.

Features related to leaves are **bracts.** These are reduced leaflike structures or scales and are often associated with flowers. Sometimes bracts are like miniature versions of the plant's leaves, sometimes they are just little pointed or rounded green scales, and sometimes they are totally different in size and shape from the leaves. Bracts may be green and leaflike in texture, thin and papery, or sometimes even colored like flowers. On some plants there are two specialized bractlike structures called **stipules** at the base of the leaf stalk. These may be large and showy, or tiny and scalelike, or they may fall off soon after the leaf emerges from the bud.

Flowers are the most complicated parts of a plant, and come in an array of shapes, sizes, and colors. Flower descriptions in this guide are intended to help in identification, so only prominent or distinctive flower characteristics are discussed. Lack of discussion of a particular feature does not mean it is lacking for that species, but only that it is not a useful character for identification.

Flowers have one main function—to facilitate pollination of the female flower parts and development of the seeds and fruits. Flowers that are insect pollinated often have showy or fragrant parts to attract suitable pollinators. On the other hand, flowers that are wind pollinated, such as many trees and grasses, have very reduced flowers suited to launching and capturing windblown pollen without the need for showy or fragrant parts. Flowers of plants such as grasses are highly modified and not discussed in detail in this book.

A diagram of a generalized flower is given in **Figure 4.** Most flowers have an outer series of flower parts, called **sepals,** surrounding the base of the flower. Sepals are often green and can be inconspicuous, but they also can be showy and colored. The sepals together form the **calyx.** The calyx may be composed of separate sepals, or the sepals may be joined or fused into a tube or cuplike calyx. If the sepals are fused, they are often represented by teeth or points around the top of the calyx.

Inside the calyx of most flowers is a series of usually showy parts called **petals;** these are what we see when we view the average flower. The petals come in a variety of shapes, sizes, and colors, and depending on the kind of plant there may be no petals or three to six or more per flower. The petals may be separate from each other or partially or wholly fused together into a cuplike, tubular, or irregular shape. The petals together, whether fused or separate, form the **corolla.** Some flowers have no corolla, and in some plants the sepals and petals are identical.

Within the flower, pollen is produced by the **stamens.** There may be one to more than a hundred stamens per flower. Stamens are typically long, thin filaments with clublike or elongate appendages at the tip. The seed-producing part of the flower is called the **pistil**—this consists of the usually swollen **ovary** where the seeds develop, above which is a usually long, tubelike **style** with a blunt, divided or elongate **stigma** at the tip that serves as a pollen receptor. In some flowers the style is absent. While most flowers have both male (stamen) and female (pistil) parts, some plants have separate male and female flowers, and in some species male and female flowers are on separate plants.

The arrangement of flowers on a plant is also useful for identification purposes. Again, botanists use many specialized terms to describe the arrangement of flowers on a plant. Because these terms are confusing and can be hard to determine, they are avoided here. Flower arrangements are described in general terms such as "open clusters" or "narrow elongate spikes."

Two families of flowers, both well represented in tallgrass prairies, have specialized flower structures that deserve comment. Most plants in the bean family (Fabaceae) have a calyx surrounding five petals that are developed into a specialized form. The upper petal, called the **standard,** is erect, spreading, and usually the largest. Below this are two protruding side petals, called **wings,** closely surrounding the **keel,** which is actually created by the fusion of the two lowest petals. A typical bean family flower is shown in **Figure 5.**

Asters, goldenrods, daisies, dandelions, and other plants in the aster family (Asteraceae) have an unusual flower arrangement. What appears at first glance to be a single flower is actually a head composed of a few to several hundred small flowers. This head of flowers is usually surrounded at the base by a series of bracts. The calyx is absent or reduced to bristles, scales, or hairs. There are two kinds of flowers produced, **disk flowers** and **ray flowers (Fig. 6)**, as described below.

The corollas of ray flowers have a single, usually brightly colored strap that looks like the petal of a conventional flower. Disk flowers have small, tubular corollas, usually with five lobes. Depending on the species, each flower head may be all disk flowers, all ray flowers, or a combination of the two. When both are present, there is usually a central circle or cone of disk flowers surrounded by one or more series of ray flowers, the whole creating the appearance of a single typical flower, although there may be more than a hundred flowers present. A typical aster family flower head is diagrammed in **Figure 6.**

Following the description of each plant is a section titled **Habitat/Range.** This provides a summary of the typical prairie habitats for the plant, and a general range where the plant grows within the tallgrass region. **These statements apply only to the tallgrass region.** Many plants characteristic of tallgrass prairies occur in other habitats elsewhere, and much of our prairie flora ranges beyond the boundaries of the tallgrass region. This guide deals exclusively with plants in the context of the prairie environments within the tallgrass region.

The Habitat/Range section also includes comments about the relative abundance of plants, using terms such as "common," "occasional," and "rare." These are general terms to give the user an idea of the relative rarity of each species, but are intended merely as range-wide guides. Species described as common throughout the tallgrass region may be rare or absent in a particular area, and rare species may be locally abundant in some areas.

Some entries also have a section labeled **Comments.** This provides information such as discussions of closely related species, historical uses for the plant, and other notes of interest. Several plants in this book are listed as having been eaten or used as medicine— this information is presented for historical perspective only, and in many cases is based on literature reports. Because of the uncertainties of plant identification, and the lack of information about the accuracy of early reports, these plants should not be eaten or used medicinally, since many edible plants have poisonous counterparts. A list of suggested readings at the back of the book provides some sources for additional information about prairies and prairie locations.

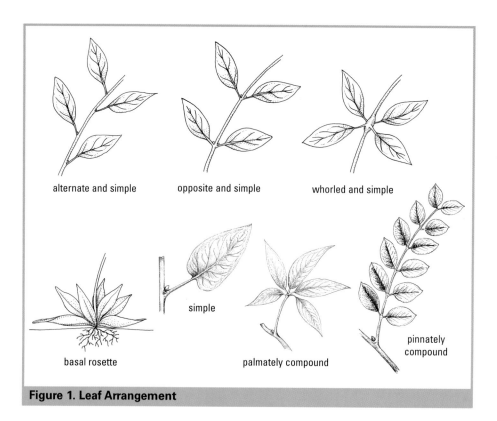

Figure 1. Leaf Arrangement

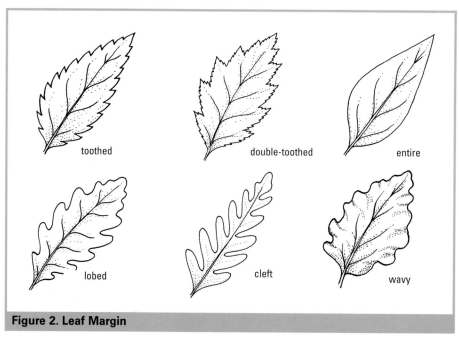

Figure 2. Leaf Margin

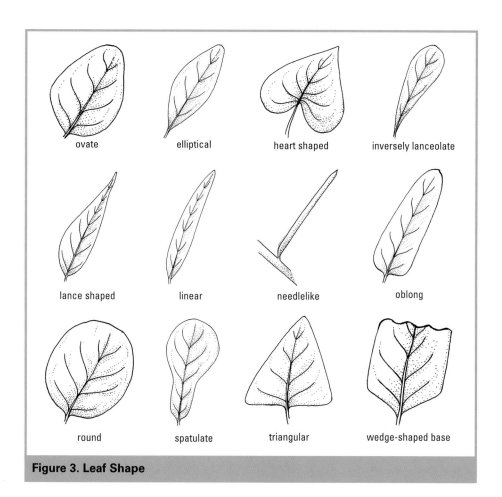

Figure 3. Leaf Shape

ovate

elliptical

heart shaped

inversely lanceolate

lance shaped

linear

needlelike

oblong

round

spatulate

triangular

wedge-shaped base

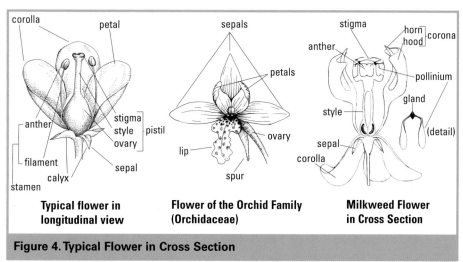

corolla

petal

sepals

stigma

horn
hood

corona

anther

petals

pollinium

gland

style

(detail)

stigma
style

pistil

ovary

sepal

anther

ovary

lip

corolla

filament

sepal

spur

stamen

calyx

**Typical flower in
longitudinal view**

**Flower of the Orchid Family
(Orchidaceae)**

**Milkweed Flower
in Cross Section**

Figure 4. Typical Flower in Cross Section

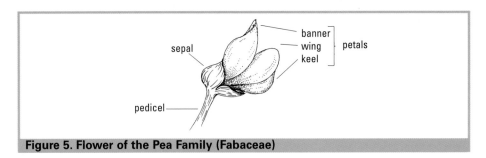

Figure 5. Flower of the Pea Family (Fabaceae)

sepal

banner
wing
keel ⎫ petals

pedicel

flower head

disk flowers

ray flowers

strap-shaped corolla

phyllaries (bracts)

disk flower

ray flower

pappus

developing seedlike fruit

Figure 6. Flowers of the Aster Family (Asteraceae)

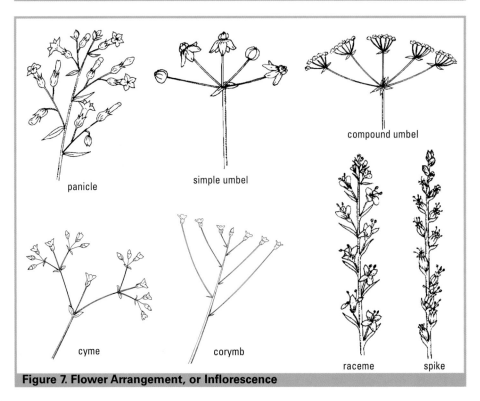

panicle

simple umbel

compound umbel

cyme

corymb

raceme

spike

Figure 7. Flower Arrangement, or Inflorescence

BLUE AND PURPLE FLOWERS

FRANK OBERLE

This section includes flowers ranging from pale blue to deep indigo and from lavender to violet. Since purple flowers grade into pink flowers, readers looking for purple flowers should check the pink section as well.

FRANK OBERLE

HAIRY WILD PETUNIA
Ruellia humilis
Acanthus family (Acanthaceae)

Description: Plants with squarish, often branched, hairy stems usually 1' or less tall, with several pairs of opposite leaves. The leaves are usually about 2" long by 1" wide and stalkless or on short stalks. The flowers are stalkless and arise in small groups at the bases of the middle and upper leaves. Each flower has 5 long, needle-like sepals and a tubular corolla, 1–2½" long, which flares into 5 broad, purple lobes. The inside of the flower is often marked with darker purple lines.

Bloom Season: Late spring–early fall.

Habitat/Range: Common in dry prairies and rocky, open woodlands from southeastern Nebraska, central Iowa, and southern Wisconsin east and south.

FRANK OBERLE

FRANK OBERLE

LEAVENWORTH ERYNGO
Eryngium leavenworthii
Parsley family (Apiaceae)

Description: Thistle-like, hairless annuals to 3
tall, with stout, erect, usually branched stems.
The leaves are alternate and usually clasping,
with the upper leaves divided into several narrow
segments like the fingers of a hand. All of the
leaves are thick and smooth-surfaced, with pale
edges and veins and many sharp spines. The
flowers are in dense, rounded, purple cylinders at
the tops of the branches, with spiny, purple,
leaflike bracts at the base and usually a few
purple to green spiny bracts at the top of the
cluster. The small flowers cover the head, and
have 5 tiny white to blue-violet petals.
Occasionally the heads and bracts are white
instead of purple.

Bloom Season: Midsummer–fall.

Habitat/Range: Local in rocky soils in prairies and
pastures, often associated with limestone; in
eastern Kansas and eastern Oklahoma.

PURPLE MILKWEED
Asclepias purpurascens
Milkweed family (Asclepiadaceae)

Description: Stout, green stems to 3' tall, with
abundant milky sap, and many pairs of large,
opposite, oval leaves. The leaves are up to 8"
long and 4" wide and on stalks up to 1" long.
There are one to a few rounded flower clusters
near the top of the plant, each on a stalk up to 4"
long. The individually stalked, deep reddish purple
flowers in each cluster are up to ¾" long, with 5
purple, reflexed petals flanking 5 erect, purple
hoods. The smooth seed pods are narrow and
taper toward the ends, ranging up to 6" long but
less than 1" wide.

Bloom Season: Late spring–midsummer.

Habitat/Range: Frequent in well-drained or rocky
sites in prairie thickets, open prairie woodlands,
and along prairie/woodland edges, from eastern
Kansas through Illinois, becoming more sporadic
north and eastward.

KENNETH DRITZ

FRANK OBERLE

SMOOTH BLUE ASTER
Aster laevis
Aster family (Asteraceae)

Description: Plants to 3' tall, with a distinctive bluish green cast to the leaves and stem. The leaves are smooth and almost waxy, with very rough edges. The basal leaves are rounded and stalked, with a narrow wing along either side of the upper leaf stalk. The stem leaves are alternate, broadest at the base, strongly clasp the stem, and taper to pointed tips. There are several individually stalked flower heads on the upper half of the plant; each head is ¾–1½" wide, with up to 25 blue, petal-like ray flowers surrounding a yellow disk.

Bloom Season: Late summer–fall.

Habitat/Range: Occasional throughout the tallgrass region in mesic to dry prairies and open upland savannas.

NEW ENGLAND ASTER
Aster novae-angliae
Aster family (Asteraceae)

Description: Showy asters to 6' tall with hairy stems and leaves. The alternate leaves are up to 4" long and 1" wide, with broad, clasping bases and pointed tips. The individually stalked flower heads are in an open, rounded cluster at the tops of the main stem branches. The flower stalks and bracts at the base of each flower head are covered with gland-tipped hairs. Each head is about 1½" wide, with 40 or more bright purple, petal-like ray flowers surrounding a central yellow disk. The ray flowers are sometimes pinkish purple or pale lavender.

Bloom Season: Late summer–fall.

Habitat/Range: Frequent throughout the tallgrass region in wet to mesic prairies and moist open areas.

Comments: This is a handsome and widely cultivated aster, which can be grown easily from seed. It has some weedy tendencies and may spread into moist ditches and open thickets. A related species, Swamp Aster *(A. puniceus)* occurs in wetter sites in wet prairies and fens; it has hairs in lines along the stems, and lacks gland-tipped hairs.

DON KURZ

FRANK OBERLE

AROMATIC ASTER
Aster oblongifolius
Aster family (Asteraceae)

Description: Fragrant, hairy plants less than 2½'
tall with spreading branches and alternate leaves.
The upper stems, leaves, and bracts of the flower
heads have small, round glands that are visible
under magnification. The leaves are up to 3" long,
and less than 1" wide, with toothless edges and
clasping bases. Flower heads are at the ends of
short branches, with numerous, small, leaflike
bracts along their length. Each head is about 1"
wide, with a series of green outer bracts and
mostly 20–35 purple, petal-like ray flowers
surrounding the yellow disk flowers.

Bloom Season: Late summer–fall.

Habitat/Range: Locally common in sparse
vegetation in areas on prairie uplands and hill
prairies; found throughout the tallgrass region,
but uncommon east of Illinois.

SKY BLUE ASTER
Aster oolentangiensis
Aster family (Asteraceae)

Description: Plants typically less than 3' tall, but
occasionally to 5', with long-stalked, sandpapery
basal leaves that have heart-shaped bases. The
leaves may be toothed or smooth along their
edges. The stem leaves are progressively smaller
upward along the stem, alternate, and seldom
heart-shaped at the base, with the upper stem
leaves small, narrow, and stalkless. There are
numerous spreading flower branches near the top
of the plant, with each flower head on a long
individual stalk that usually has a few, small,
narrow bracts along its length. Flower heads are
about 1" wide, with up to 25 blue to lavender,
petal-like ray flowers surrounding a yellow disk.

Bloom Season: Late summer–fall.

Habitat/Range: Common in mesic to dry prairies
and savannas through most of the tallgrass
region; becoming rare north of east-central
Nebraska.

27

SOUTHERN PRAIRIE ASTER

Aster paludosus ssp. *hemisphericus*
Aster family (Asteraceae)

Description: This species has the most spectacular flower heads of any prairie aster. The stems are usually less than 2' tall with most of the leaves tapering to narrow, clasping bases. The leaves are up to 6" long and only about ¼" wide, with the leaves progressively smaller upwards along the stem. There are typically several flower heads clustered along the upper stem, with each head up to 2" wide, including 15–35 deep violet, petal-like ray flowers surrounding a central disk.

Bloom Season: Late summer–fall.

Habitat/Range: Occasional in high-quality mesic to dry prairies from southeastern Kansas and southwestern Missouri southward.

WILLOW ASTER

Aster praealtus
Aster family (Asteraceae)

Descriptions: Plants to 5' tall often growing in dense colonies. The stems are roughly hairy on the upper parts, with long, narrow, alternate leaves that are widest near the middle. The leaves are up to 5½" long and about ¾" wide, and are nearly the same size along the length of the main stems. There are many flower heads near the top of the plant, forming a tall, pyramid-like cluster. Each head is up to 1" wide, with 20–40 pale lavender, petal-like ray flowers surrounding a small yellow disk.

Bloom Season: Late summer–fall.

Habitat/Range: Frequent in moist places, including wet prairies, streambanks, and open thickets, from northeastern Nebraska south and eastward.

FRANK OBERLE

SILKY ASTER
Aster sericeus
Aster family (Asteraceae)

Description: Widely branching plants to 2½' tall, with alternate leaves up to 1¾" long and ½" wide. The leaves are densely covered with fine silky hairs that lie flat on the leaf surface, giving them a distinctive silvery green color and slippery texture. Flower heads are usually numerous in an open branching cluster at the tops of the stems. Each flower head is about 1¼" wide, with 16–25 purple, petal-like ray flowers surrounding a yellow disk.

Bloom Season: Late summer–fall.

Habitat/Range: Occasional in dry or sandy prairies from Indiana westward, often associated with limestone or calcium-rich soils.

FRANK OBERLE

PASTURE THISTLE
Cirsium discolor
Aster family (Asteraceae)

Description: Branched spiny plants up to 8' tall. The leaves are alternate, very spiny, and deeply divided into narrow lobes. The underside of each leaf is densely covered with white hairs, so the bottom appears bright white. The edges of the leaves are slightly downturned and thickened. Flower heads are up to 2½" wide and on individual leafy stalks. Each head has numerous, overlapping, spiny, green bracts cupping many pale pinkish purple disk flowers. Each narrow, tubular flower is about 1½" long, with 5 narrow corolla lobes, each about ¼" long, and 2 protruding, threadlike style branches.

Bloom Season: Midsummer–fall.

Habitat/Range: Common in dry pastures, upland old fields, and prairies with a history of grazing or other disturbance; found in the eastern tallgrass region west through Missouri.

Comments: A closely related species, Tall Thistle *(C. altissimum)*, occurs throughout the tallgrass region in prairies, growing in the western parts and more commonly in woodlands and thickets in the eastern parts. Tall Thistle is less spiny, with mostly undivided leaves or leaves with only a few lobes. The upper surfaces of the leaves of Tall Thistle are often lighter green, and the leaf edges are not downturned. Wavy-Leaved Thistle *(C. undulatum)* has densely white-hairy stems, and the upper surfaces of the leaves are often white-hairy as well. It occurs on upland prairies in the western tallgrass region. These and several other native thistles in prairie areas should not be confused with introduced weedy thistles.

FRANK OBERLE

PALE PURPLE CONEFLOWER
Echinacea pallida
Aster family (Asteraceae)

Description: Plants to 3' tall, with coarse, bristly hairs on the stout stems and leaves. The leaves are rough, up to 10" long and 1½" wide, and tapering at either end, with several parallel veins running along their lengths. The basal leaves are on long stalks, while the stem leaves are few, alternate, and usually lack long stalks. There is a single showy flower head at the top of each stem, with many drooping, pale purple, petal-like ray flowers, each up to 3½" long, surrounding a broad, purplish brown, cone-shaped central disk.

Bloom Season: Late spring–midsummer.

Habitat/Range: Locally common and widely distributed in dry and mesic prairies and open savannas from southeastern Nebraska and north-central Iowa south and east to southwestern Arkansas and northwestern Indiana. Farther east

it is rare, with most populations representing escapes from cultivation.

Comments: A related plant, Narrow-Leaved Purple Coneflower *(E. angustifolia),* occurs in upland prairies throughout the western tallgrass region and westward; it is a shorter plant with smaller ray flowers and yellow pollen–typical Pale Purple Coneflower has white pollen. Some scientists think that the two types are varieties of a single species. All of the Purple Coneflowers were used as medicinal plants by Native Americans. There is still a market for the roots, which are used to make herbal medicines and tonics. Illegal root digging poses a major threat to the plants in some areas.

FRANK OBERLE

FRANK OBERLE

PURPLE CONEFLOWER
Echinacea purpurea
Aster family (Asteraceae)

Description: Plants to 5' tall with much-branched stems, although plants are fewer-branched and shorter in exposed sites. The rough leaves are coarsely toothed, alternate, mostly stalked, up to 8" long and 5" wide, and widest near the base. Flower heads are on individual stalks near the tops of the stems, with each head 2½–5" wide and consisting of up to 20 purple, petal-like ray flowers surrounding a cone-shaped head of disk flowers.

Bloom Season: Late spring–fall.

Habitat/Range: Occasional in prairies and open woodlands, usually in moister sites than Pale Purple Coneflower; scattered through the tallgrass region west to southeastern Kansas.

Comments: This plant is a popular ornamental, and many populations are escapes from cultivation. The plants are typically branched, with much wider leaves than Pale Purple Coneflower.

FLAX-LEAVED ASTER
Ionactis linariifolius
Aster family (Asteraceae)

Description: Plants usually less than 2' tall with abundant alternate, narrowly tapered, stiff leaves up to 1½" long and about ⅛" wide. The leaves taper to sharp points and break rather than bend when folded. Numerous flower heads occur at the tops of the stems on short individual stalks among the leaves. Each flower head is about 1–1¼" wide, with about 10-15 purple, petal-like ray flowers surrounding a yellow disk.

Bloom Season: Late summer–fall.

Habitat/Range: Occasional in acidic, well-drained sand prairies or prairies in sandstone regions, and locally common in open upland savannas in acidic soils; found through much of the eastern tallgrass region, west through southern Missouri to southeastern Kansas.

FRANK OBERLE

FRANK OBERLE

ROUGH BLAZING STAR
Liatris aspera
Aster family (Asteraceae)

Description: Unbranched hairy or smooth stems to about 4' tall, with numerous alternate, smooth-edged leaves. The basal leaves are widest near the middle, tapering gradually to each end, and up to 2" wide and 16" long, including their long stalks. Middle and upper leaves on the stem are smaller and narrower, with rounded tips and leaf stalks short or lacking. The flower heads are alternate along the upper stem, and each head has a series of overlapping rounded bracts with white to purplish, papery tips. Each flower head is about ¾–1" wide, with 16–35 small, purple disk flowers, each with a tiny 5-lobed corolla and 2 conspicuous, threadlike style branches.

Bloom Season: Midsummer–fall.

Habitat/Range: Common throughout the tallgrass region in dry, rocky prairies and open upland savannas, usually in acidic soils and typically in areas of relatively sparse vegetation.

CYLINDRICAL BLAZING STAR
Liatris cylindracea
Aster family (Asteraceae)

Description: Smooth, unbranched plants to 2' tall, with shiny, grasslike leaves. Rarely, there are short hairs on the stem and leaves. The longest leaves on the stem are up to 10" long and ½" wide, with the leaves becoming progressively smaller upward along the stem. The cylindrical flower heads are alternate along the upper stems, with each head about ½" wide. Each head has an overlapping series of smooth, short-pointed bracts, with the tips of the bracts flat and not spreading outward. Inside the bracts are 10–35 small purple disk flowers. Each individual flower has a corolla with 5 narrow, pointed tips that curl backward and have long hairs on their inner sides, and a long style divided into 2 threadlike, purple branches that protrude ½" from the flower.

Bloom Season: Midsummer–early fall.

Habitat/Range: Frequent in dry or sandy prairies and rocky areas, often associated with limestone or calcium-rich soils; found in the eastern tallgrass region west to southwestern Missouri.

FRANK OBERLE

DOTTED BLAZING STAR
Liatris punctata
Aster family (Asteraceae)

Description: Unbranched stems usually in dense clusters, with each stem less than 3' tall. Plants are smooth and hairless except for a line of tiny hairs usually along the edges of the stiff, narrow leaves. Leaves are abundant along the stem, giving the plant a bushy appearance. Each leaf is usually less than 5" long and less than ¼" wide, with a central vein and many tiny round dots on the underside. Flower heads are in dense leafy spikes at the tops of the stems. Each head is surrounded at the base by an overlapping series of flat-tipped, resinous, dotted bracts. There are 3–8 tiny purple disk flowers in each head, with each flower having a small 5-lobed corolla and 2 long threadlike style branches.

Bloom Season: Midsummer–fall.

Habitat/Range: Common to locally abundant in dry prairies through the western tallgrass region, east to central Iowa and western Missouri.

Comments: In hard times, the tough underground parts were a food of last resort for Native Americans. Narrow-Leaf Gayfeather *(L. mucronata)* is a very similar species that occurs in the southwestern tallgrass region into southwestern Missouri. It has a large bulblike base and smooth leaf edges, in contrast to the long taproots and hairy-edged leaves of Dotted Blazing Star.

FRANK OBERLE

FRANK OBERLE

PRAIRIE BLAZING STAR
Liatris pycnostachya
Aster family (Asteraceae)

Description: Slender, spikelike plants to 5' tall, with abundant grasslike leaves and usually hairy stems. The lowest leaves can be well over 1' long and up to ½" wide, with the stem leaves smaller and progressively reduced upward. The flower heads are in a dense spike at the top of the plant. Each small head is about ¼" wide, with an overlapping series of bracts that have hairy, outward-curving, pointed tips. There are mostly 5–10 small, 5-lobed, purple disk flowers per head, with 2 prominent threadlike style branches protruding from each flower. Forms of this plant with white flowers occasionally occur among groups of purple-flowered plants.

Bloom Season: Midsummer–early fall.

Habitat/Range: Common throughout the tallgrass region in seepage areas in upland prairies, moist prairie depressions, and mesic to dry prairies.

MARSH BLAZING STAR
Liatris spicata
Aster family (Asteraceae)

Description: Plants similar to Prairie Blazing Star, except that the stems are smooth and hairless, even on their flowering portions, and the overlapping bracts at the base of each flower head have their tips flat against the head and are often bluntly rounded. These contrast with the pointed, outward-curved bracts of Prairie Blazing Star.

Bloom Season: Midsummer–early fall.

Habitat/Range: Locally frequent in mesic to wet prairies in the eastern tallgrass region from central Illinois through the Great Lakes.

FRANK OBERLE

FRANK OBERLE

SCALY BLAZING STAR
Liatris squarrosa
Aster family (Asteraceae)

Description: Unbranched plants to about 2½' tall, with firm, pointed, grasslike leaves up to 10" long and ½" wide. The leaves are progressively smaller upward along the stem. Flower heads are about ½" wide and widely spaced along the leafy upper stems; each head has a base of overlapping pointed bracts that bend sharply outward at their tips, creating an almost spiny appearance. There are 20–40 small disk flowers in each head. The larger head at the top of the stem sometimes has more flowers. Like all the blazing stars, each purple flower has a small, 5-lobed, tubular corolla and 2 protruding, threadlike style branches.

Bloom Season: Midsummer–early fall.

Habitat/Range: Frequent in dry, often rocky prairies and upland open woods, often in acidic soils; found through the southern half of the tallgrass region.

WESTERN IRONWEED
Vernonia baldwinii
Aster family (Asteraceae)

Description: Hairy plants to 5' tall, with alternate leaves up to 7" long and 2½" wide. The leaves are broadest near the middle, toothed along the edges, and densely hairy underneath with long, crooked hairs. Flower heads are in rounded to flat-topped, branching clusters at the tops of the stems, with each flower head cupped by a series of small overlapping bracts with pointed, often spreading, tips. Each flower head is up to ½" wide, with up to 34 small, purple disk flowers. Each flower has a tiny, 5-lobed corolla and 2 threadlike style branches.

Bloom Season: Summer–fall.

Habitat/Range: Frequent in dry prairies in the southern tallgrass region from northeastern Nebraska to central Illinois and southward.

Comments: This plant is avoided by cattle, and is often abundant in pastures and old fields. There are several similar Ironweeds in the prairie region. Although Ironweeds can be very difficult to identify, only Western Ironweed has bracts on the flower heads with short, outward-pointing tips.

FRANK OBERLE

FRANK OBERLE

COMMON IRONWEED
Vernonia fasciculata
Aster family (Asteraceae)

Description: Stout plants to 4' tall with smooth, hairless stems and leaves. The leaves are alternate, finely and regularly toothed along their edges, widest at the middle and gradually tapering to narrow bases and pointed tips. The largest leaves can be 6" long and over 1" wide, but are often much narrower. There are numerous tiny pits on the underside of each leaf. Flower heads are in a dense, rounded cluster at the top of the plant. Each head is typically about ⅜" wide with 15–25 radiating, purple disk flowers. Each flower has a tiny, 5-petaled, tubular corolla and 2 protruding, threadlike style branches.

Bloom Season: Midsummer–fall.

Habitat/Range: Common in wet prairies and moist prairie depressions, often growing with Prairie Cord Grass. Distributed through most of the tallgrass region.

HAREBELL
Campanula rotundifolia
Bellflower family (Campanulaceae)

Description: Delicate plants to 20" tall, with slender, alternate leaves. The stem leaves are up to 4" long and less than ½" wide, and become grasslike on the upper part of the stem. The long-stalked basal leaves are almost round, with toothed edges and heart-shaped bases. Flowers occur at the top of the plant on slender, flexible stalks. Each flower has 5 small, narrow, green sepals and a cuplike, blue corolla about ¾" long, with 5 flaring, triangular lobes.

Bloom Season: Late spring–early fall.

Habitat/Range: Local in several habitats, including dry hill prairies over limestone, open sandy woodlands, exposed cliffs, and along streams; mostly found in the northern half of the tallgrass region.

GREAT BLUE LOBELIA
Lobelia siphilitica
Bellflower family (Campanulaceae)

Description: Plants usually no more than 3' tall, with yellowish-milky juice, mostly unbranched stems, and finely toothed alternate leaves. The leaves are up to 6" long and 1½" wide, widest near the middle and taper to pointed tips and stalkless bases. Flowers are numerous in a crowded alternate array on short individual stalks at the tops of the main stems. Each flower has a small, green calyx with 5 pointed lobes and a deep blue, 2-lipped, tubular corolla, ¾–1½" long, with pale stripes on the tube. The upper corolla lip is split into 2 erect lobes, and the lower lip is divided into 3 spreading lobes.

Bloom Season: Midsummer–fall.

Habitat/Range: Occasional throughout the tallgrass region in prairie swales and wet prairies, along streams, and in seepage areas, generally in sites with minimal competition from dense vegetation.

PALE SPIKED LOBELIA
Lobelia spicata
Bellflower family (Campanulaceae)

Description: Slender, single-stemmed plants to 3' tall, with narrow, alternate, toothed leaves up to 3½" long and 1" wide. The sap is a watery milk white. The small, pale blue flowers are alternate along the upper part of the stem. Each flower is on a short, slender stalk, with a tiny leaflike bract at the base of each flower stalk. Flowers are less than ½" long, with 5 narrow, pointed, green sepals and a 2-lipped tubular corolla with 2 narrow erect lobes above 3 larger, spreading lobes.

Bloom Season: Midspring–midsummer.

Habitat/Range: Common in moist to dry prairies throughout the tallgrass region.

KITTY KOHOUT—MORTON ARBORETUM

VENUS' LOOKING GLASS
Triodanis perfoliata
Bellflower family (Campanulaceae)

Description: Small, usually unbranched or slightly branched, annuals mostly less than 1' tall, but occasionally up to 3'. The alternate, nearly circular leaves are seldom more than 1" long, with toothed edges and bases that strongly clasp the angular stems. Flowers arise in groups of 1-3 on the stem just above the leaf bases. When more than one flower occurs at a spot, usually only one develops and opens. Each stalkless flower has a small, green, cylindrical ovary topped by 5 small, pointed, green sepals and a cup-shaped, 5-lobed, blue corolla up to ¾" wide. The ovary develops into a capsule filled with tiny seeds. The seeds are released through small holes in the sides of the capsule.

Bloom Season: Midspring–midsummer.

Habitat/Range: Common in sterile, often sandy or gravelly, soils in prairies, pastures, old fields, open woodlands, and along roadsides, often in sites with a history of previous disturbance; found through all but the extreme northwest tallgrass region, but uncommon and scattered north of Iowa.

39

FRANK OBERLE

DON KURZ

COMMON SPIDERWORT
Tradescantia ohiensis
Spiderwort family (Commelinaceae)

Description: Smooth, bluish green, spindly plants to 3' tall, with long, pointed, alternate leaves that sheath the stem at their bases. The leaves are up to 15" long and usually less than 1" wide. The individually stalked flowers are 1–1½" wide and emerge in a spidery cluster above 2 leaves at the top of the stems, with each flower composed of 3 smooth green sepals, 3 broadly rounded, blue to purple petals, and 6 yellow-tipped stamens covered with long, colored hairs.

Bloom Season: Late spring–fall.

Habitat/Range: Common in savannas and prairies ranging from dry to mesic, and in pastures and along roadsides and railroads; found in all but the northwest part of the tallgrass region.

Comments: Spiderwort flowers last for just a single day before decaying into a sticky, liquified mass.

VIRGINIA SPIDERWORT
Tradescantia virginiana
Spiderwort family (Commelinaceae)

Description: Unbranched plants up to 2' tall, with long, alternate, straplike leaves that clasp the stem at their bases. There are usually 2–5 leaves per plant, with each leaf less than 1" wide and up to 1' long. The individually stalked flowers are in a dense cluster at the top of the stem, just above two leaflike bracts. Each flower is a little more than 1" wide, with 3 small, hairy, green sepals and 3 rounded, purple petals surrounding 6 yellow-tipped stamens with purple hairs along their length.

Bloom Season: Mid–late spring.

Habitat/Range: Occasional in sandy or rocky prairies and open, rocky oak woodlands; from the eastern tallgrass region west into Missouri.

Comments: A similar species, Long-Bracted Spiderwort *(T. bracteata)* occurs from the western tallgrass region east to western Illinois and rarely eastward. The hairs on the sepals of Long-Bracted Spiderwort are glandular and somewhat sticky, while those of Virginia Spiderwort are smooth and pointed. The sepals of Common Spiderwort are smooth and hairless.

FRANK OBERLE

G. YATSKIEVYCH

LEAD PLANT
Amorpha canescens
Bean family (Fabaceae)

Description: Single-stemmed to few-branched, scarcely woody, grayish hairy shrubs to 3' tall, with alternate compound leaves. The leaves are stalked and divided into as many as 51 narrow leaflets, with each leaflet up to ¾" long and ½" wide. The small flowers are in several dense, stalked, spikelike clusters along the upper stem. Each flower has a tiny, hairy, green calyx with 5 teeth and a single ¼"-long, deep purple petal curling around the 10 protruding orange-tipped stamens.

Bloom Season: Late spring–summer.

Habitat/Range: Widely distributed and locally frequent in dry to mesic prairies and open upland savannas through most of the tallgrass region, east through northern Indiana.

Comments: Parts of the plant have been used in folk medicines, and a yellow tea can be made from the leaves. Because of its long, stringy roots, Lead Plant is also called Prairie Shoestring.

INDIGO BUSH
Amorpha fruticosa
Bean family (Fabaceae)

Description: Large, bushy shrubs sometimes more than 10' tall, but often 5–6', with alternate, compound leaves. The oval leaflets are paired along a central axis, with an additional leaflet at the tip, so there are always an odd number of leaflets, ranging from 11–31. Each leaflet is up to 2" long and just over 1" wide, with a small, bristlelike point at the rounded tip. The flowers are in dense spikes on the upper part of the plant, often with several spikes clustered together. Each flower has a single, ¼"-long, dark indigo-purple petal wrapped around 10 protruding, yellow-tipped stamens.

Bloom Season: Late spring–midsummer.

Habitat/Range: Common in moist prairie thickets and along streams and rivers in prairies throughout the tallgrass region, but sporadically distributed east of Illinois.

MORTON ARBORETUM

GROUND PLUM
Astragalus crassicarpus
Bean family (Fabaceae)

Description: Plants usually have several trailing or sprawling stems from a single root, ranging up to 2' long, but often 1' or less. The leaves are alternate, compound, and on short stalks. There are 15–27 leaflets per leaf, arranged along a central axis like the rays of a feather, with an additional leaflet at the tip. The leaflets are up to ¾" long and ⅓" wide and are often slightly folded lengthwise, with hairy undersides. The flowers are in small clusters at the ends of branches and side stalks; each flower is about ¾" long, with a small, pale green, 5-toothed calyx and a nearly tubular set of petals. The upper petal is larger and flaring at the tip, below which are 2 side petals and a lower lip. The fruits are succulent, shiny, round pods up to 1" in diameter that become dry and hard with age.

Bloom Season: Midspring–early summer.

Habitat/Range: Frequent in dry prairies in the western tallgrass region, east to Minnesota and western Missouri, often in limestone or calcium-rich soils.

Comments: The new fruits are green with a reddish cast and were extensively used as food by Native Americans and pioneers. They are very juicy, with a taste like raw peas. A subspecies with creamy white flowers, called Mexican Plum (variety *trichocalyx),* occurs in prairies and rocky open woodlands from southwestern Illinois south and westward.

FRANK OBERLE

DON KURZ

BLUE WILD INDIGO
Baptisia australis variety *minor*
Bean Family (Fabaceae)

Description: Plants to 4' tall, with smooth, hairless stems and alternate compound leaves divided into 3 rounded to oblong leaflets, each less than 2" long. The lower leaves are distinctly stalked, while the upper leaves are usually almost stalkless. The erect flowering stems extend above the leaves, with scattered, alternate, deep blue flowers. The flowers are sometimes more than 1" long, and each flower has a notched, upright, blue upper petal, below which are 2 smaller blue side petals close against the protruding, pale, keel-like lower lip. The seed pods are black, hairless, and about 2–2½" long, with a thin point at the tip.

Bloom Season: Midspring–early summer.

Habitat/Range: Occasional in rocky or clayey soil in prairies, often associated with limestone, throughout the southwestern tallgrass region, from southern Iowa and southeastern Nebraska to eastern Missouri.

Comments: This handsome plant does well in cultivation, even beyond its native range.

PURPLE PRAIRIE CLOVER
Dalea purpurea
Bean family (Fabaceae)

Description: Slender, erect plants to about 2' tall, with alternate compound leaves. Each leaf has 3-9 shiny, narrow leaflets usually less than 1" long and about ⅛" wide, with a slight fragrance when crushed. The flowers, each about ¼" long, are in dense cylindrical spikes at the tops of the stem branches. Flowers are bright purple-magenta, each with a large petal and 4 smaller petals, with 5 protruding orange stamens. The flowers at the bottom of each spike bloom first, forming a brilliant wreath that climbs the spike as flowering progresses.

Bloom Season: Late spring–summer.

Habitat/Range: Characteristic in dry to mesic prairies throughout the tallgrass region.

Comments: Intolerant of overgrazing. Like the related White Prairie Clover, this plant was used by Native Americans to brew tea.

FRANK OBERLE

CARL KURTZ

SILKY PRAIRIE CLOVER
Dalea villosa
Bean family (Fabaceae)

Description: Densely hairy plants seldom over 1'
tall, with alternate compound leaves each
composed of 9–25 leaflets. The grayish green
leaflets are less than ½" long and compactly
arranged along the leaf axis. The flowers are at
the ends of the stems in dense cylindrical heads
up to 4" long. Individual flowers are pinkish
purple to pink, or sometimes white, and less than
¼" long. Each flower has a small, 5-toothed,
green calyx, one large upper petal, 4 smaller
petals, and 5 protruding, yellow stamens.

Bloom Season: Summer.

Habitat/Range: Local in sandy prairies and
pastures, particularly in areas of loose sand with
sparse vegetation; scattered in the northwestern
tallgrass region from eastern Nebraska to
Wisconsin and northward.

SHOWY TICK TREFOIL
Desmodium canadense
Bean family (Fabaceae)

Description: Plants mostly 2–4' tall, with each
alternate, short-stalked, beanlike leaf composed
of 3 leaflets. These short-stalked leaflets are
1½–4" long and two or more times longer than
broad. Elongate clusters of bright purple flowers
occur at the ends of the branches. Each flower is
about ½" long, with a flaring, erect upper petal
and two small side petals flanking a keel-like
lower lip. The fruits are 3- to 5-segmented pods
resembling a flattened chain of beads.

Bloom Season: Mid–late summer.

Habitat/Range: Frequent throughout the tallgrass
region in moist to dry sites in prairies, pastures,
thickets, and along streams.

Comments: Several other species of tick trefoil
occur in prairies, but all have smaller flowers.
Tick trefoils are also known as Sticktights,
because the flattened, rough fruit segments cling
tenaciously to clothing, shoelaces, and hair.

K. YATSKIEVYCH

MARSH VETCHLING
Lathyrus palustris
Bean family (Fabaceae)

Description: Sprawling or low-climbing plants with angled or narrowly winged stems up to 3' long and alternate compound leaves with conspicuous stipules at the base of the leaf stalk. Each leaf has 2–3 (rarely 4) pairs of leaflets and ends in a branched tendril. The leaflets can be up to 3" long and about ¾" wide, but are often much smaller. The flowers occur in clusters of 2–8 on long stalks arising at the bases of the upper leaves. Each red-purple flower is about ½–¾" long, with an erect, fanlike upper petal, and 2 side petals flanking a keel-like lower lip. The fruits are narrow pods up to 2½" long.

Bloom Season: Late spring–summer.

Habitat/Range: Occasional in moist to wet prairies, sedge meadows, and along shores; found through the northern tallgrass region from eastern Nebraska eastward, becoming uncommon south of Iowa and central Illinois.

Comments: Veiny Pea *(L. venosus)*, a related plant, occurs in drier prairies and savannas scattered through the tallgrass region—it has 4–7 pairs of leaflets per leaf and usually 10 or more flowers per cluster.

JOHN PALIS

DON KURZ

VIOLET BUSH CLOVER
Lespedeza violacea
Bean family (Fabaceae)

Description: Thin-stemmed, bushy-branched plants seldom more than 18" tall, with stalked, alternate, compound leaves. Each leaf is divided into 3 oval leaflets, each about 1–1½" long and half as wide. The individually stalked flowers are in sparse clusters at the ends of slender branches. Each flower is less than ¼" wide, with 5 small, pointed calyx lobes and a purple corolla. The corolla has a flaring upper petal, 2 smaller side petals, and a lower lip. The fruits are small, flattened, single-seeded pods up to ¼" long.

Bloom Season: Mid–late summer.

Habitat/Range: Occasional in dry rocky prairies and open woodlands in the southern tallgrass region, from southeastern Nebraska eastward.

SLENDER BUSH CLOVER
Lespedeza virginica
Bean family (Fabaceae)

Description: Slender-stemmed, hairy, upward-branching plants to 3' tall. The alternate compound leaves are divided into 3 narrow leaflets, each of which is less than ¼" wide and usually less than 1½" long. The leaves are on stalks up to 1" long. The flowers are in dense clusters among the leaves on the upper stems. Each purple flower is about ¼" long, with a spreading upper petal and 2 smaller side petals along a protruding lower lip.

Bloom Season: Late spring–early fall.

Habitat/Range: Common in dry to mesic sites in prairies and open savannas through the southern half of the tallgrass region.

Comments: An extremely rare relative, the federally listed threatened Prairie Bush Clover *(L. leptostachya)*, occurs in well-drained prairies in Illinois, Iowa, Minnesota, and Wisconsin. Prairie Bush Clover plants have a silver cast, with widely spaced, slender leaflets and open clusters of pale pink to creamy white flowers that bloom in midsummer. Slender Bush Clover plants are green, with closely spaced leaves and dense clusters of purple flowers.

WILD LUPINE
Lupinus perennis
Bean family (Fabaceae)

Description: Hairy-stemmed plants to 2' tall, with alternate, stalked, compound leaves and elongate flower clusters at the tops of the stems. Each leaf has 7–11 smooth-edged leaflets radiating from a common point, with each leaflet up to 2" long but less than ½" wide. Each individually stalked blue flower is about ½" long, with an erect, fanlike upper petal and a protruding lower lip flanked by 2 side petals. The fruits are small, hairy pods up to 2" long.

Bloom Season: Midspring–midsummer.

Habitat/Range: Locally common in sandy open woodlands with other prairie plants, sometimes in sterile sand prairies. Found in the northeastern tallgrass region from northern Illinois and Minnesota eastward.

Comments: The federally listed endangered Karner Blue butterfly is dependent on this plant as a larval food source.

SAMPSON'S SNAKEROOT
Orbexilum pedunculatum
Bean family (Fabaceae)

Description: Erect or sprawling plants with stems to 3' long with alternate compound leaves. The leaves are stalked, with each leaf divided into 3 individually stalked leaflets up to 3" long and ¾" wide. Flowers are in elongate clusters at the tops of stalks arising at the bases of main stem leaves. The individual flowers are about ¼" long, with a fanlike upper petal and 2 smaller side petals flanking a keel-like lower lip. The fruits are hairy, flat pods less than ¼" long, with wrinkled surfaces.

Bloom Season: Midspring–midsummer.

Habitat/Range: Common in dry, acidic sites in upland prairies and open woodlands in the southern tallgrass region, from southeastern Kansas east through southern Illinois to Ohio.

CARL KURTZ

PURPLE LOCOWEED
Oxytropis lambertii
Bean family (Fabaceae)

Description: Low, gray-hairy plants usually less than 8" tall, with compound leaves. The stem of each plant is reduced to a small crown at ground level, so that the plant appears stemless. The leaves have about 7–19 widely separated, narrow leaflets, each usually less than ⅛" wide and seldom more than 1" long. Flowers are in a dense cluster on a leafless stalk extending above the leaves. Each flower is about ¾" long, with a hairy, rounded, green calyx with 5 narrow lobes and a purple (sometimes pale yellowish) corolla with a hooded to spreading, notched upper petal and two side petals flanking a pointed, keel-like lower lip. The fruits are smooth, round, tapering pods less than 1" long.

Bloom Season: Late spring–midsummer.

Habitat/Range: Locally frequent in dry, often rocky or gravelly, prairies in the northwestern tallgrass region from northwestern Missouri north and westward.

Comments: Unlike Ground Plum, Purple Locoweed lacks a well-developed, leafy stem, and the lower lip of the flower has a distinctly pointed tip. Locoweeds accumulate selenium from the soil; this toxic mineral causes bizarre behavior and even death when eaten in sufficient quantities. It is usually avoided by livestock, but in overgrazed sites animals may become addicted to it.

SILVERY SCURF PEA
Pediomelum argophyllum
Bean family (Fabaceae)

Description: Bushy-branched plants to 3' tall. The stems and leaves are densely covered with white hairs, creating a silvery-whitened appearance. The leaves are alternate, stalked, and compound, with each leaf consisting of 3–5 narrow to oval, pointed leaflets up to 2" long and ¾" wide and radiating from a single point. The flowers are in open spikes along the tops of the branches, with 2-8 flowers and 1–5 narrow, hairy bracts at each point along the spike. Each deep blue flower is less than ¼" wide, with a flaring upper petal and 2 side petals flanking a pro-truding lower lip. The flowers gradually fade to yellowish or brownish.

Bloom Season: Summer.

Habitat/Range: Frequent in dry, often rocky prairies in the western tallgrass region, becoming rare eastward to Wisconsin, Iowa, and Missouri.

Comments: Silvery Scurf Pea was used by Native Americans to treat wounds and fevers and was thought by pioneers to be a remedy for snakebite.

PRAIRIE TURNIP
Pediomelum esculentum
Bean family (Fabaceae)

Description: Plants with large, tuberous roots and branched flowering stems to about 1½' tall. The stem is covered with long, spreading, white hairs. The leaves are alternate and compound, with each leaf on a hairy stalk up to 3½" long. Each leaf is divided into 5 narrow, hairy leaflets arranged like the fingers on a hand, with each leaflet up to 2" long. Cylindrical flower clusters occur at the ends of stem branches, with each dark bluish flower about ½" long, including an erect, fanlike upper petal and two smaller side petals flanking a keel-like lower lip. The flowers become pale with age. The fruits are small, beanlike pods covered with silky hairs.

Bloom Season: Late spring–midsummer.

Habitat/Range: Occasional in dry, often rocky, prairies in the western half of the tallgrass region east to Wisconsin.

Comments: This plant is known by many common names, including Prairie Apple, Indian Breadfruit, and Pomme de Prairie. The large, starchy root was a favored food among Native Americans and was also used by pioneers. Roots were eaten raw, boiled, roasted, or pounded into meal and mixed with other foods. They are said to taste like turnips.

FRANK OBERLE

SCURFY PEA
Psoralidium tenuiflorum
Bean family (Fabaceae)

Description: Open, bushy plants to about 3' tall, with widely spaced, alternate, stalked leaves, each divided into 3–5 narrow, rounded leaflets. The leaflets radiate from a common point, and are each up to 2" long and less than ½" wide. Flowers are in elongate clusters on small branches arising where the leaf stalks join the stems. Each flower has a 5-toothed, hairy, green calyx and a blue corolla up to ⅓" long, with a slightly flaring, hooded upper petal and 2 similar side petals flanking a keel-like lip.

Bloom Season: Late spring–midsummer; also in fall.

Habitat/Range: Occasional in dry to mesic prairies from western Indiana through the Illinois River basin into Missouri and Iowa, and westward.

JOHN TAFT

FRANK OBERLE

CLOSED GENTIAN
Gentiana andrewsii
Gentian family (Gentianaceae)

Description: Plants to 2½' tall, typically with unbranched stems and stalkless opposite leaves, with the upper leaves usually the largest. The leaves are up to 5" long and 1½" wide, with pointed tips and several parallel veins along their lengths. Flowers occur in 1-3 clusters at the tops of the stems, with a whorl of leaves and small leaflike bracts under each cluster. Each stalkless flower is deep blue, 1–1½" long, and closed even at maturity, appearing like a large blue flower bud with a tiny opening at the tip.

Bloom Season: Late summer–fall.

Habitat/Range: Scattered and local through most of the tallgrass region in mesic to moist prairies, seepage areas, and fens.

Comments: The roots of this and other gentians have been used medicinally and to flavor beverages. This plant is also called Bottle Gentian.

DOWNY GENTIAN
Gentiana puberulenta
Gentian family (Gentianaceae)

Description: Usually unbranched stems less than 20" tall, with shiny, smooth, pointed, opposite leaves. The leaves are stalkless with rounded bases, usually broadest just below the middle, up to 2" long and nearly 1" wide, with a prominent vein along the middle. Flowers are stalked or stalkless, usually in a cluster at the top of the plant, sometimes with additional flowers arising from the bases of the upper leaves. Each deeply cup-shaped flower is up to 1½" broad, deep blue, and often marked with white and pale green lines within, and has 5 pointed, spreading lobes alternating with small fringed segments.

Bloom Season: Late summer–fall.

Habitat/Range: Locally frequent through most of the tallgrass region in mesic to dry upland prairies and open savannas.

Comments: The flowers of Downy Gentian are one of the last to appear on the prairie and often survive hard frosts.

FRANK OBERLE

FRANK OBERLE

STIFF GENTIAN
Gentianella quinquefolia
Gentian family (Gentianaceae)

Description: Annual plants usually less than 1' tall, with stalkless opposite leaves and numerous erect branches. The leaves are up to 2½" long, widest near the bases and tapering to pointed tips, with several parallel veins along their lengths. Several upright flowers are clustered at the tips of the upper branches. Each flower is up to 1" long, with a small, green, 5-lobed calyx and a tubular blue corolla with 5 teeth at the nearly closed mouth.

Bloom Season: Late summer–fall.

Habitat/Range: Infrequent in moist to dry prairies with limestone, calcium-rich soil, or seepage of mineralized ground water; scattered through the eastern tallgrass region west to Minnesota and Missouri.

FRINGED GENTIAN
Gentianopsis crinita
Gentian family (Gentianaceae)

Description: Annual or biennial plants usually less than 2' tall, with opposite, stalkless leaves that clasp the stem at their rounded bases. Each leaf is up to 3" long and 1" wide, with a prominent central vein and pointed tip. Flowers are on long individual stalks near the top of the plant. Each deep blue flower is about 1" wide, with a cuplike green calyx with 4 triangular lobes and a corolla with 4 broadly rounded, spreading lobes that are finely fringed along the edges.

Bloom Season: Late summer–fall.

Habitat/Range: Uncommon and local in high-quality wet sites, including prairie swales and along streams, often in calcium-rich waters; found in the northern tallgrass region from North Dakota and southwestern Michigan east into Ohio.

FRANK OBERLE

FRANK OBERLE

BLUE FLAG
Iris virginica variety *shrevei*
Iris family (Iridaceae)

Description: This iris typically forms large colonies with stiff, pale green, swordlike leaves that taper to pointed tips. The flower stems are up to 3' tall, often with 1 or 2 branches. The flowers occur on short stalks along the tops of the stems. Each flower is up to 3½" wide, and usually deep blue-violet, with yellow and white markings. What appear to be 6 petals are actually 3 downward-curving sepals, each with a hairy, yellowish central line near the base, and 3 shorter erect petals, with pale streaks along their narrow bases. There are 3 stamens and 3 petal-like style branches within the flower. The fruits are roundly 3-angled capsules up to 3½" long.

Bloom Season: Late spring–midsummer.

Habitat/Range: Locally frequent throughout the tallgrass region in marshes and wet prairies where water levels are relatively stable.

Comments: The roots are poisonous to humans, but have been used in small amounts in folk medicines.

PRAIRIE IRIS
Nemastylis geminiflora
Iris family (Iridaceae)

Description: Plants growing from bulbs, with 2-4 alternate, narrow, sword-shaped main stem leaves up to 1' long and less than ½" wide. The flowers emerge in groups of 1-3 from paired sheathing bracts at the top of short stalks. Each flower is 1½–2½" wide, with 6 spreading, lavender blue, petal-like segments (actually 3 petals and 3 similar sepals) that are widest near the middle and taper to pointed tips and narrow bases. The bases of the flower parts are white. A 6-branched style and 3 orange stamens are in the center of the flower. The flowers open in late morning and close by early afternoon.

Bloom Season: Mid–late spring.

Habitat/Range: Uncommon in dry to moist prairies, usually over limestone, from southeastern Kansas and southern Missouri south to Oklahoma and Arkansas.

ROBERT TATINA

PRAIRIE BLUE-EYED GRASS
Sisyrinchium campestre
Iris family (Iridaceae)

Description: Light green plants mostly less than 1' tall, with pointed, erect, grasslike leaves. The flower stems are narrow, flattened, less than ⅛" wide, and longer than the leaves. There are several flowers on delicate individual stalks emerging from 2 overlapping, long-pointed, leaflike bracts at the top of the stem. Each light to dark blue flower is about ½" wide, with 3 petals and 3 sepals, all similar, giving the appearance of 6 petals. The sepals and petals are sometimes shallowly notched at the tips, with hairlike points, and are yellowish at the base.

There are 3 yellow- or orange-tipped stamens joined together in the center of the flower.

Bloom Season: Midspring–early summer.

Habitat/Range: Frequent in dry upland prairies and well-drained prairie slopes through most of the tallgrass region, east to eastern Illinois.

Comments: Eastern Blue-Eyed Grass *(S. albidum)* occurs from the eastern tallgrass region west into Missouri; it has 3–4 bracts surrounding the flower cluster at the top of the stem.

MORTON ARBORETUM

FRANK OBERLE

FALSE PENNYROYAL
Isanthus brachiatus
Mint family (Lamiaceae)

Description: Low, branching, opposite-leaved, aromatic annual plants less than 18" tall and finely hairy at least in the upper half. The leaves are up to 2" long and ¾" wide, broadest near the middle and tapering to pointed tips and short stalks. Each leaf has 3 parallel veins along its length. Flowers are on individual stalks up to ⅝" long, with 1–3 flowers per cluster at the bases of the upper stem leaves. Each flower is less than ¼" wide, with 5 tiny, green, pointed calyx lobes, 5 tiny, blue corolla lobes, 4 protruding purple stamens, and a slender style that is split at the tip.

Bloom Season: Midsummer–early fall.

Habitat/Range: Associated with limestone in dry, rocky prairies, upland pastures, and areas of sparse vegetation and shallow soil; found through the tallgrass region north and west to eastern South Dakota and southwestern Minnesota.

WILD BERGAMOT
Monarda fistulosa
Mint family (Lamiaceae)

Description: Fragrant mints with branching, square stems to 5' tall, with the upper stems usually finely hairy. The leaves are opposite, up to 5" long and 2" wide, sharply toothed, broadest near the base and tapering to long pointed tips, and on stalks about ½–1" long. Flowers are in dense, rounded heads at the tops of the stems, with each head surrounded by a whorl of pale, leafy bracts. The calyx is a narrow tube less than ½" long, with 5 spiny points and numerous white hairs at the mouth. The tubular, lavender corolla has 2 long lips at the summit, the upper of which is narrow and hairy and the lower 3-lobed. Two threadlike stamens and the style protrude below the upper lip.

Bloom Season: Late spring–early fall.

Habitat/Range: Common throughout the tallgrass region in prairie thickets, pastures, old fields, and occasionally in open dry prairies.

FRANK OBERLE

DON KURZ

BLUE SAGE
Salvia azurea
Mint family (Lamiaceae)

Description: Plants with hairy, angular, 4-cornered stems to 5' tall, unbranched or with a few branches. The leaves are widely spaced along the stem, opposite, narrow, and usually toothed, with the largest leaves up to 4½" long and 1" wide. The leaves have a riblike pattern of raised veins on the undersides. The flowers are in an elongated series of whorls along the upper stems, with up to 8 flowers per whorl. Each flower has a small green calyx with 3 triangular teeth, and a blue, tubular corolla up to 1" long, ending in a broadly flaring, lobed lower lip and a narrow, hairy, hooded upper lip containing the 2 stamens.

Bloom Season: Summer–fall.

Habitat/Range: Common in dry prairies and pastures, often in rocky or sandy soils, in the southwestern tallgrass region. Found from southeastern Nebraska through western Missouri and southward, occurring farther east as an escape from cultivation.

SMALL SKULLCAP
Scutellaria parvula
Mint family (Lamiaceae)

Description: Small, square-stemmed plants usually less than 8" tall, with stalkless, opposite leaves. The leaves are less than 1" long and mostly less than ½" wide, with rounded bases and bluntly triangular tips. The middle and lower leaves usually have a few shallow teeth along the edges. The small flowers occur on short, individual stalks paired at the bases of the stem leaves on the upper half of the plant. Each flower is about ⅓" long, with a tubular blue corolla that ends in a hooded upper lip and a weakly lobed lower lip with dark purple spots. The calyx has a prominent crest on the upper side.

Bloom Season: Midspring–midsummer.

Habitat/Range: Common throughout the tallgrass region, in upland prairies, pastures, and open woodlands, often in rocky or sandy sites.

FRANK OBERLE

FRANK OBERLE

WOUNDWORT
Stachys palustris
Mint family (Lamiaceae)

Description: Mostly unbranched plants to 3' tall with square, hairy stems and opposite leaves. The leaves are up to 5" long and 2" wide and stalkless or nearly so, with toothed edges; they have broadly rounded bases and taper to pointed tips. Flowers occur in several whorls at the top of the stem. Each whorl is typically 6-flowered, with several small leaves just below the flowers. Each flower is about ½" long, with a 5-toothed, hairy, green calyx and a tubular, mottled, pinkish purple corolla with 2 lips. The upper lip is hooded and 2-lobed, while the broader lower lip is 3-lobed.

Bloom Season: Summer.

Habitat/Range: Occasional in wet prairies and along exposed shores and streams, primarily in the northern half of the tallgrass region from northeastern Kansas eastward.

Comments: The large middle lobe of the lower lip serves as a landing pad for pollinating insects. This plant was formerly used in folk medicine to heal wounds. The tubers are reportedly edible.

GERMANDER
Teucrium canadense
Mint family (Lamiaceae)

Description: Finely hairy, usually unbranched plants to 4' tall, with square stems. The leaves are stalked, opposite, widest near the broadly rounded bases, coarsely toothed along the edges, and up to 6" long by 2½" wide with pointed tips and strongly raised veins on their undersides. Tiny shoots with reduced leaves often arise just above the bases of the main stem leaves. Flowers are in an elongate cluster at the top of the plant, with each flower on a ⅛"-long stalk just above a tiny, pointed bract. Each flower has a hairy, 5-toothed calyx about ¼" long, and a lavender to pinkish corolla about ¾" long with 2 small, erect projections on top and a lower lip with a larger bottom lobe and 2 small side lobes.

Bloom Season: Late spring–late summer.

Habitat/Range: Common throughout the tallgrass region in moist soil in wet prairies, thickets, along streams, low areas in pastures, and low disturbed open ground.

57

FRANK OBERLE

JOHN TAFT

WILD HYACINTH
Camassia scilloides
Lily family (Liliaceae)

Description: Spring-flowering bulbs with long, strap-shaped basal leaves, which are often folded along their lengths, and leafless stems typically about 1' tall. The leaves are usually less than ½" wide and may be more than 1' long. The individually stalked flowers are clustered along the upper stem, with each flower appearing to have 6 blue to lavender petals (actually 3 petals and 3 sepals) that taper to delicate, narrow bases, and 6 yellow-tipped stamens surrounding a green ovary with a single slender style. The flowers are up to 1" wide, with the lowest flowers blooming first. The fruits are rounded, triangular capsules about ¼–⅜" tall, with shiny black seeds.

Bloom Season: Spring.

Habitat/Range: Common in mesic and dry prairies, open rocky slopes, glades, and open woodlands through the eastern tallgrass region, north and west to Wisconsin, Iowa, and eastern Kansas.

Comments: A closely related species, Prairie Hyacinth *(C. angusta)*, occurs in prairies from Oklahoma to Indiana. It has taller stems with 5 or more bracts, and flowers in late spring to early summer. Wild Hyacinth typically has up to 3 bracts on a stem.

WINGED LOOSESTRIFE
Lythrum alatum
Loosestrife family (Lythraceae)

Description: Smooth, hairless plants to 2' tall, with squarish stems. The leaves are usually opposite on the lower stem and alternate above, shiny green on the upper surface, up to 2" long, broadly rounded at the base, and tapering to pointed tips. Leaves on the upper stems are much smaller. The flowers are about ½" wide and solitary on short stalks at the bases of the upper leaves. Each flower has a narrow, greenish tube with 6 purple petals. Some flowers have a protruding style, some have 6 protruding stamens, and some have all the parts inside the corolla tube.

Bloom Season: Late spring–late summer.

Habitat/Range: Frequent in marshes, seepage areas, wet swales, and along streams in upland prairies, as well as in wet prairies and wet pastures, often in sandy soils; throughout the tallgrass region except for the northwestern corner.

Comments: This is a native prairie plant, and should not be confused with the introduced Purple Loosestrife *(L. salicaria)*—a taller, usually hairy plant with almost all of the leaves opposite or whorled and showy spikes of purple flowers at the tops of the stems. Purple Loosestrife is an aggressive weed of wetlands.

FRANK OBERLE

FRANK OBERLE

FRINGED POPPY MALLOW
Callirhoe digitata
Mallow family (Malvaceae)

Description: Spindly plants to 3' tall, smooth to slightly hairy, often with a pale bluish coating on the stems. The leaves are alternate, stalked, and divided into 5–7 very narrow lobes arranged like the fingers on a hand. Each lobe may be further lobed or divided and is usually less than ¼" wide. Flowers are on long individual stalks at the top of the plant; each flower is up to 2" wide, with 5 bright magenta petals with ragged outer edges surrounding a central column containing the stamens and style branches.

Bloom Season: Midspring–late summer.

Habitat/Range: Locally common in upland prairies in the southwestern tallgrass region, from southwestern Missouri and southeastern Kansas south into Arkansas and Oklahoma.

PURPLE POPPY MALLOW
Callirhoe involucrata
Mallow family (Malvaceae)

Description: Low plants with hairy stems trailing along the ground and growing up to 3' long. The long-stalked leaves are about 3" long and deeply divided into 3–5 lobes arranged like the fingers on a hand, with each lobe further lobed or toothed. There are large, rounded stipules at the base of each leaf stalk. The flowers are on long stalks arising from the junction of the stem and a leaf stalk. Each cup-shaped flower is deep reddish purple and about 2–2½" wide, with 5 large petals tapering to narrow pale bases surrounding a central columnlike structure containing the stamens and style branches.

Bloom Season: Midspring–midsummer.

Habitat/Range: Dry, open soil in prairies, especially in sandy areas, from southwestern Minnesota south and west, and occasional as an introduced weed eastward.

Comments: The roots have been used as a food source.

ROBERT TATINA

MORTON ARBORETUM

WILD FOUR O'CLOCK
Mirabilis nyctaginea
Four O'Clock family (Nyctaginaceae)

Description: Plants with branching, angular stems 2–4' tall, with widely spaced pairs of stalked, opposite leaves. The broad, triangular leaves are up to 4" long with pointed tips and usually heart-shaped bases. The stem is usually slightly swollen where the leaves are attached. Flowers are on hairy stalks in open, branched clusters near the tops of the stems. At the end of each flower stalk is a broadly 5-lobed, green to purplish, calyx-like bract surrounding 2-5 flowers. Each flower is less than ½" wide, with no petals and a pink, 5-lobed, corolla-like calyx and 3–5 protruding, yellow-tipped stamens. The flowers open in late afternoon.

Bloom Season: Late spring–early fall.

Habitat/Range: A common, weedy species in disturbed open ground, especially in sandy soils, also in pastures, old fields, and upland prairies; found throughout the tallgrass region, but probably introduced in all but the western parts.

PINK MILKWORT
Polygala incarnata
Milkwort family (Polygalaceae)

Description: Slender annuals with a distinctive bluish green cast, usually growing less than 1' tall, but occasionally up to 2'. The tiny, alternate leaves are extremely narrow, less than ½" long, and widely spaced along the stem. Flowers are in dense, cylindrical clusters at the tops of the stems. Each pinkish purple to magenta flower is about ⅛" wide and ¼" long, with 3 tiny green sepals, 2 larger petal-like sepals, and 3 petals united into a tube that flares into 6 lobes that are themselves fringed and cleft.

Bloom Season: Midspring–fall.

Habitat/Range: Occasional in dry upland prairies and savannas, less common in moist prairies, from eastern Kansas, Iowa, and Wisconsin eastward.

FRANK OBERLE

PRAIRIE LARKSPUR
Delphinium carolinianum
Buttercup family (Ranunculaceae)

Description: Finely hairy plants to 3½' tall, with stalked alternate leaves mostly on the lower half of the stem. The basal and lower stem leaves are divided into 3–7 segments arranged like the fingers on a hand, and these are toothed or further divided once or twice more. The upper stems usually have a few smaller, stalkless leaves. The individually stalked flowers are arranged alternately along the upper stem, with each irregularly cornucopia-shaped flower about 1" long and consisting of 5 white to deep blue, petal-like sepals, with the upper sepal curved back and upward in a long, tubular spur, and 4 smaller white to pale bluish petals, the lower 2 of which are each split into 2 hairy lobes.

Bloom Season: Late spring–early summer.

Habitat/Range: Frequent in dry upland prairies and prairie pastures; found in the western tallgrass region, sporadically eastward to western Illinois.

Comments: Most prairie plants are subspecies *virescens,* with pale flowers, scaly seeds, and persistent basal leaves. Plants with blue flowers, papery-winged seeds, and with most of the basal leaves withered by flowering time are subspecies *carolinanum;* they occur from Arkansas and eastern Kansas sporadically eastward.

FRANK OBERLE

PASQUE FLOWER
Pulsatilla patens
Buttercup family (Ranunculaceae)

Description: These are one of the first and most spectacular prairie flowers of spring. Shortly after the winter snows melt, low, delicate stems covered with soft, spreading hairs emerge from the ground, and leaves and flowers unfold soon after. The long-stemmed basal leaves are deeply divided into several narrow, lobed and toothed, segments originating from a common point. The whorl of leaves below the flower is similar to the basal leaves, but stalkless and smaller. The single flower on each stem has 5–8 showy, pale lavender to purple, petal-like sepals, each up to 1½" long and covered on the outer surface with long, soft hairs. The flattened, seedlike fruits are tipped with a plume of feathery hairs up to 1½" long, giving the seed head a smoky appearance.

Bloom Season: Early–midspring.

Habitat/Range: Occasional in dry, rocky, or gravelly sites in the northern tallgrass region, south to central Iowa and northern Illinois; found mostly on hill prairies in the eastern region.

Comments: The plant was used medicinally by Native Americans, although the juice is reported to cause blistering.

FRANK OBERLE

SMALL BLUETS
Houstonia pusilla
Madder family (Rubiaceae)

Description: Tiny annual plants usually less than 4" tall, typically with several stems from a cluster of small basal leaves. Each stem has a few pairs of small opposite leaves that are widest near the middle and less than ½" long. The stems typically branch once near the middle, with a single flower on each branch. The flowers are about ¼" wide. Each flower has a small, green calyx with 4 pointed lobes and a tubular corolla with 4 white to bluish purple lobes and a reddish purple center. There are 4 short stamens within the tube.

Bloom Season: Late winter–midspring.

Habitat/Range: Common in open, sandy soils of prairies, pastures, hay meadows, and old fields in the southern half of the tallgrass region, north sporadically into northern Illinois.

BLUETS
Houstonia caerulea
Madder family (Rubiaceae)

Description: Delicate, smooth, annuals up to 6" tall and often branched at the base. The small, opposite leaves are up to ½" long, with several leaves in a rosette at the base of the plant, and a pair of leaves below the middle of the stem. The few leaves above the middle of the stem are typically much smaller than the lower leaves. Flowers are single at the ends of the upright branches, with each flower about ½" wide. The flowers have 4 narrow, pointed, green sepals and a tubular corolla flaring at the top into 4 sky blue lobes with a yellow center.

Bloom Season: Midspring–midsummer.

Habitat/Range: Occasional, sometimes locally abundant, in moist to dry, sandy prairies with sparse vegetation from Arkansas to Wisconsin and eastward.

EARED FALSE FOXGLOVE
Agalinis auriculata
Snapdragon family (Scrophulariaceae)

Description: Rough-hairy, unbranched to slightly branched, partially parasitic annuals typically up to 2' tall, with stalkless, opposite leaves. The leaves are up to 2" long and ¾" wide, broadest near the base and pointed at the tip, with many of the upper leaves having 1 or 2 small, outward-pointing lobes near their rounded bases. The flowers are stalkless and single at the bases of the upper stem leaves. Each flower is up to 1" wide, with a 5-lobed, green, hairy calyx more than ½" long, a cuplike purple corolla with 5 flaring lobes and dark purple spots inside, and 4 stamens and a style slightly protruding from the top of the flower.

Bloom Season: Mid–late summer.

Habitat/Range: Rare and local in dry to moist prairies at scattered locations in the tallgrass region, from Minnesota south and eastward.

FRANK OBERLE

DON KURZ

FASCICLED FALSE FOXGLOVE
Agalinis fasciculata
Snapdragon family (Scrophulariaceae)

Description: Stems angular and rough to the touch, 2–3' tall, with numerous short side branches. The leaves are up to 1½" long and less than ⅛" wide, with a prominent vein along the middle. There are usually clusters of smaller leaves where some of the main leaves join the stem. Flowers are on very short individual stalks at the bases of leaves or tips of the stem branches. Each flower stalk is shorter than the 5-toothed green calyx. The flower has a showy, pinkish purple corolla up to 1" wide, with 5 broad, fuzzy-fringed lobes and a flaring, tubular base. The upper 2 lobes are slightly smaller than the 3 lower lobes. The upper part of the flower tube is hairy within, while the lower half is pale and purple spotted. A pale stigma lies against the upper flower tube and protrudes slightly.

Bloom Season: Late summer–fall.

Habitat/Range: Frequent in somewhat dry to mesic prairies in the southwestern tallgrass region from southeastern Kansas to southern Illinois and southward.

SLENDER FALSE FOXGLOVE
Agalinis tenuifolia
Snapdragon family (Scrophulariaceae)

Description: Annual plants usually less than 2' tall with abundant opposite branches and narrow ridges along the main stem. The leaves are very narrow, up to 3" long but often less than ⅛" wide and smooth-edged. Each leaf has a prominent raised middle vein along the length of its underside. The upper leaves are smaller and often have small clusters of tiny leaves where each leaf joins the stem. Flowers are usually numerous and on individual stalks about ½" long. Each flower has a green, 5-toothed calyx with an obliquely funnel-shaped, 5-lobed, purple corolla about ¾" wide. There are 4 hairy stamens of unequal lengths inside the flower. The fruits are shiny round capsules.

Bloom Season: Midsummer–fall.

Habitat/Range: Occasional throughout the tallgrass region in moist to dry prairies, moist sandy areas, wet thickets, along streams, and in woodlands.

Comments: This species is partially parasitic on the roots of other flowering plants.

JOHN TAFT

BLUE HEARTS
Buchnera americana
Snapdragon family (Scrophulariaceae)

Description: Single-stemmed, grayish green plants to 3' tall, with conspicuous spreading hairs. The leaves are stalkless, opposite, and progressively smaller along the stem, with a few large, coarse teeth along their edges and 3 distinct veins radiating upward from the base. At the top of the stem is a dense spike of paired, opposite flower buds, each directly above a small leaflike bract. As the flowers bloom, starting at the bottom of the spike, the flower stalk elongates. Each deep purple flower is about ⅝" wide with 5 petals that are united in their lower portions into a tube about ½" long.

Bloom Season: Summer–early fall.

Habitat/Range: Local in dry to moist prairies and open savannas from eastern Kansas and northeastern Oklahoma through southern Missouri into western Illinois, and rarely in prairies eastward around the Great Lakes.

Comments: Partially parasitic, Blue Hearts live on the roots of other plants. The plants turn black when dried.

BILL SUMMERS

BLUE TOADFLAX
Nuttallanthus canadensis
Snapdragon family (Scrophulariaceae)

Description: Smooth-stemmed, slender annual plants to 18" tall, often with several small creeping leafy shoots at the base. The narrow leaves are seldom more than 1" long and always less than ⅛" wide. The main stem leaves are alternate, but the leaves of the basal shoots are smaller and opposite or in threes. Flowers occur on short individual stalks in an elongate cluster along the top of the stem, and are up to ½" long. Each flower has a small green calyx with 5 pointed teeth, and a light blue, 2-lipped, tubular corolla with a narrow, reflexed spur. The upper corolla lip is erect and 2-lobed, and the lower lip is spreading and 3-lobed.

Bloom Season: Spring–summer.

Habitat/Range: Frequent in well-drained, open, sandy areas, including sandy prairies, old fields, and pastures; found throughout the tallgrass region, but uncommon in the northern half.

Comments: A form with larger flowers up to nearly 1" is sometimes separated as a different species, Southern Blue Toadflax *(N. texanus)*. Southern Blue Toadflax is more common in the western tallgrass region and has bumpy seeds, as opposed to the ridged seeds of Blue Toadflax.

FRANK OBERLE

SHOWY BEARD TONGUE
Penstemon cobaea
Snapdragon family (Scrophulariaceae)

Description: Finely hairy plants to 3' tall, with opposite leaves. The largest leaves near the base of the stem are up to 8" long and 3" wide, with strongly to weakly toothed edges, broad bases, and somewhat pointed tips. The upper stem leaves are smaller and tend to clasp the stem. Flowers are on short individual stalks in a series of 4- to 12-flowered groups along the tops of the stems, with a pair of reduced leaves below each group. Each flower has a 5-lobed, green calyx about ½" long and a large, inflated, tubular corolla up to 2¼" long. The corolla flares at the end into 2 upper lobes and 3 lower lobes. The flowers are sticky-hairy on the outside and range from deep purple to pale lavender with purple lines inside.

Bloom Season: Midspring–early summer.

Habitat/Range: Occasional in well-drained prairies, especially in areas with limestone, in the southwestern tallgrass region from southeastern Nebraska and western Missouri southward.

Comments: The form with deep purple flowers, pictured here, is restricted to rocky open glades in southwestern Missouri and adjacent Arkansas. Populations of this plant in the prairies west of Missouri have white to pale lavender flowers. This showy plant sometimes escapes from cultivation outside its native range.

FRANK OBERLE

DON KURZ

LARGE-FLOWERED BEARD TONGUE
Penstemon grandiflorus
Snapdragon family (Scrophulariaceae)

Description: Smooth, stout plants to 3½' tall, with a distinctive bluish green color. The broadly rounded opposite leaves are thick, waxy, stiff, and up to 4" long and 2" wide, with somewhat clasping bases. Flowers are on short, individual stalks in several groups of 2-6 at the tops of the stems, with each group just above a pair of small leaves. The purple, tubular, hairless flowers are about 2" long and flare at their ends into 2 upper lobes and 3 lower lobes.

Bloom Season: Midspring–midsummer.

Habitat/Range: Locally common in upland prairies, often in sandy sites, in the Great Plains and western tallgrass region, ranging east to northwestern Missouri and rarely eastward. This plant is cultivated and sometimes escapes into rocky or sandy waste ground.

Comments: Native Americans prepared a toothache remedy from this plant.

PALE BEARD TONGUE
Penstemon pallidus
Snapdragon family (Scrophulariaceae)

Description: Hairy-stemmed plants to 3' tall, but often 2' or less, typically with several unbranched stems from the same point. The velvety-hairy, stalkless stem leaves are opposite, usually somewhat toothed, widest near the bases and tapering to pointed tips, and up to 4" long and 1" wide. Flowers are in stalked clusters along the top of the stem, with 2 small leaflike bracts at the base of each cluster. Each tubular flower is about 1" long, with a small, 5-toothed, green calyx, and a tubular corolla flaring at the end into a 2-lobed upper lip and a 3-lobed lower lip. The flowers are usually white and marked with lavender lines. At the mouth of the flower is a sterile stamen with bright yellow hairs.

Bloom Season: Midspring–midsummer.

Habitat/Range: Common in dry, often rocky, upland prairies and open woodlands from eastern Oklahoma, Missouri, and Iowa eastward.

FRANK OBERLE

FRANK OBERLE

BLUE VERVAIN
Verbena hastata
Vervain family (Verbenaceae)

Description: Narrow plants to 6' tall with erect branches and opposite leaves. The leaves are stalked, pointed, coarsely toothed, and up to 7" long and 2" wide. The larger leaves often have 2 small, toothed lobes at their bases. Many erect spikes of small, blue flowers occur in a loose cluster near the top of each plant. Each flower is less than ¼" wide, with a tiny, 5-toothed, green calyx and a 5-lobed, blue to pink or purple corolla.

Bloom Season: Summer–fall.

Habitat/Range: Very common in open wet areas, including wet prairies, low pastures, shores, marshes, low muddy depressions, and streambanks; found throughout the tallgrass region, but becoming uncommon at the southern edge.

Comments: The plants have been used in a variety of folk medicines.

HOARY VERVAIN
Verbena stricta
Vervain family (Verbenaceae)

Description: Plants to 4' tall, unbranched or branched in the upper half, with spreading hairs on the stems. The leaves are gray-hairy, broadly rounded, toothed along the edges, mostly stalkless, and up to 4" long and 2½" wide. Flowers occur in one to several erect, narrow spikes at the top of the plant. Each purple flower is about ¼" wide, with a small, hairy, 5-toothed calyx and a purple corolla with 5 spreading, rounded lobes.

Bloom Season: Late spring–early fall.

Habitat/Range: Common throughout the tallgrass region in disturbed upland sites, including pastures, old fields, degraded prairies, and roadsides.

Comments: This bitter-tasting plant is avoided by livestock and can become abundant in overgrazed uplands.

FRANK OBERLE

FRANK OBERLE

BIRD'S FOOT VIOLET
Viola pedata
Violet family (Violaceae)

Description: Delicate plants to about 6" tall, with each leaf divided into 3 narrow segments radiating from a single point. Each main leaf segment is usually further lobed and divided. All of the leaves are on individual stalks coming from the base of the plant. The flowering stems extend well above the leaves, and are bare except for a pair of narrow pointed bracts near the middle. Each flower stem is sharply curved at the top, with a single flower. Each flower is about 1½" wide, with 5 sepals and 5 pale lavender to vivid purple petals. All of the petals are hairless on the inside. The 5 large, orange stamens are prominent in the center of the flower. Two color forms are common—one with 5 uniformly purple petals and one with the upper 2 petals dark purple and the lower 3 pale lavender to white with lavender streaks.

Bloom Season: Spring; also in fall.

Habitat/Range: Common in well-drained acid soils in prairies, glades, oak savannas, and other exposed sites, and often in sandy or rocky soils, but also in mesic, black soil prairies. Found through the tallgrass region from central Iowa and eastern Kansas south and eastward.

PRAIRIE VIOLET
Viola pedatifida
Violet family (Violaceae)

Description: Similar to those of Bird's Foot Violet, the leaves of Prairie Violet are all stalked, basal, and divided into 3 main segments, with the segments further divided into narrow lobes. The flowering stems are usually taller than the leaves, bare except for a pair of small pointed bracts near the middle, with a single, 5-petaled, purple to blue-violet flower up to 1½" wide. The 3 lower petals of each flower are densely bearded with hairs on the lower half of their inside surfaces, and the stamens are not exposed as compared with the hairless petals and prominent stamens of Bird's Foot Violet.

Bloom Season: Spring; also in fall.

Habitat/Range: Local in high-quality prairies, often in fertile soils, throughout the tallgrass region but rarer south and east of southeastern Missouri and northern Indiana.

FRANK OBERLE

ARROW-LEAVED VIOLET
Viola sagittata
Violet family (Violaceae)

Description: Generally less than 6" tall, these violets have long-stalked, arrowhead-shaped basal leaves up to 3" long and always longer than they are wide. The leaves have blunt to heart-shaped bases with a few large lobes or teeth. The leaf edges have small, shallow teeth and the flowering stalks are about as long as the leaves, with a single pair of small bracts near the middle. The single flower on each stalk has 5 purple petals and is about 1" wide.

Bloom Season: Spring–early summer.

Habitat/Range: Common in moist to dry prairies and open woodlands, often in clayey soils. Found through much of the tallgrass region, west to southeastern Kansas; rare and sporadic north of northwestern Missouri.

PINK FLOWERS

FRANK OBERLE

This section includes flowers ranging from pale pinkish white to vivid electric pink and pinkish magenta. Since pink flowers grade into purple flowers or white flowers, readers looking for pink flowers should check the purple and white sections as well.

MORTON ARBORETUM

FRANK OBERLE

SHOWY MILKWEED
Asclepias speciosa
Milkweed family (Asclepiadaceae)

Description: Stout, hairy plants to 3' tall with white, milky sap. The stems have pairs of opposite, broadly oval leaves up to 8" long and sometimes more than half as wide. The flowers are larger than those of most milkweeds and occur in a few round, 10–40-flowered clusters on stout stalks near the top of the plant. Each flower can be over 1" long, with 5 spreading to reflexed purplish petals, and 5 prominent, erect, long-pointed, pinkish hoods. The seed pods are about 3" long and 1½" thick and covered with soft projections.

Bloom Season: Late spring–midsummer.

Habitat/Range: Common in the Great Plains, ranging east to western portions of Minnesota and Iowa, south through eastern Kansas; typically in moist sites and along prairie streams.

Comments: Pioneers used the downy-plumed seeds of this and other milkweeds as cushion stuffing.

PRAIRIE MILKWEED
Asclepias sullivantii
Milkweed family (Asclepiadaceae)

Description: Robust, thick-stemmed, smooth, hairless plants to 3½' tall, with milky sap. The thick, oval, opposite leaves are up to 7" long and 3½" wide and stalkless, with broad bases and pointed tips. One to several rounded flower clusters occur near the top of the plant, with each cluster having up to 40 flowers. Flowers are individually stalked, and just under 1" long and ½" wide. Each flower has 5 reflexed, deep reddish pink petals and 5 erect, pink hoods. The seed pods are about 4" long and 1½" thick, and usually have soft, pointed projections on the upper half.

Bloom Season: Early–midsummer.

Habitat/Range: Occasional in moist to wet prairies through much of the tallgrass region, becoming rare north of Iowa.

Comments: Prairie Milkweed is often confused with the weedy Common Milkweed, which differs in having hairy, dull leaves, seed pods usually with abundant pointed projections over their entire surfaces, and slightly smaller flowers.

FRANK OBERLE

COMMON MILKWEED
Asclepias syriaca
Milkweed family (Asclepiadaceae)

Description: Mostly unbranched, finely hairy plants usually 3–4' tall, but occasionally up to 6', with white, milky sap. The large, mostly opposite, thick, oval, short-stalked leaves are up to 8" (rarely 12") long and 4½" wide, usually with pinkish veins. Flowers are in rounded clusters of 25–140 at the tops of the stems or on stalks arising from the bases of the upper leaves. Each pinkish purple flower is about ¼" wide, with 5 purplish, reflexed petals surrounding 5 spreading, pinkish purple hoods, each with a tiny, pointed horn arising from it. The fruits are 2–4" long, fat pods covered with many tiny projections and filled with fluffy seeds.

Bloom Season: Late spring–summer.

Habitat/Range: Abundant in open disturbed areas, including fields, upland pastures, roadsides, and even planted fields, as well as occasionally in prairies, especially degraded prairies; found throughout the tallgrass region, but becoming less common at the extreme southern edge.

Comments: Young shoots and pods of this plant have been used as a vegetable, although the cooking water must be changed several times to remove toxins. The fluffy seed hairs formerly were used to stuff life jackets. Native Americans used milkweeds for medicine and made sugar from the flowers. Common Milkweed is similar to Prairie Milkweed, which is smooth and hairless, has slightly larger flowers, and grows in high-quality, moist prairies.

JIM NACHEL—MORTON ARBORETUM

FRANK OBERLE

PRAIRIE THISTLE
Cirsium hillii
Aster family (Asteraceae)

Description: Coarse, spiny plants to 3' tall, with large alternate leaves that are usually hairy on the underside, but not whitened. The leaves are irregularly lobed and toothed along the edges, with many spines. Flower heads are single at the tops of hairy stem branches, with each 2–4" wide head containing many overlapping, green, spiny bracts surrounding numerous, small, pale purple disk flowers each with a 5-lobed tubular corolla and 2 protruding, threadlike style branches.

Bloom Season: Early–midsummer

Habitat/Range: Occasional in dry prairies in the northeastern tallgrass region, south and west to west-central Illinois and Minnesota.

Comments: This plant is also called Hollow-Rooted Thistle, because the thick roots have long, hollow internal chambers.

SPOTTED JOE PYE WEED
Eupatorium maculatum
Aster family (Asteraceae)

Description: Stems unbranched and up to 5' tall, usually with purple spots or purplish throughout, with widely spaced whorls of 4-6 coarsely toothed leaves. Each leaf is broadest near the middle, up to 9" long and 2½" wide, and tapers to a long, pointed tip. The numerous flower heads are in a flat to shallowly rounded cluster from numerous branches near the top of the plant. Each narrow flower head is about ⅓" tall, with 8–22 small, pinkish purple disk flowers; there are no petal-like ray flowers. Conspicuous threadlike, purple styles extend from the flowers.

Bloom Season: Late spring–early fall.

Habitat/Range: Locally common in permanently moist sites, often in spring-fed, mineral-rich waters; found in the northern tallgrass region south to northwestern Missouri.

SKELETON WEED
Lygodesmia juncea
Aster family (Asteraceae)

Description: Smooth, hairless grooved stems to about 18" tall, with upright branches and milky to yellowish sap. The name comes from the bare appearance of the stems, since the small, narrow, alternate leaves are inconspicuous and scalelike. The flower heads are single at the tops of stem branches, with each head up to 1" wide and consisting of 5 pink, petal-like ray flowers, each with a 5-toothed tip. The plants frequently have round, green, pea-like balls on the stems—these are galls caused by a small wasp that lays its eggs in the stems.

Bloom Season: Summer.

Habitat/Range: Common in dry upland prairies in the western tallgrass region, east to

Minnesota, western Iowa, and northwestern Missouri.

Comments: Native Americans used the plant medicinally for eye ailments and while nursing children. The hardened sap was used as chewing gum, and is reported to turn bright blue when chewed.

BARBARA'S BUTTONS
Marshallia caespitosa
Aster family (Asteraceae)

Description: Delicate plants usually no more than 10" tall, but occasionally up to 20", with basal clusters of small, narrow leaves and hairy, nearly leafless, unbranched stems, each with a single flower head. The leaves are grasslike, hairless, toothless, up to 6" long and ½" wide, with pointed tips and tapering bases. Numerous parallel veins run along their length. Flowers are in dense, buttonlike heads up to 1½" wide, with numerous long, very thin, pointed, green bracts under a rounded head of many tiny, pink to white, tubular flowers. Each individual flower has 5 narrow, strap-shaped lobes and 2 protruding style branches.

Bloom Season: Midspring–early summer.

Habitat/Range: Uncommon in dry, often sandy or limestone-rich prairies from southeastern Kansas and southwestern Missouri southward.

KEVIN MAGEE

KITTY KOHOUT—MORTON ARBORETUM

HEDGE BINDWEED
Calystegia sepium
Morning Glory family (Convolvulaceae)

Description: Smooth, twining vines with stems up to 10' long, but usually shorter. The alternate leaves are widely spaced along the stem, with each individually stalked leaf up to 4" long and 2½" wide and arrowhead-shaped, with a pointed tip. The leaf base has 2 prominent, angular lobes and an indented notch where the stalk is attached. The long-stalked flowers arise singly at the bases of the leaf stalks, with 2 broad green bracts at the base of each flower. Each flaring, funnel-shaped flower is about 2–2½" wide at the mouth, with 5 small, nearly transparent sepals and a shallowly 5-lobed corolla which may be white, pink, or a combination of the two.

Bloom Season: Late spring–early fall.

Habitat/Range: Frequent in open thickets and fencerows, as well as in moist tangles of vegetation along streams, in prairies, fields, pastures, and disturbed areas throughout the tallgrass region.

ILLINOIS TICK TREFOIL
Desmodium illinoense
Bean family (Fabaceae)

Description: Plants typically 3' tall, occasionally taller, with alternate, stalked compound leaves. Each leaf is composed of 3 leaflets, with the middle leaflet on a stalk shorter than the leaf stalk. The stem and leaves are covered with curved, hook-shaped hairs, so that the undersides of the leaves stick to clothing. The leaflets are up to 4" long and 2½" wide, although usually smaller. The individually stalked flowers are loosely clustered along an elongate, usually unbranched stalk at the top of the plant. Each pale pink flower is about ⅓" wide, with an erect, flaring upper petal and 2 smaller side petals flanking a protruding lower lip. The fruits are a beadlike chain of 3–6 flattened, hairy segments each about ¼" long.

Bloom Season: Late spring–summer.

Habitat/Range: Common in upland prairies and pastures, as well as along roadsides in prairie areas, from southeastern South Dakota south and eastward to Ohio.

FRANK OBERLE

ROBERT TATINA

SENSITIVE BRIAR
Mimosa nuttallii
Bean family (Fabaceae)

Description: Distinctive sprawling or trailing vines with angular stems covered with abundant, hooked prickles. These stems are up to 4' long, with alternate, doubly compound leaves on prickly stalks. The numerous individual leaflets are less than ½" long, with prominent raised veins on their undersides. Ball-shaped flower heads resembling miniature fireworks explosions occur on 2–3" prickly stalks along the stems. These heads are a dense cluster of flowers whose showiness is largely due to the 8-10 protruding, magenta-pink, yellow-tipped stamens per flower.

Bloom Season: Late spring–summer.

Habitat/Range: Common in dry prairies and savannas, often in acidic soils; in the south-western tallgrass region, north to central South Dakota, becoming rare and local eastward to central Illinois.

Comments: The sensitive leaflets rapidly fold together when contacted. The stem prickles are painful if caught between the toes of those running barefoot, prompting rural children to call this plant Devil's Shoestrings.

SMALL WILD BEAN
Strophostyles leiosperma
Bean family (Fabaceae)

Description: Small, hairy, twining, annual vines with stalked, mostly alternate, compound leaves. Each leaf is composed of 3 leaflets, with the middle leaflet on a short stalk. The leaflets are up to 2" long and usually less than ½" wide, with smooth edges. Flowers are on long stalks arising at the bases of the upper leaf stalks, with one to several flowers at the end of each stalk. Each pinkish flower is about ¼" wide, with a small, hairy, green, 4-lobed calyx, an erect upper petal, and 2 smaller side petals flanking a protruding lower lip. The fruits are narrow, hairy pods about 1–1½" long.

Bloom Season: Late spring–fall.

Habitat/Range: Frequent in open, well-drained areas including prairies, especially in sandy soils; found throughout the tallgrass region, but uncommon east of Illinois and north of Iowa.

Comments: Trailing Wild Bean *(S. helvula)* is a similar species with broader, often lobed, leaflets, a hairless calyx, and larger flowers; it occurs in moister sites.

FRANK OBERLE

CARL KURTZ

GOAT'S RUE
Tephrosia virginiana
Bean family (Fabaceae)

Description: Stems single or branched only at the base, hairy, up to 2½' tall, with numerous alternate, compound leaves. The leaves are divided, featherlike, into as many as 31 narrow leaflets, each up to 1¼" long and ⅓" wide. The leaflets may be pointed or square at the end, but always have a small, hairlike tip, and are usually gray-hairy. Flowers are in dense clusters at the tops of the stems, with each flower about ¾" long and consisting of a flaring, pale yellow upper petal and two smaller pink petals flanking a protruding, keel-like lip. The fruits are hairy, flattened pods up to 2" long.

Bloom Season: Late spring–midsummer.

Habitat/Range: Frequent in upland prairies and especially savannas, often in sandy soil, through the southern tallgrass region, north into Iowa and Wisconsin.

Comments: Goat's Rue has been used medicinally by Native Americans and pioneers, and the rotenone in the roots has been used to stun fish.

AMERICAN VETCH
Vicia americana
Bean family (Fabaceae)

Description: Sprawling vines with alternate compound leaves and stems up to 3' long. Each leaf typically has 5-10 pairs of narrowly oval leaflets each up to about 1½" long, with a twining tendril at the end of the leaf. There are promi-nent, sharply toothed stipules at the bases of the leaf stalks. Long-stalked clusters of several flowers arise from the junction of leaf stalks with the stems. Each flower is up to 1" long with a small, greenish, unevenly 5-toothed calyx and a somewhat tubular corolla with an erect, flaring upper petal and two smaller side petals flanking a keel-like lower lip. The fruits are small pods 1–1½" long.

Bloom Season: Midspring–midsummer.

Habitat/Range: Occasional in prairies, thickets, and open woodlands, usually in somewhat moist areas; scattered through most of the northern and western tallgrass region.

G. YATSKIEVYCH

PRAIRIE ROSE GENTIAN
Sabatia campestris
Gentian family (Gentianaceae)

Description: Annual or biennial plants to 15" tall, but often less than 8", with alternate branches in the flower cluster. The leaves are up to 1" long and ½" wide, opposite, broadest near the middle, broadly rounded at the base, and tapering to pointed tips. Flowers are on individual branches in a nearly flat cluster at the top of the plant. Each flower is about 1–1¾" wide and consists of a winged, green calyx with 5 narrow, pointed lobes each more than ½" long, 5 rounded, pink corolla lobes that taper to pointed tips and usually have a yellow mark at the base, and 5 stamens.

Bloom Season: Summer.

Habitat/Range: Locally frequent in dry upland prairies, often in sandy soil, and occasionally in mesic sand prairies; found in the southern tallgrass region from eastern Kansas to Illinois, and southward.

Comments: Common Rose Gentian *(S. angularis)* is a closely related species found in similar habitats, although more commonly in moister sites, from southeastern Kansas eastward. Unlike Prairie Rose Gentian, it has opposite branches in the flower cluster and an unwinged calyx.

CARL KURTZ

OBEDIENT PLANT
Physostegia virginiana
Mint family (Lamiaceae)

Description: Plants to 4' tall, with thick, narrow, sharply toothed, opposite leaves. These leaves are stalkless and up to 6" long and 1½" wide, but usually much smaller. Flowers are in spikelike clusters along the upper stems, with each short-stalked flower accompanied by a small leaflike bract. Each flower has a cuplike, 5-toothed, green calyx, and a large, tubular, 2-lipped pink or lavender corolla up to 1" long. The lowest flowers bloom first, with flowering proceeding upward along the stem.

Bloom Season: Midsummer–early fall.

Habitat/Range: Common throughout the tallgrass region in wet prairies, along streams, and in low marshy areas, as well as in mesic and sometimes in upland prairies.

Comments: The common name comes from the fact that the flowers can be rotated around the stem, and remain where they are placed. Another common name for this plant is False Dragonhead. Botanists have described several varieties and subspecies of this variable plant.

FRANK OBERLE

LEMON MINT
Monarda citriodora
Mint family (Lamiaceae)

Description: Finely hairy, square-stemmed annuals to 3' tall, with opposite, toothed leaves. The leaves are up to 3" long and about ¾" wide and broadest at or below the middle. They taper to pointed tips and have short to long stalks. The leaves on the upper part of the stem below the flower heads are often in whorls. The flowers are in 2–6 dense heads arranged one above another along the upper stem. Each head is surrounded at the base by hairy, leaflike bracts that have pointed tips and are whitish to pinkish lavender on the upper surface. Each flower is ⅝–1" long, with a narrow tubular calyx with 5 spiny teeth and a 2-lipped, widely spreading, pinkish lavender corolla resembling an open snake's mouth.

Bloom Season: Late spring–midsummer.

Habitat/Range: Frequent in open sandy or rocky upland prairies and pastures of the southwestern tallgrass region, from eastern Kansas and Missouri southward.

CLARK SCHAACK

NODDING WILD ONION
Allium cernuum
Lily family (Liliaceae)

Description: Plants usually less than 1½' tall, arising from a small bulb. The smooth stems are round and leafless, with several shorter, grass-like, flattened leaves at the base. The stem is sharply curved near the top, so that the single head of flowers is nodding downward. Each flower is on a stalk up to 1" long and has 6 petal-like, pinkish segments up to ¼" long and 6 prominent, yellow-tipped stamens. The flowers develop into small, rounded seed capsules.

Bloom Season: Summer.

Habitat/Range: Locally frequent in mesic and dry prairies in widely scattered areas, including the southern Great Lakes region, south-central Missouri, and, rarely, eastern South Dakota.

Comments: This plant is especially common in prairie remnants around southern Lake Michigan, where it was used as a food by Native Americans. It has a mild onion fragrance and taste.

FRANK OBERLE

PRAIRIE ONION
Allium stellatum
Lily family (Liliaceae)

Description: Very similar to Nodding Wild Onion, except that the stems are erect, and the flower heads are not drooping or nodding. The leaves are all basal, but typically wither and disappear before flowering time. The flowers of Prairie Onion are often a deep reddish pink, contrasting with the pale pink hue of Nodding Wild Onion.

Bloom Season: Midsummer–fall.

Habitat/Range: Frequent in dry prairies and on hill prairies, especially in rocky sites associated with limestone; found from western Ontario and scattered sites in Illinois westward.

FRANK OBERLE

LARGE-FLOWERED GAURA
Gaura longiflora
Evening Primrose family (Onagraceae)

Description: Branched, slender, annual or biennial plants to 7' tall, with alternate leaves and finely hairy stems. The leaves are up to 6" long and 1½" wide, broadest near the middle, and usually have some widely separated teeth along the edges and small, silky hairs lying flat against the upper surface. Flowers are about 1" long and scattered alternately along the upper stem branches. Each flower has 2 sets of paired reddish sepals which angle back along the long tubular flower base. There are 4 narrow-based, pinkish petals arranged in an upward-pointing semicircle, below which are 8 downward-pointing stamens and a threadlike style with 4 narrow lobes at the tip.

Bloom Season: Late spring–fall.

Habitat/Range: Locally frequent in dry and rocky prairies and pastures, especially in somewhat disturbed areas, and also along roadsides and in waste ground; found from Illinois to southeastern Nebraska and southward.

Comments: A closely related species, Biennial Gaura *(G. biennis),* occurs in similar sites mostly east of the Mississippi River. Biennial Gaura is usually smaller and has some straight hairs spreading away from the main stem, contrasting with the always-curled hairs of Large-Flowered Gaura, which lie against the stem.

FRANK OBERLE

FRANK OBERLE

SHOWY EVENING PRIMROSE
Oenothera speciosa
Evening Primrose family (Onagraceae)

Description: Plants with sparsely hairy stems up to 2' tall, but usually lower and sprawling, often in large colonies. The leaves are alternate, up to 3½" long and 1" wide, with wavy or weakly toothed edges, and occasionally a few small lobes near the tapering bases. The upper leaves are smaller, with flowers arising singly from where the leaves join the stem. Each flower is up to 3" wide when fully open, with a small ovary and a long, slender tube under the sepals and petals. There are 4 pointed sepals bent sharply backward and united at their tips. Four large, round, pink to white petals surround 8 stamens and a longer style with a narrowly 4-lobed tip. The petals are often tinged yellow toward the base and marked with fine, dark pink lines.

Bloom Season: Midspring–midsummer.

Habitat/Range: Locally frequent in rocky prairies, pastures, and along roadsides, often in disturbed areas with low vegetation; found in the southwestern tallgrass region from southeastern Nebraska and Missouri southward, and occasionally introduced elsewhere.

PRAIRIE GRASS PINK ORCHID
Calopogon oklahomensis
Orchid family (Orchidaceae)

Description: Delicate, smooth, single-stemmed plants less than 2' tall, usually with a single, long, narrow, pointed, grasslike leaf at the base of the plant. This leaf can be up to 10" long but is less than ¾" wide. The top of the stem has up to 10 individually stalked flowers, each with a small leaflike bract at its base. The flowers are vivid electric pink to pale pink or even white, with 3 petal-like sepals, each about ¾" long, and 3 petals. Two petals are narrower and slightly shorter than the sepals, and the upper petal is flared into a rounded triangular lobe at the end, with dense, yellow to purple hairs along its length.

Bloom Season: Midspring–midsummer.

Habitat/Range: Occasional in moist sand prairies and acifdic upland prairies that are wet during the spring; from central Missouri and Kansas southward.

Comments: A related species, Grass Pink Orchid *(C. tuberosus),* occurs in bogs, fens, and other wetlands through much much of the tallgrass region except Nebraska and the Dakotas. It has brighter magenta flowers that open in midsummer and extend well above the leaflike bracts, and the hairs of the upper petal are yellow or white.

FRANK OBERLE

VIOLET WOOD SORREL
Oxalis violacea
Wood Sorrel family (Oxalidaceae)

Description: Small plants to about 6" tall, with all leaves basal and long-stalked. Each leaf is up to 1" wide and divided into 3 leaflets radiating from a common point. Each leaflet is folded, notched at the tip, and heart-shaped, frequently with a dark reddish spot near the base. The undersides of the leaflets are sometimes tinged with purple. The flower stems are taller than the leaves, with several individually stalked flowers at the top. Each flower is ½" wide or slightly wider, with 5 small, pointed, orange-tipped, green sepals and 5 pink or purple petals enclosing 10 stamens and 5 styles.

Bloom Season: Late spring–early summer; also in fall.

Habitat/Range: Common in dry to mesic prairies and open woodlands throughout the tallgrass region.

ROBERT TATINA

FRANK OBERLE

MARSH PHLOX
Phlox glaberrima
Phlox family (Polemoniaceae)

Description: Smooth, usually hairless plants typically less than 2' tall, with stalkless, opposite leaves. The leaves are up to 5" long and ⅝" wide, widest near the rounded bases and gradually tapering to pointed tips. The individually stalked flowers are in a branching, rounded cluster at the top of the plant. Each flower is ½–¾" wide, with a narrow, tubular, green calyx with 5 bristlelike teeth, and a deep magenta tubular corolla flaring into 5 broad lobes.

Bloom Season: Late spring–summer.

Habitat/Range: Occasional in moist prairies in the eastern tallgrass region, west into Missouri and Arkansas.

PRAIRIE PHLOX
Phlox pilosa
Phlox family (Polemoniaceae)

Description: Hairy-stemmed plants to about 2' tall, with widely spaced pairs of opposite, stalkless leaves. The hairs on the stem can be smooth or sticky. The leaves taper to pointed tips and are up to 4" long and ¾" wide, with prominent central veins along their length. Flowers are in a branching, rounded cluster at the tops of the stems. Each flower is about ¾" wide, with 5 pink, petal-like lobes at the top of a narrow tube about ½" tall. The base of each lobe often has darker pink markings. The tops of the 5 yellow-tipped stamens can be seen at the top of the flower tube.

Midspring–midsummer; also in fall.

Habitat/Range: Common in dry to mesic, often rocky or sandy, prairies and open oak savannas throughout the tallgrass region.

89

FRANK OBERLE

FRANK OBERLE

FIELD MILKWORT
Polygala sanguinea
Milkwort family (Polygalaceae)

Description: Small annuals less than 1' tall with unbranched to few-branched, angular stems. The leaves are alternate and up to 1¾" long and about ⅛" wide, with nearly microscopic teeth along the edges. Flowers are in dense, short, cylindrical heads at the tops of the branches. The individual flowers are small, pinkish purple to whitish, and less than ¼" long. The flowers have an unusual structure of 5 sepals, with the upper 1 and lower 2 small and green. The 2 side sepals are larger and colored deep pink to white like the 3 small petals, which are united into a small tube.

Bloom Season: Late spring–fall.

Habitat/Range: Frequent in sterile or sandy upland sites and open moist sandy areas; found through the southern tallgrass region, becoming rare north of southern Minnesota.

SHOOTING STAR
Dodecatheon meadia
Primrose family (Primulaceae)

Description: All leaves are basal, smooth, up to 8" long and 3" wide at the middle, on long stalks, and taper to rounded tips. The smooth flower stalk grows up to 2' tall from the middle of the cluster of basal leaves. At the top of the stalk is a whorl of small bracts, from which a spray of individually stalked flowers arises. Each dangling flower has 5 small, green sepals hidden by 5 reflexed petals, each up to 1" long. The petals are light to dark pink with yellow and white at the base, and are joined at their bases by a small yellowish tube. There are 5 prominent stamens projecting from the center of the flower; these usually have dark brown bases. The flower stalks become upright during fruiting.

Bloom Season: Mid–late spring.

Habitat/Range: Common in moist to dry prairies, open savannas, and rocky hill prairies from eastern Kansas and Iowa south and eastward.

FRANK OBERLE

QUEEN OF THE PRAIRIE
Filipendula rubra
Rose family (Rosaceae)

Description: Smooth plants to 7' tall, but typically 4', with alternate compound leaves and large, toothed stipules at the base of the leaf stalks. The leaves are sometimes more than 2' long and divided into several narrow, irregularly toothed segments of varying size on the same leaf. The end leaflet is large and deeply divided into 7–9 leafletlike lobes up to 4" long, which themselves are sometimes further lobed and divided. The flowers are in branching, spraylike clusters at the tops of the stems. The deep pink flowers are about ⅓–½" wide, with 5 small, blunt, reflexed sepals and 5 pink petals surrounding many small stamens.

Bloom Season: Early–midsummer.

Habitat/Range: Rare and local in moist prairies, swampy prairie seeps, and fens, often in areas of mineralized groundwater seepage; scattered from Minnesota to Missouri and eastward.

Comments: Native Americans and early European settlers used this plant for a variety of medicinal roles, including treatment of arthritis, fevers, and skin ailments.

FRANK OBERLE

PRAIRIE SMOKE
Geum triflorum
Rose family (Rosaceae)

Description: Plants with hairy stems, usually less than 1' tall, with numerous basal leaves. The basal leaves are up to 7" long and divided into as many as 19 toothed segments. There is usually a pair of smaller, opposite, deeply segmented leaves near the middle of the stem. The stems have 3–6 individually stalked, nodding flowers. Each flower is less than ¾" wide, with 5 somewhat triangular, reddish purple sepals alternating with narrow threadlike bracts, and 5 smaller, creamy white to pinkish or purplish petals. The fruits are the showiest part of the plant, and have long, feathery plumes up to 2" long, giving the fruiting heads a wispy, smoky appearance.

Bloom Season: Mid–late spring.

Habitat/Range: Common westward, becoming rare eastward, on dry prairies, especially on gravelly hill prairies; found in the northwestern tallgrass region, from northeastern North Dakota and adjacent Canada south and east to northern Illinois.

Comments: Native Americans and European settlers made a medicinal tea from the roots of Prairie Smoke.

MARY KAY SOLECKI

PASTURE ROSE
Rosa carolina
Rose family (Rosaceae)

Description: Low, prickly shrubs usually less than 2' tall, with alternate compound leaves and slender spines. The leaves usually have 3–7 oval leaflets, with each leaflet up to 2" long and sharply toothed along the edges. There are 2 prominent, pointed stipules along the base of the leaf stalk. Flowers occur on bristly individual stalks on the upper part of the plant. Each flower is about 2½–3" wide, with 5 green, long-pointed sepals, 5 broad, pink petals, and numerous yellow stamens. The fruits are red, rounded "hips" that develop below the sepals.

Bloom Season: Midspring–summer.

Habitat/Range: Common and widely distributed in dry to mesic open sites including prairies, pastures, old fields and open woodlands; found through all but the northwestern tallgrass region, reaching western Iowa and Minnesota.

Comments: The hips are rich in vitamin C and have been used for food and medicine. A very similar species, Prairie Wild Rose *(R. arkansana)*, is common on prairies in the western tall-grass region and has 9–11 leaflets per leaf.

Unlike the bristly-hairy flower stalks and fruits of Pasture Rose, those of Prairie Wild Rose are smooth. Early Wild Rose *(R. blanda)* has almost spineless new branches, 5–7 leaflets per leaf, and smooth flower stalks and fruits; it occasionally occurs in prairies.

DON KURZ

FRANK OBERLE

ROUGH BUTTONWEED
Diodia teres
Madder family (Rubiaceae)

Description: Small, branched annuals with squarish stems that sometimes creep along the ground. The stalkless, narrow, smooth-edged leaves are opposite and typically up to 1¼" long and less than ¼" wide, with pointed tips and a prominent central vein. Each pair of leaves is joined across the stem by a pair of small, whitish, papery stipules which usually have numerous erect bristles along the edges. The flowers are in groups of 1–3 from the junction of the leaf bases and the stem, with each flower less than ¼" wide and consisting of 4 small, green sepals and a pink tubular corolla with 4 spreading lobes and 4 small, round-tipped stamens.

Bloom Season: Summer–fall.

Habitat/Range: Frequent in dry, sterile sites, usually in acid soils, such as sand or thin soil over sandstone, in dry prairies and pastures; found in the southern tallgrass region from northeastern Kansas through southern Ohio, and introduced as a weed in open sandy soil northward.

NARROW-LEAVED BLUETS
Hedyotis nigricans
Madder family (Rubiaceae)

Description: Low, slender plants usually less than 8" tall, typically with several stems arising from the base. The leaves are opposite and up to 1½" long and about ⅛" wide, with a single middle vein and sharply pointed tips. There are often small clusters of tiny leaves where the main leaves join the stem. Each pair of leaves is joined across the stem by a pair of pale, papery, pointed stipules. Flowers are numerous in small clusters at the tops of the branches; each flower has a 4-toothed, green calyx and a small, pink to white, tubular corolla with 4 pointed lobes, 4 slightly protruding stamens, and a protruding style. The flowers are less than ¼" wide, with hairy upper surfaces on the corolla lobes.

Bloom Season: Late spring–fall.

Habitat/Range: Occasional in exposed hill prairies and dry rocky prairie sites, usually areas with limestone or calcium-rich soils; found in the southern tallgrass region from eastern Nebraska to Ohio and southward.

FRANK OBERLE

ROSE VERVAIN
Glandularia canadensis
Vervain family (Verbenaceae)

Description: Sprawling to erect plants with stems to 2' long, usually with numerous stems arising from a single point. The leaves are stalked, opposite, up to 4" long and 1½" wide, and usually divided into several lobed segments that are coarsely toothed along the edges. Flowers are in dense, cylindrical clusters at the tops of the stems, with each flower just above a small, narrow, pointed bract. Each flower is about ½" wide, with a narrow, tubular calyx with 5 bristle-like teeth. The deep pink corolla tapers into a narrow tube below 5 spreading lobes with notched tips.

Bloom Season: Spring–fall.

Habitat/Range: Frequent in open well-drained sites with sparse vegetation, including rocky prairies, pastures, bluff summits, and along roadsides; found from southeastern Nebraska to central Illinois and southward, and occasionally escaping from cultivation elsewhere.

RED AND ORANGE FLOWERS

FRANK OBERLE

This section includes red and orange flowers. Since red flowers grade into both pink flowers and purple flowers, readers looking for red flowers should check the pink and purple sections as well.

FRANK OBERLE

FRANK OBERLE

SWAMP MILKWEED
Asclepias incarnata
Milkweed family (Asclepiadaceae)

Description: Milky-sapped plants to 5' tall, with narrow, opposite leaves that taper to pointed tips. The leaves are up to 6" long and seldom over 1" wide. The stems are branched above, with one or more flower clusters at the tips of the branches. Each cluster is a flattened to shallowly rounded head of numerous individually stalked, reddish pink flowers, often with whitish centers. Each flower is less than ¼" wide, with 5 reflexed, reddish pink petals flanking 5 erect, pink hoods. The seed pods are paired, narrow, up to 4" long, and gradually tapered at both ends.

Bloom Season: Summer.

Habitat/Range: Common in wet prairies, marshes, and along streams, ponds, and shores throughout the tallgrass region.

Comments: This is the only milkweed commonly found in prairies that have saturated soils.

BUTTERFLY MILKWEED
Asclepias tuberosa
Milkweed family (Asclepiadaceae)

Description: Stout plants to 3' tall, often somewhat sprawling, and sometimes even appearing bushy. While other milkweeds have white, milky juice, this plant has clear sap. The stems are covered with coarse, spreading hairs. The narrow, stalkless, hairy leaves are shaped like dagger blades about 4" long and seldom over 1" wide. The leaves are alternate, but occasionally opposite along the upper part of the stem. Flower clusters arise where the leaves join the stem. Each cluster is relatively flat, with up to 25 individually stalked flowers, each less than ¾" long. The flowers are typically brilliant orange, but can range from pale yellow to deep red, with 5 reflexed petals below 5 erect hoods. The seed pods are about 6" long and less than ¾" thick, smooth, and usually finely hairy.

Bloom Season: Late spring–summer.

Habitat/Range: Common in well-drained prairies, open savannas, and particularly in sandy sites throughout the tallgrass region.

Comments: Native Americans used the roots as food, and both Native Americans and European settlers used the roots as medicine. Another common name for the plant is Pleurisy Root.

FRANK OBERLE

BLANKET FLOWER
Gaillardia pulchella
Aster family (Asteraceae)

Description: Hairy annuals to 2' tall, with stalkless, alternate leaves up to 4" long and seldom over 1" wide. The leaves are variable and may be smooth-edged, toothed, or even lobed. Flower heads are single at the tops of the branches, with each head 1½–3" wide, and consisting of 6-16 petal-like ray flowers surrounding a reddish purple, rounded, central disk with numerous tubular flowers. Each broadly fanlike ray flower is 3-lobed and deep red, usually with a yellow tip. In rare cases the ray flowers may be all red or all yellow.

Bloom Season: Late spring–early fall.

Habitat/Range: Widely distributed in dry, usually sandy, soil in the southern Great Plains, but occurring in tallgrass prairies as a native plant only in the southwesternmost tallgrass region, from northeastern Oklahoma southward; commonly cultivated and escaping as a weed through much of the tallgrass region.

Comments: This is the state wildflower of Oklahoma.

FRANK OBERLE

FRANK OBERLE

CARDINAL FLOWER
Lobelia cardinalis
Bellflower family (Campanulaceae)

Description: Usually single-stemmed plants, typically less than 4' tall with alternate leaves and milky juice. The leaves are finely toothed along the edges, up to 7" long and 2" wide, widest near the middle, and tapered to pointed tips and short-stalked bases. Flowers are brilliant red and alternately arranged on small individual stalks in a close cluster at the top of the stems. Each flower is about 1½" long, with 5 green, needlelike sepals at the base of a vivid red, tubular, 2-lipped corolla. The lower corolla lip is 3-lobed, and the upper lip has 2 smaller, narrow lobes. The stamens and style are in a red central column.

Bloom Season: Midsummer–early fall.

Habitat/Range: Locally frequent in wet sites, including marshy depressions in prairies, borders of prairie streams, moist thickets, and moist open woodlands. Found mostly in the southern tallgrass region, becoming rare in the north.

ROYAL CATCHFLY
Silene regia
Pink family (Caryophyllaceae)

Description: Stems usually unbranched below the flowers, up to 4' tall, and usually somewhat clammy-hairy. Plants typically have 10–20 pairs of opposite leaves along the stem, with each leaf up to 5" long and 3" wide, slightly pointed at the tip, and with stalkless bases that weakly clasp the stem. The flowers are on individual stalks on the upper part of the plant. Each flower has a 1"-long, tubular, 5-toothed calyx covered with sticky hairs, 5 bright red petals with scalelike flaps near the base and often with ragged tips, and 10 protruding pale stamens.

Bloom Season: Late spring–fall.

Habitat/Range: Uncommon and local in dry to mesic prairies and open oak savannas; scattered in the southern tallgrass region, from southeastern Kansas and southern Missouri to Ohio, north to northern parts of Illinois and Indiana.

FRANK OBERLE

FRANK OBERLE

MICHIGAN LILY
Lilium michiganense
Lily family (Liliaceae)

Description: Stout, smooth plants to 6' tall with most of the stem leaves in whorls of 4–7, but with the upper stem leaves usually alternate. The leaves are thick and waxy, broadest near the middle, up to 6" long and less than 1" wide, with pointed tips and several parallel veins along their lengths. Each flower is on a spreading to drooping stalk, usually with several stalks above a whorl of leaves at the top of the plant. The flowers typically face downward. Each flower is up to 3" wide and has 6 petal-like, orange segments with many dark purple spots. These segments curl back away from the flower, exposing the 6 prominent, reddish brown-tipped stamens and a central style.

Bloom Season: Early–midsummer.

Habitat/Range: Occasional in moist prairies, prairie swales, and open seepage areas; scattered through the tallgrass region.

Comments: This plant is also called Turk's Cap Lily.

PRAIRIE LILY
Lilium philadelphicum
Lily family (Liliaceae)

Description: Vivid orange flowers are uncommon among our prairie flora, and Prairie Lily is one of the most spectacular of these. The stems arise from a small bulb and are ½–3' tall. Narrow, pointed leaves, 2–4" long, occur in whorls of 4-7 on the upper part of the stem; the lower leaves are opposite or alternate. Each stem is topped by a single large, upright flower about 3–4" wide. The flowers have 6 orange-red "petals" (actually 3 petals and 3 similar sepals), usually with purplish spots on the lower parts of the inner side, and taper to narrow, stalklike bases. Inside the flower are 6 prominent, erect stamens surrounding a central style.

Bloom Season: Early–midsummer.

Habitat/Range: A rare and exquisitely beautiful plant of rich, moist prairies in the northern tallgrass region, ranging south to central Illinois.

Comments: The only other true lily of the prairies, Michigan Lily, has smaller, less reddish, downward-pointing flowers, with several flowers on each stem.

FRANK OBERLE

ORANGE FRINGED ORCHID
Platanthera ciliaris
Orchid family (Orchidaceae)

Description: A spectacular orchid growing up to 2' tall, with up to 3 large, smooth, alternate leaves on the lower part of the stem. These leaves are up to 6" long and 1½" wide, with pointed tips and clasping bases. Above the main leaves are several smaller, alternate leaves. At the top of the plant is a short cluster of numerous orange to yellow flowers. Each flower is about 1" long, with 3 rounded orange sepals, 2 narrow, slightly fringed upper petals, and a larger lower petal with a delicate fringe of long orange segments and a reflexed, tubelike spur.

Bloom Season: Summer–early fall.

Habitat/Range: Primarily a species of wet acid sand flats and bogs in the eastern and southern states, ranging to western Arkansas and southeastern Missouri; rare in moist, acidic prairies in the southern Great Lakes region.

FRANK OBERLE

INDIAN PAINTBRUSH

Castilleja coccinea
Snapdragon family (Scrophulariaceae)

Description: Annuals with unbranched, hairy stems to 2' tall, but usually 1' or less. The leaves are alternate, yellowish green, and usually divided into 3 narrow, widely spreading lobes. The flowers are at the top of the plant in a dense spike which elongates as the season progresses. The actual flowers are inconspicuous, each with a thin, tubular, 2-lipped calyx about 1" long and a greenish, tubular corolla. The showiness of the plant comes from the brightly colored, leafy bract that grows under each flower. These are often divided like the stem leaves and are typically bright vermilion, although yellow forms also occur.

Bloom Season: Spring–summer.

Habitat/Range: Common in mesic, dry, and sandy prairies, usually in sites that have some seepage during the spring; found through the tallgrass region from western Minnesota and eastern Kansas eastward.

Comments: Indian Paintbrush is a partial parasite, attaching to the roots of several species of prairie plants.

YELLOW FLOWERS

FRANK OBERLE

This section includes flowers ranging from bright golden yellow and yellow-orange to pale, creamy yellow. Some flowers have mixed colors, such as yellow and red, or yellow and pink. Those multiple-colored flowers that are predominantly yellow are included in this section. Readers looking for flowers with multiple colors should check the red and pink sections as well.

FRANK OBERLE

PRAIRIE PARSLEY
Polytaenia nuttallii
Parsley family (Apiaceae)

Description: Plants to 3' tall, with thick, long-stalked, alternate, light green, compound leaves. The leaf stalks have wide, clasping bases. The leaves are divided into several segments, each of which is again once or twice divided or lobed. Flowers are in a flat, umbrella-like group of many stalked clusters near the top of the plant, typically with 15-25 flowers at the end of each stalk. Each pale yellow flower is about ⅛" wide, with 5 minute greenish sepals, 5 tiny petals, 5 protruding stamens, and 2 slightly longer styles. The fruits are rounded and about ¼" long.

Bloom Season: Midspring–early summer.

Habitat/Range: Occasional in dry prairies and open savannas from western Indiana westward; absent in the extreme northwestern tallgrass region.

DON KURZ

GOLDEN ALEXANDERS
Zizia aurea
Parsley family (Apiaceae)

Description: Smooth, branched plants to 3' tall, with stalked, alternate compound leaves. Each leaf is divided into 3 parts, and each part is often further divided into 3 leaflets. The leaflets are up to 3" long and a little over 1" wide, with evenly toothed edges. There are several shallowly domed flower clusters, with each cluster having small heads of flowers at the ends of 10–20 stalks radiating from the top of a branch. The central flower in each small head is stalkless. Each yellow flower is less than ⅛" wide, with 5 tiny, incurved petals and 5 protruding yellow stamens.

Bloom Season: Midspring–early summer.

Habitat/Range: Common throughout the tallgrass region in moist prairies, wet thickets, and along streams.

Comments: Early pioneers thought the plant would cure syphilis. Two close relatives also occur in prairies. Heart-Leaved Meadow Parsnip *(Z. aptera)* occurs in drier prairies and has most or all of its basal leaves undivided and heart-shaped at the base. Meadow Parsnip *(Thaspium trifoliatum variety aureum)* is nearly identical to Golden Alexanders, except that the central flower in each small cluster is on a tiny stalk. Meadow Parsnip is usually found in upland prairies and savannas.

BUR MARIGOLD
Bidens aristosa
Aster family (Asteraceae)

Description: Smooth-stemmed annuals to about 3' tall, occasionally with a few long hairs on the stems near the leaf bases. The leaves are opposite, stalked, and divided into 5–11 narrow, coarsely toothed segments. Flower heads are on individual stalks at the top of the plant, with each head about 1½–2½" wide, including about 8 bright golden yellow, petal-like ray flowers surrounding a central disk. The flattened, black fruits have 2 sharply barbed needlelike teeth at the top are the familiar "beggar's ticks."

Bloom Season: Late summer–fall.

Habitat/Range: Common in wet prairies and prairie marshes, and becoming weedy and spreading abundantly into ditches and low fallow fields; found through the central and southern tallgrass region, becoming rare north of central Iowa.

LARGE-FLOWERED COREOPSIS
Coreopsis grandiflora
Aster family (Asteraceae)

Description: Delicate plants to 2' tall, with mostly opposite leaves. The leaves are divided into slender, threadlike segments less than ¼" wide, although the lowest pair of leaves is sometimes undivided. Flower heads are on individual erect stalks above the leaves. Each flower head typically has about 8 fan-shaped, golden yellow, petal-like ray flowers, each up to 1" long, and with 4–5 ragged teeth at the tip.

Bloom Season: Midspring–midsummer.

Habitat/Range: Locally frequent in dry prairies, especially in soils associated with sandstone and flint; found in the southwestern tallgrass region, from northeastern Kansas through Missouri and southward.

KEITH BOARD

FRANK OBERLE

SAND COREOPSIS
Coreopsis lanceolata
Aster family (Asteraceae)

Description: Showy plants typically 1–2' tall, with mostly basal leaves and a few pairs of opposite leaves on the stem. The leaves are up to 8" long and less than 1" wide, varying from hairy to smooth and hairless. Most leaves lack teeth or lobes, but rarely there are a few small lobes along the edges of some basal leaves. Flower heads are on individual stalks above the rest of the plant, often with a single head per plant. Each head has 8–10 golden yellow, petal-like ray flowers. These are wide and fan-shaped, with 4–5 jagged teeth at the tip.

Bloom Season: Midspring–midsummer.

Habitat/Range: Locally common in dry, sandy soils in the southwestern tallgrass region, through the southern half of Missouri and Illinois into northwestern Indiana, and sporadically eastward; also becoming established as a weed in disturbed sandy soils.

Comments: This species often grows in sites with less vegetation than the related Large-Flowered Coreopsis.

PRAIRIE COREOPSIS
Coreopsis palmata
Aster family (Asteraceae)

Description: Plants usually 1–2½' tall and unbranched below the flower stalks. There are no basal leaves, and the stem leaves are opposite, with each leaf divided into 3 long, narrow segments, and the central segment often itself divided into 1–2 segments. The leaves have prominent veins along the lengths of the segments. Flower heads are at the tops of individual erect stalks, typically with 8 yellow, petal-like ray flowers per head. The ray flowers are not as fan-shaped or coarsely toothed at the tips as other species of Coreopsis found on prairies, and the flowers are paler yellow.

Bloom Season: Late spring–midsummer.

Habitat/Range: Frequent in dry prairies and open savannas, typically in sandy, gravelly, or rocky sites; scattered through all but the northernmost tallgrass region, from eastern South Dakota to northeastern Oklahoma and east through northwestern Indiana into Michigan.

FRANK OBERLE

FRANK OBERLE

TALL COREOPSIS
Coreopsis tripteris
Aster family (Asteraceae)

Description: Smooth, usually hairless plants, typically 2–4' tall, but occasionally reaching 8'. The leaves are opposite and stalked, with all or most divided into 3 long, narrow leaflets resembling the leaves of plants in the Bean family (Fabaceae). The leaf veins are arranged like the rays of a bird feather. Individual flower heads occur on numerous erect, slender stalks on the upper part of the plant. Each head is 1–2" wide, typically with 8 yellow, petal-like ray flowers surrounding a brown central disk.

Bloom Season: Summer–early fall.

Habitat/Range: Occasional in moist to mesic prairies, often in deep soils, from eastern Kansas and southern Iowa eastward. This species is characteristic of prairies in the eastern tallgrass region, but occurs more typically in thickets and moist sites in the western tallgrass region.

YELLOW CONEFLOWER
Echinacea paradoxa
Aster family (Asteraceae)

Description: Shiny, smooth to inconspicuously hairy plants typically 2–3' tall, with stout erect stems. The narrow alternate leaves are mostly near the base of the plant, and up to 9" long, but less than 2" wide, each with several parallel lengthwise veins. Each stem is topped with a spectacular head that resembles a single flower up to 5" across, with many golden yellow petal-like ray flowers which usually angle downward, and a rounded central brown cone of disk flowers and sharp bracts.

Bloom Season: Late spring–early summer

Habitat/range: Local in exposed, well-drained, calcium-rich soil in glades and prairies in the Ozarks from central Missouri to northern Arkansas.

Comments: This unusual yellow-flowered relative of the purple coneflower has a restricted native range, but is hardy, commercially available, and should be used more in gardens because of its stunning appearance. A variant with pinkish to white ray flowers, variety neglecta, occurs in southwestern tallgrass sites in Oklahoma and Texas.

FRANK OBERLE

FRANK OBERLE

PLAINS GRASS-LEAVED GOLDENROD
Euthamia gymnospermoides
Aster family (Asteraceae)

Description: Spindly plants to 3' tall, branched in the upper half. The leaves are alternate along the hairless stems, less than ⅛" wide, hairless, and covered on the undersides with minute, resinous spots. There is a prominent vein along the center of the leaf, sometimes with a less prominent vein on each side of the main vein. The flower heads are about ¼" wide and occur in small, flattened, branching clusters at the tips of the stem branches. Each head has fewer than 15 yellow, petal-like ray flowers surrounding 4–6 small, tubular disk flowers.

Bloom Season: Late summer–fall.

Habitat/Range: Locally frequent in sandy soils and upland prairies from northern Indiana south and westward; rare north of Iowa.

Comments: Grass-Leaved Goldenrod *(E. graminifolia)* is a similar species of prairies and fields through much of the tallgrass region, but is rare at the southern edge of the area. It has hairy stems and leaves with at least 3 well-defined main veins along their length, with some of the leaves more than ⅛" wide.

SPINY-TOOTHED GUMWEED
Grindelia lanceolata
Aster family (Asteraceae)

Description: Alternate-leaved plants to about 3' tall, usually branched in the upper half. The leaves are smooth, up to 4" long and 1" wide, with bases that slightly clasp the stem, and scattered bristlelike teeth along the edges. The ends of the leaves taper abruptly to pointed tips. Flower heads are about 1½" wide and on individual stalks on the upper branches. Each head has many gummy or sticky green bracts around its base. These bracts have long, wiry tips that spread outward, giving the head a burlike appearance. There are about 20–30 yellow, petal-like ray flowers surrounding a flat, yellow disk.

Bloom Season: Late summer–fall.

Habitat/Range: Locally common in dry, rocky sites with exposed limestone, including prairies, glades, pastures, and along roadsides; found in the southwestern tallgrass region from eastern Kansas and Missouri southward, and occasionally introduced as a weed eastward.

FRANK OBERLE

COMMON SUNFLOWER

Helianthus annuus
Aster family (Asteraceae)

Description: Tall, coarsely hairy annuals with stout stems and broad alternate leaves, sometimes with the lowest leaves opposite. Although cultivated plants can exceed 10', wild plants are usually less than 5' tall. The long-stalked, rough leaves are typically up to 8" long and half to fully as wide, with toothed edges, broad bases, and triangular tips. At the ends of branches on the upper part of the plant are one to several large flower heads. Each head has a reddish brown central disk 1" or more in diameter, surrounded by 20 or more yellow, petal-like ray flowers. Each ray flower is 1–2" long, usually with impressed parallel lines along its length.

Bloom Season: Midsummer–fall.

Habitat/Range: Dry prairies, pastures, and disturbed open sites throughout the tallgrass region. Although probably native near the western edge of the tallgrass region, most of the plants seen today are introduced populations.

Comments: This species was first cultivated by Native Americans. Many forms of Common Sunflower are now cultivated throughout the world for ornament, seed, forage, and oil. Some of these strains escape and become established. A similar annual sunflower, Plains Sunflower *(H. petiolaris)*, is a smaller plant with smaller flower heads, usually with darker brown disks containing scales with white hairs at their tips.

FRANK OBERLE

FRANK OBERLE

SNEEZEWEED
Helenium autumnale
Aster family (Asteraceae)

Description: Branching plants to 5' tall with opposite, somewhat fleshy leaves and narrow wings of leafy green tissue extending downward along the stem from the leaf bases. The leaves are widest near the middle and taper at each end. They are up to 6" long and 1½" wide, usually with small, widely spaced teeth along the edges. Flower heads are on individual stalks. Each head is 1–1¾" wide, with several long, thin, pointed green bracts underlying 10-20 broadly fan-shaped, yellow, petal-like ray flowers which surround a rounded central yellow disk up to ¾" wide. The ray flowers are each cleft into 3–4 lobes at their tips.

Bloom Season: Midsummer–fall.

Habitat/Range: Locally frequent in moist areas in prairies, wet pastures, along streams, and especially common in areas with seepage of mineralized water throughout the tallgrass region.

Comments: Sneezeweed is poisonous to livestock, but is usually not eaten. The dried flower heads were reportedly used as snuff by the pioneers.

PURPLE-HEADED SNEEZEWEED
Helenium flexuosum
Aster family (Asteraceae)

Description: Plants to 3' tall, with winged stems and alternate, stalkless leaves up to 3" long and less than 1" wide. The bases of the leaves continue down the stem as wings of green tissue. Flower heads are in a flattish cluster on individual stalks at the top of the plant. Each head is about 1" wide, with a round, brownish purple central disk surrounded by 8–14 fan-shaped, yellow, petal-like ray flowers, each with 3 lobes.

Bloom Season: Summer–fall.

Habitat/Range: Frequent in dry to moist sites in prairies, pastures, and old fields, often in acidic soils; found through the southern tallgrass region from southeastern Kansas eastward, and introduced as a weed northward.

Comments: Like Sneezeweed, this plant is poisonous when grazed by livestock, but is usually avoided because of its bitter taste.

FRANK OBERLE

SAWTOOTH SUNFLOWER
Helianthus grosseserratus
Aster family (Asteraceae)

Description: Tall, colony-forming sunflowers with many large, narrow, alternate leaves along the stem, which is hairless below the flowers. The leaves commonly have at least a few teeth along their edges, and have hairy undersides. The largest leaves are about 8" long and nearly 2" wide near the middle, tapering to pointed tips and short, winged leaf stalks. The upper part of the plant has numerous flower heads on individual stalks or branch tips. Each head is 2–3½" wide, with 10–20 yellow, petal-like ray flowers surrounding a yellow disk.

Bloom Season: Midsummer–fall.

Habitat/Range: Common in draws and thickets in dry to wet prairies and pastures, also along roadsides, ditches, and streams; found throughout the tallgrass region.

FRANK OBERLE

MAXIMILIAN SUNFLOWER
Helianthus maximilianii
Aster family (Asteraceae)

Description: Coarse plants to 9' tall, with densely white-hairy stems and narrow, alternate, toothed leaves. The largest leaves are up to 12" long, only 2" wide, and are usually curved and folded together along the middle. There are usually many flower heads in a tall, narrow cluster near the top of the plant. Each head is up to 4" wide, with 10–25 yellow, petal-like ray flowers, each up to 1½" long, surrounding a yellow disk.

Bloom Season: Midsummer–fall.

Habitat/Range: Frequent on exposed rocky slopes, dry prairies, and sometimes in moister sites; often in sandy soil. Found through most of the tallgrass region, but many of the populations east of Missouri are recent introductions or escapes from cultivation.

Comments: Another sunflower with extreme-ly narrow leaves, Willow-Leaved Sunflower *(H. salicifolius)*, has reddish disks, leaves less than ½" wide, and occurs in limestone prairies in eastern Kansas, western Missouri, and northeastern Oklahoma.

FRANK OBERLE

DON KURZ

ASHY SUNFLOWER
Helianthus mollis
Aster family (Asteraceae)

Description: Grayish green plants to 3' tall, with conspicuously hairy stems and leaves. The leaves are stiff, opposite, and up to 6" long and 3" wide, with rounded to notched, stalkless bases. The leaves taper to pointed tips, and the edges of the leaves often have small teeth. There are one to few individually stalked flower heads at the top of the plant, with each head 2½–4" wide. Each head has many thin, narrow, overlapping, green bracts at its base, up to 30 yellow, petal-like ray flowers, and a central disk with yellow disk flowers and brown bracts.

Bloom Season: Midsummer–fall.

Habitat/Range: One of the most widespread and characteristic species of upland prairies in the southern half of the tallgrass region, from northern Illinois southward.

WESTERN SUNFLOWER
Helianthus occidentalis
Aster family (Asteraceae)

Description: Stems of this sunflower are covered with spreading white hairs. The plants are usually 2–3' tall, with up to 5 sets of opposite or 3-whorled leaves along the stem. Below the stem is usually a conspicuous cluster of long-stalked basal leaves 3–6" long and 1–2½" wide. The stem leaves are smaller, with shorter stalks or no stalks at all. Flower heads occur on small stalks near the top of the plant. Each head is 1½–2" wide, with about 15 narrow, yellow, petal-like ray flowers surrounding a ½"-wide yellow disk. The bracts at the base of the flower heads are narrow and long-pointed, with tips that tend to curve outward.

Bloom Season: Midsummer–fall.

Habitat/Range: Occasional in dry sandy or rocky prairies, as well as in hill prairies, typically in areas with sparse vegetation; found in the eastern tallgrass region west to western Missouri.

FRANK OBERLE

FRANK OBERLE

PRAIRIE SUNFLOWER
Helianthus pauciflorus
Aster family (Asteraceae)

Description: This sunflower has a few widely spaced, narrow, mostly opposite leaves which are progressively smaller toward the top of the unbranched to sparsely branched stems. The leaves are thick, rough, long-pointed, broadest below the middle, and up to 12" long and 2½" wide. There are one to several flower heads per plant, with each individually stalked head 2½–4" wide and containing overlapping, broadly triangular, green bracts at the base, with 10–23 yellow, petal-like ray flowers surrounding a dark reddish purple disk.

Bloom Season: Midsummer–fall.

Habitat/Range: Widespread and locally frequent in dry prairies throughout the tallgrass region.

JERUSALEM ARTICHOKE
Helianthus tuberosus
Aster family (Asteraceae)

Description: This tall sunflower has opposite leaves on the lower half of the stem, often with alternate leaves on the upper half. The leaves are roughly hairy and up to 10" long and about a third as wide, with the widest part near the base. The flower heads are on individual stalks at the tops of branches, with each head up to 4" wide. There are 10–20 yellow, petal-like ray flowers surrounding a yellow disk that is ¾–1" wide.

Bloom Season: Midsummer–fall.

Habitat/Range: Frequent in moist thickets, along streams, and in prairie draws throughout the tallgrass region, but usually occurring along the edges of prairie vegetation.

Comments: The native range of Jerusalem Artichoke is uncertain since the plant has been cultivated for centuries for its edible tubers, which are marketed commercially today.

117

FRANK OBERLE

FRANK OBERLE

FALSE SUNFLOWER
Heliopsis helianthoides
Aster family (Asteraceae)

Description: Branching plants to 4' tall, with opposite, stalked, triangular leaves. The leaves are coarsely and regularly toothed along the edges, and up to 6" long and 3½" wide. Flower heads are on individual stalks, with the stalks slightly thickened just below the heads. Each pale to golden yellow flower head is 2–4" wide, with up to 20 petal-like ray flowers and a cone-shaped yellow disk.

Bloom Season: Late spring–fall.

Habitat/Range: Common in moist draws and seepage areas in upland prairies, on prairie slopes with exposed limestone, and in open thickets in prairies and woodlands; throughout the tallgrass region.

LONG-BEARDED HAWKWEED
Hieracium longipilum
Aster family (Asteraceae)

Description: Slender stems 3' or more tall arise from a dense cluster of long-hairy basal leaves. These leaves are up to 10" long and typically about 1" wide, broadest just above the middle, and taper to bluntly pointed tips and long-tapering bases. The stem leaves are mostly on the lower half of the plant and progressively smaller upward along the stem. The stem is densely furry with long hairs, with at least some of the hairs more than ½" long. Flower heads are in an open cylindrical cluster at the top of the stem, usually with tiny, stalked black glands along the flower stalks. The flower heads are about ¼" wide, with up to 90 small, yellow, petal-like flowers per head, resembling a miniature dandelion head.

Bloom Season: Mid-late summer.

Habitat/Range: Frequent in dry prairies and open sandy sites in the southern half of the tallgrass region, from Iowa east to Indiana and rarely northward.

DON KURZ

KEITH BOARD

DWARF DANDELION
Krigia virginica
Aster family (Asteraceae)

Description: Small annuals usually less than 8" tall, with milky juice, and resembling miniature Potato Dandelions (above), which are larger and perennial. The roots of Dwarf Dandelion are fibrous, with no tubers. Leaves are all basal or on the lower parts of the stems, usually less than 4½" long and ½" wide, and often scalloped into numerous, pointed lobes. The flower heads are single at the tops of the stems, with each yellow-orange head about ½" wide and consisting of numerous small, yellow-orange, petal-like ray flowers.

Bloom Season: Midspring–midsummer.

Habitat/Range: Occasional in a variety of sandy sites, including prairies, pastures, fields, and disturbed areas in much of the tallgrass region, west through Missouri and north to northern Illinois.

Comments: A closely related species, Western Dwarf Dandelion *(K. occidentalis),* occurs in sandy prairies from southwestern Missouri south and westward. It differs in having 8 or fewer ribbed bracts at the base of each flower head, as opposed to the 9 or more flat bracts at the base of each head in Dwarf Dandelion.

POTATO DANDELION
Krigia dandelion
Aster family (Asteraceae)

Description: Dandelion-like plants with milky juice, bulbous underground tubers, and bare stems to about 15" tall, each topped with a single flower head. The leaves are all basal, with each leaf evenly scalloped into several wide, sharp-toothed lobes. The leaves are up to 8" long and 1" wide. The flower heads are about 1½" wide with 25-35 small, yellow-orange, petal-like ray flowers.

Bloom Season: Midspring–early summer.

Habitat/Range: Frequent in prairies, rocky open woodlands, and sandy areas in the southern tallgrass region, from southeastern Kansas east through southern Indiana.

Comments: False Dandelion *(K. biflora)* is a similar species occurring in most of the tallgrass region; it grows in open woodlands, as well as prairies in the eastern half of the region, and can be distinguished by the presence of a few leaves on the stem and 2 or more flower heads per stem.

K. YATSKIEVYCH

DON KURZ

WILD LETTUCE

Lactuca canadensis
Aster family (Asteraceae)

Description: Light green, biennial plants to 8'
tall, with alternate leaves and milky, orange-tan
sap. The leaves are up to 12" long and 6" wide,
but in prairies are usually about 3–6" long and
less than 2½" wide. Leaves vary from deeply
lobed to rounded and unlobed, with edges that
may be toothed or smooth. The small flower
heads are on individual stalks in a large,
branching cluster at the tops of the main stem
branches. Each head is less than ½" wide when
fully opened, with several pointed, green bracts
surrounding 15–22 yellow, petal-like ray flowers
resembling a miniature Dandelion.

Bloom Season: Summer.

Habitat/Range: Common throughout the tallgrass
region in pastures, upland prairies, open thickets,
and along woodland edges, usually in sites with a
history of previous disturbance.

PRAIRIE DANDELION

Nothocalais cuspidata
Aster family (Asteraceae)

Description: Although similar to the introduced,
weedy Common Dandelion found in lawns, Prairie
Dandelions are native prairie plants with a very
restricted habitat. The base of each plant has a
cluster of long, narrow, wavy-edged leaves, each
less than 1" wide and up to 1' long. A leafless
stalk originates from the center of the basal leaf
cluster, growing to about 1' tall, and topped with
a single, showy, bright yellow flower head to 2"
wide, with numerous, petal-like ray flowers.

Bloom Season: Spring.

Habitat/Range: Uncommon and local in dry
prairies, often in gravelly or rocky sites with
sparse vegetation, from central Illinois north and
westward.

Comments: This species often grows with Pasque
Flower.

KENNETH DRITZ

FRANK OBERLE

RIDDELL'S GOLDENROD
Oligoneuron riddellii
Aster family (Asteraceae)

Description: Stout, showy goldenrods to 3' tall, with smooth, hairless stems and leaves. The leaves are toothless, shiny, somewhat folded lengthwise, and tend to curve away from the stem, with rough edges. Flowers are in a short, dense, domed cluster at the top of the stem, with numerous heads on all sides of the branches. Each small head is up to ⅜" wide, with 7–9 yellow, petal-like ray flowers surrounding up to 20 tiny, tubular disk flowers.

Bloom Season: Late summer–fall.

Habitat/Range: Restricted to mesic and wet prairies and seepage areas through all but the westernmost tallgrass region; rare in western Minnesota and eastern North Dakota, and absent west of Missouri.

STIFF GOLDENROD
Oligoneuron rigidum
Aster family (Asteraceae)

Description: Coarse plants to 5' tall, usually somewhat hairy, with unbranched lower stems and broad, thick leaves. The large basal leaves are on long stalks and up to 10" long and 5" wide, sometimes with weakly toothed edges. The alternately arranged stem leaves are progressively smaller upward, with shorter stalks or stalkless. The flower heads are in a rounded to flattened cluster at the top of the plant, with the branch below each head having many small leaflike bracts. Each flower head is about ½" wide, with 7–14 yellow, petal-like ray flowers surrounding the central disk flowers, which have protruding threadlike stigmas. This species has larger flower heads than most of our goldenrods.

Bloom Season: Late summer–fall.

Habitat/Range: Frequent in well-drained prairies throughout the tallgrass region.

Comments: The deep roots of Stiff Goldenrod allow it to survive severe overgrazing and other disturbances. It can become abundant in old fields and pastures that were formerly prairie.

121

FRANK OBERLE

PRAIRIE RAGWORT
Packera plattensis
Aster family (Asteraceae)

Description: Stems mostly unbranched and up to 2' tall, with alternate leaves and usually with patches of white, cobweblike hairs on the leaves and flower heads. The basal leaves are up to 3" long and 1½" wide (less than 3 times as long as wide), long stalked, toothed, and sometimes have lobed edges. The few stem leaves are smaller, mostly stalkless, and usually divided into lobes. Up to 10 (rarely 20) flower heads occur in a flattened cluster at the top of the stem. Each head is ½–1" wide, with about 6–15 yellow, petal-like ray flowers surrounding the small, yellow-orange disk flowers.

Bloom Season: Midspring–early summer.

Habitat/Range: Frequent in dry upland prairies and sandy or gravelly areas throughout the tallgrass region, but less common eastward.

Comments: The plants are poisonous to humans and livestock but were used in folk medicines. Balsam Ragwort *(P. paupercula)* occurs in moist prairies through all but the southern tallgrass region; the blades of the basal leaves are mostly more than 3 times as long as they are wide.

FRANK OBERLE

GRAY-HEADED CONEFLOWER
Ratibida pinnata
Aster family (Asteraceae)

Description: Hairy, slender-stemmed, branching plants to about 4' tall. All leaves are alternate; most are divided into 1–4 pairs of narrow lobes, with an additional lobe at the tip. Each lobe is widest near the middle, tapers to a narrow base and pointed tip, and may have a few teeth or small side lobes. The basal leaves are on long stalks, with the blade of the leaf up to 7" long. The upper leaves are smaller and often undivided. Flower heads are about 3" wide and on long individual stalks. Each head has a brown, bullet-shaped central disk less than 1" tall and usually taller than wide, surrounded by up to 13 downward-pointing, yellow, petal-like ray flowers. The seed heads are sharply aromatic when crushed.

Bloom Season: Late spring–fall.

Habitat/Range: Common in mesic to dry prairies, especially in sites with a history of previous disturbance, as well as in open thickets and along banks and draws in prairies; found through the tallgrass region north to northeastern South Dakota.

Comments: Prairie Coneflower *(R. columnifera)* is a similar species at the western edge of the tallgrass region. It has the ray flowers surrounding an elongate central disk more than twice as long as it is wide, and the ray flowers sometimes marked with dark red.

FRANK OBERLE

FRANK OBERLE

BLACK-EYED SUSAN
Rudbeckia hirta
Aster family (Asteraceae)

Description: Plants up to 3' tall, but typically 1–2' tall, with bristly-hairy leaves and stems. The leaves are alternate, sometimes toothed, widest at the middle and tapering to pointed tips, with the lowest leaves usually stalked, and most of the stem leaves less than 4" long. There are several parallel veins running along the length of each leaf. Flower heads are single at the top of each stem branch, with each head about 2–3" wide and composed of a dark brown, rounded to conical, buttonlike central disk surrounded by 8–20 yellow, petal-like ray flowers.

Bloom Season: Midspring–fall.

Habitat/Range: Widely distributed, but never abundant, in high-quality dry to mesic prairies, more common in grazed prairies, dry pastures, hay meadows, old fields, and along roadsides throughout the tallgrass region.

Comments: A tea made from the leaves of Black-Eyed Susan was used in folk medicines, and a yellow dye can be made from the plant.

SWEET BLACK-EYED SUSAN
Rudbeckia subtomentosa
Aster family (Asteraceae)

Description: Plants to 6' tall, with at least some fine hairiness on the upper stems, although usually smooth below. The leaves are alternate and softly hairy, but not bristly, with the basal leaves on long stalks and the stem leaves on short stalks or stalkless. Some of the stem leaves are deeply divided into 3 lobes. There are usually several individually stalked flower heads at the top of the plant, with each head about 2½–3" wide and composed of 6–20 yellow, petal-like ray flowers surrounding a bluntly conical central disk that is as tall or taller than it is wide.

Bloom Season: Summer.

Habitat/Range: Locally frequent in mesic prairies, low swales in upland prairies, and in thickets along prairie streams; found from Indiana through eastern Nebraska and southward.

Comments: This plant is also called Sweet Coneflower.

KENNETH DRITZ

FRANK OBERLE

BROWN-EYED SUSAN
Rudbeckia triloba
Aster family (Asteraceae)

Description: Bushy-branched plants to 5' tall, with spreading hairs on the stems. The leaves are alternate, with the main stem leaves about 4" long, including their narrowly winged to clasping bases. The leaves are rough and bristly on both sides, with coarsely toothed edges and pointed tips. Some of the main leaves are divided into 3 forklike lobes. Flower heads are abundant over the upper part of the plant and are on individual stalks spreading away from the main stems. Each head is up to 1¾" wide, with about 6–12 yellow, petal-like ray flowers surrounding a cone-shaped to rounded, brown center. The ray flowers are grooved along their lengths and narrowly notched at the tips.

Bloom Season: Summer–fall.

Habitat/Range: Common in moist thickets, low woods, and along streams from Iowa south and eastward, but also found in prairies and low prairie pastures, particularly in Ohio.

ROSIN WEED
Silphium integrifolium
Aster family (Asteraceae)

Description: Stout plants usually 2–3' tall. The leaves are rough and sandpapery on the top surface, up to 6" long and 2½" wide, and stalkless. Rosin Weed is extremely variable— the leaves may be narrow or broad and round, toothless or toothed along the edges, and are usually opposite, although occasionally alternate or even whorled. There are several large flower heads on the ends of short, stout stalks at the top of the plant, with each head surrounded by a series of broad, green, sepal-like bracts. The flower heads are about 3" wide, with numerous yellow, petal-like ray flowers surrounding a disk of small, sterile, disk flowers.

Bloom Season: Summer–fall.

Habitat/Range: A characteristic plant of mesic, deep-soil prairies of the tallgrass region, north and west to southeastern South Dakota.

Comments: This plant is similar to Ashy Sunflower, but the sunflower has many narrow, needlelike bracts at the base of each flower head, and the surface of the sunflower leaf is less rough, and can be rubbed with the fingers, whereas the leaf of Rosin Weed is so rough that it cannot easily be rubbed.

FRANK OBERLE

COMPASS PLANT
Silphium laciniatum
Aster family (Asteraceae)

Description: One of the largest-leaved plants of the prairie, Compass Plant has huge basal leaves, and a 3–8' tall flower stalk with a few similar, but progressively smaller, alternate leaves along its length. The basal leaves are broadly triangular in general outline and can be over 1' long. They are deeply divided into a series of narrow segments that are themselves sometimes divided. At the top of the hairy stalk are several alternate, green-bracted flower heads. Each head is 2½–4½" wide, with many yellow, petal-like ray flowers surrounding a yellow center with many sterile disk flowers.

Bloom Season: Late spring–summer.

Habitat/Range: Common in mesic and drier prairies, often along roadsides and in slightly disturbed sites; from southeastern South Dakota southward, becoming more sporadic from Indiana eastward.

Comments: Native American children used the dried resinous sap as chewing gum.

FRANK OBERLE

FRANK OBERLE

CUP PLANT
Silphium perfoliatum
Aster family (Asteraceae)

Description: Distinctive plants with smooth, square stems growing up to 8' tall. The large, coarsely toothed, opposite leaves are joined around the stem, forming a cup that actually holds rainwater. The flower heads are on individual branches in the upper part of the plant. Each head is 2½–4" wide, with several broad, green, pointed bracts flanking 18–40 yellow, petal-like ray flowers. The small, tubular disk flowers in the middle of the flower are sterile and do not produce fruits.

Bloom Season: Summer–fall.

Habitat/Range: Locally frequent in moist areas along prairie streams, low thickets, floodplains, and along the edges of wet woodlands. Found throughout the tallgrass region, but more sporadic northward.

PRAIRIE DOCK
Silphium terebinthinaceum
Aster family (Asteraceae)

Description: Prairie Dock is easily recognized by its clusters of large, sandpapery, spade-shaped basal leaves, which are up to 16" long. The flower heads are in an open cluster at the top of a smooth, shiny, nearly leafless 2- to 10'-tall stalk. The individually stalked flower heads are 2–3" wide. Each head has several broad, shiny, green, rounded bracts and 12–25 yellow, petal-like ray flowers with notched tips; these surround several small, tubular, sterile, yellow disk flowers with protruding, threadlike styles. This is a drought-resistant, long-lived perennial with fragrant, resinous sap.

Bloom Season: Summer–fall.

Habitat/Range: Characteristic in deep-soil and loamy prairies and also in rocky sites; found in the eastern half of the tallgrass region, but rare or absent from western Missouri westward.

Comments: Prairie Dock is among the tallest and largest-leaved of our prairie plants. Just as with Compass Plant, in open prairies the leaves of Prairie Dock often orient themselves along a north-south axis, facilitating maximum leaf exposure to sunlight.

FRANK OBERLE

TALL GOLDENROD
Solidago altissima
Aster family (Asteraceae)

Description: Hairy-stemmed plants to 7' tall, usually unbranched in the lower half. There are many alternate leaves, with the largest leaves on the middle part of the stem. These leaves are narrow and up to 6" long and 1¼" wide, usually with a few scattered, sharp teeth near the tips. The underside of the leaf is hairy, with 3 prominently raised veins running the length of the leaf. Tiny flower heads are in a cluster of radiating branches at the top of the plant, with the flower heads all occurring on the upper side of a branch. The individual heads are up to ¼" wide, each with about 10–15 narrow, yellow, petal-like ray flowers and a few disk flowers; the protruding styles are tipped with spear-pointed yellow stigmas.

Bloom Season: Midsummer–fall.

Habitat/Range: Common throughout the tallgrass region and locally abundant in moist to dry open sites, especially areas with a history of previous disturbance.

Comments: This is the weediest goldenrod in the region, and is rare in undisturbed prairies. A close relative, Canada Goldenrod *(S. Canadensis)* is also common through the region. It has the green bracts under the flower heads less than ⅛" tall, while in Tall Goldenrod they are more than ⅛" tall.

KENNETH DRITZ

EARLY GOLDENROD
Solidago juncea
Aster family (Asteraceae)

Description: Most goldenrods bloom in late summer through fall, but this species is often in full bloom by early summer, and is one of the earliest goldenrods to flower. Plants grow to 3' tall, with the largest leaves at the base of the plant usually more than 1" wide, and up to 8" long. The stem leaves are alternate, progressively smaller upward, and have a single prominent vein and numerous smaller side veins. Flower heads are on the top sides of arching branches, with less than 14 very small, yellow, petal-like ray flowers and about 10 tiny disk flowers per head.

Bloom Season: Summer–fall.

Habitat/Range: Frequent in dry open fields and prairies in the eastern tallgrass region, becoming rare at its western limits in southern Missouri.

Comments: A related early-blooming goldenrod, Missouri Goldenrod *(S. missouriensis)* occurs through the western two-thirds of the tallgrass region. It has prominently 3-veined leaves and basal leaves less than 1" wide which often wither before flowering time.

KENNETH DRITZ

FRANK OBERLE

OLD-FIELD GOLDENROD
Solidago nemoralis
Aster family (Asteraceae)

Description: Distinctive goldenrods with the stems unbranched below the flower heads, alternate leaves progressively reduced upward along the stem, and the stems and leaves covered with dense, short gray hairs, giving the entire plant a gray-green appearance. The flowers are in a narrow, elongate spray at the top of the plant, with small heads along the tops of short, arching side branches. Each head is less than ¼" wide, with fewer than 10 yellow, petal-like ray flowers surrounding about 3-6 small, tubular, yellow disk flowers.

Bloom Season: Late summer–fall.

Habitat/Range: Common in dry prairies, prairie pastures, and old fields, especially in sandy and rocky soils; throughout the tallgrass region.

SHOWY GOLDENROD
Solidago speciosa
Aster family (Asteraceae)

Description: Unbranched stems to 4' tall, with alternate, thick, smooth leaves. The lower leaves are up to 8" long and 4" wide, or rarely larger, with the middle and upper leaves smaller. The flowers are in an elongate, cylindrical cluster at the top of the stem, with numerous small heads on short lateral branches. Each head is up to ½" wide, with typically 5–6 (but up to 10) yellow, petal-like ray flowers and usually 4–5 small disk flowers.

Bloom Season: Late summer–fall.

Habitat/Range: Occasional in prairies and open savannas throughout the tallgrass region, but less common south of Missouri and southern Illinois.

FRANK OBERLE

FRANK OBERLE

HOARY PUCCOON
Lithospermum canescens
Borage family (Boraginaceae)

Description: Dark green plants to about 15" tall with softly hairy stems and leaves, typically with several stems per plant. The leaves are stalkless, smooth-edged, and alternate, with a prominent vein along the middle. Each leaf is up to 2½" long and ½" wide, often with a rounded tip. Flowers are in a flattened cluster at the top of the plant, with each flower about ½" wide. There are 5 narrow, pointed, green sepals and a tubular, deep golden yellow corolla with 5 spreading, rounded lobes.

Bloom Season: Spring–early summer.

Habitat/Range: Common in mesic to dry prairies and open upland savannas; often in rocky soils, particularly limestone, but seldom in sandy sites, throughout the tallgrass region.

Comments: The roots of this plant have been used medicinally and to produce a reddish dye. A similar species, Rough Puccoon *(L. caroliniense)* occurs in sand prairies, sand savannas, and open sandy sites and has pointed leaf tips and a coarse, rough hairiness.

FRINGED PUCCOON
Lithospermum incisum
Borage family (Boraginaceae)

Description: Hairy plants less than 15" tall, with narrow, alternate leaves up to 3" long and usually less than ¼" wide. Flowers are in clusters at the tops of the stems, with each flower up to 1" wide and consisting of a green calyx with 5 narrow, pointed lobes and a pale yellow corolla with a thin tube flaring to 5 spreading lobes with distinctive, crinkle-fringed edges.

Bloom Season: Midspring–early summer.

Habitat/Range: Occasional in dry upland prairies, often on sterile slopes or hill prairies, and in open woodlands; found in the western tallgrass region east to western Indiana and southern Ontario.

Comments: The earliest flowers are large and often sterile, while later flowers are selfpollinated and have a tiny corolla that is smaller than the calyx.

FRANK OBERLE

PRICKLY PEAR
Opuntia humifusa
Cactus family (Cactaceae)

Description: This cactus has enlarged, succulent, spiny, green stems that often occur in sprawling colonies. The flattened stem segments, called pads, are usually 3–5" long and 2–3" wide. Scattered, stiff, needlelike spines usually occur singly or in pairs on the pad surface, along with abundant clusters of tiny, bristly hairs associated with the spines. Sometimes the spines are absent, with only bristles on the pads. The bright yellow flowers grow singly from buds on ther pads. They are up to 4" wide and sometimes have reddish centers. Each flower has several sepals, 8-12 petals, numerous stamens, and a stout central style. The flowers develop into cylindrical, red fruits up to 2" long.

Bloom Season: Late spring–midsummer.

Habitat/Range: Frequent in dry, often rocky or sandy sites, including prairies, pastures, and open savannas, typically growing in areas with sparse vegetation; found from eastern Kansas and southern Minnesota south and eastward.

Comments: The fruits are edible fresh or cooked and are sometimes used to make syrup and jam. The peeled pads have been used as vegetables. Care must be taken to remove all the tiny bristles, which can become painfully embedded in the skin or mouth. A closely related species, Plains Prickly Pear *(O. macrorhiza),* occurs in the western tallgrass region, and can be identified by its bluish green color and usually more than 2 stout spines per cluster.

ROBERT MOHLENBROCK

FRANK OBERLE

SPOTTED ST. JOHN'S WORT
Hypericum punctatum
St. John's Wort family (Clusiaceae)

Description: Smooth, hairless, light green plants to 3' tall, usually unbranched in the lower half. The sepals, petals, and undersides of the leaves are covered with tiny black dots. The leaves are opposite, stalkless, bluntly oval, and up to 2½" long and ¾" wide, with rounded to bluntly pointed tips. Flowers are in dense heads at the ends of stems and side branches near the top of the plant. Each flower is about ½" wide, with 5 small green sepals, 5 yellow petals, and numerous stamens surrounding a flask-shaped central ovary.

Bloom Season: Summer.

Habitat/Range: Common in moist areas in low prairies, prairie swales, along streams and shores, moist sandy areas, and in thickets, fields and pastures; found through the southern two-thirds of the tallgrass region, north to southern Minnesota.

NITS AND LICE
Hypericum drummondii
St. John's Wort family (Clusiaceae)

Description: Slender annuals usually less than 1' tall, with reddish brown lower stems and many pairs of tiny, pointed, opposite leaves. Each leaf is less than ¾" long and less than ⅛" wide. The flowers are usually single at the tops of branches or on side stalks arising from the bases of main stem leaves. Each flower is up to ⅓" wide, with 5 pointed, green sepals which are slightly longer than the 5 orange-yellow petals.

Bloom Season: Summer.

Habitat/Range: Frequent in sterile, dry areas in acidic soils, especially in sand and clay in prairies, pastures, and glades through the southern tallgrass region, from eastern Kansas through central Illinois and eastward.

133

FRANK OBERLE

ROUND-FRUITED ST. JOHN'S WORT
Hypericum sphaerocarpum
St. John's Wort family (Clusiaceae)

Description: Plants with brownish lower stems arising from woody bases; typically less than 1' tall, but occasionally up to 2'. The leaves are opposite, smooth-edged, stalkless, and up to 3" long and ⅝" wide. The edges of the leaves are often turned downward. There are usually branches with numerous smaller leaves arising at the bases of the main leaves. Flowers are in compact, branched clusters at the tops of the stem branches, with each flower about ½–¾" wide and consisting of 5 small, green sepals and 5 deep yellow petals surrounding many yellow stamens and a flask-shaped ovary.

Bloom Season: Midspring–summer.

Habitat/Range: Common in dry rocky prairies and upland pastures, often associated with limestone, and usually growing in areas where the vegetation is somewhat sparse and low; found in the southern half of the tallgrass region, from eastern Nebraska eastward.

FRANK OBERLE

CREAM WILD INDIGO
Baptisia bracteata variety *leucophaea*
Bean family (Fabaceae)

Description: Large, finely hairy, somewhat sprawling plants about 2' tall. Each alternate compound leaf is divided into 3 leaflets. These leaflets are larger than those of other Indigos, ranging up to 3½" long, widest at or above the middle, and tapering at either end. There are frequently 2 large, leaflike stipules at the base of the leaves, giving the initial appearance of 5 leaflets per leaf. The flower stems are usually drooping or reclining and have alternate, creamy yellow flowers, with small, leaflike bracts at the base of each flower stalk. Each flower is about 1" wide with an erect, fanlike, notched upper petal and two protruding side petals flanking a keel-like lip. The seed pods are fat, black, finely hairy, and up to 2" long, with pointed tips.

Bloom Season: Mid-late spring.

Habitat/Range: Common in prairies and savannas, often in acidic soils, from eastern Nebraska and southeastern Minnesota south and eastward to western Indiana and Kentucky.

FRANK OBERLE

PARTRIDGE PEA
Chamaecrista fasciculata
Bean family (Fabaceae)

Description: Annuals to 3½' tall, with slightly hairy stems and numerous, alternate, compound leaves. Each leaf is divided, featherlike, into as many as 20 pairs of leaflets, without a lone leaflet at the tip of the leaf. The leaflets are narrow, less than 1" long, and rounded on both ends, with a small, pointed, bristlelike tip. There is a small, saucer-shaped gland near the middle of each leaf stalk. The flowers are single or in small groups on stalks arising from where the main leaves join the stem. Each flower is up to 1½" wide, with 5 pointed, narrow, green sepals alternating with 5 rounded, bright yellow petals and 10 yellow to dark reddish stamens. The 4 upper petals have dark reddish bases. The fruits are small, flat pods up to 2½" long.

Bloom Season: Summer–fall.

Habitat/Range: Common to abundant in pastures, fields, prairies, and along roadsides, often in disturbed sandy soil; found in the tallgrass region north to west-central Minnesota.

Comments: Wild Sensitive Plant *(C. nictitans)* is a similar species commonly occurring in open upland woods and savannas and occasionally in prairies and pastures. It has flowers less than ¾" wide, with 5 stamens and a stalked, saucer-shaped gland on the leaf stalk.

FRANK OBERLE

RATTLEBOX
Crotalaria sagittalis
Bean family (Fabaceae)

Description: Usually annual plants up to 1' tall, rarely taller, with softly hairy stems and leaves. The leaves are alternate, stalkless or on short stalks, narrow, and up to 3" long and ¾" wide. Flowers are in groups of 1–4 on the ends of short side branches. Each flower is on a slender stalk with tiny leaflike bracts, and has 5 long, pointed, hairy, green sepals and a yellow corolla with a flaring upper petal and 2 smaller side petals bordering a protruding, keel-like lip. The seeds are in a smooth, fat pod that is about 1" long.

Bloom Season: Late spring–early fall.

Habitat/Range: Locally common in open sandy or rocky soils in prairies, fields, and pastures, often in zones of sparse vegetation and also a weed in disturbed sand; found in the southern tallgrass region from southeastern South Dakota south and eastward, although most common in prairie habitats in the southwest part of the region.

Comments: The pods turn black when ripe, at which time the seeds rattle freely within the pod. The roasted seeds reportedly have been used as a coffee substitute, but the plants are poisonous to livestock.

FRANK OBERLE

ROBERT TATINA

PENCIL FLOWER
Stylosanthes biflora
Bean family (Fabaceae)

Description: Small, wiry-stemmed plants usually less than 8" tall. Each alternate leaf is divided into 3 narrow, pointed leaflets each less than 2" long and ½" wide. There are usually widely scattered bristles along the edges of each leaflet. The distinctive, large stipules with long, pointed tips are attached to the leaf stalks and surround the stem. Flowers occur in small, leafy clusters at the tops of the branches; each bright orange-yellow flower is about ¼" long, with a spreading upper petal and 2 smaller side petals flanking a keel-like lower lip.

Bloom Season: Late spring–summer.

Habitat/Range: Common in dry prairies and savannas from the southern tallgrass region north to central Missouri, southern Illinois, and southern Indiana.

Comments: This species is often overlooked. Although small, the flowers have a unique dark yellow hue, resembling the paint on a standard wooden pencil.

MARYLAND SENNA
Senna marilandica
Bean family (Fabaceae)

Description: Plants to 6' tall, with large, alternate, compound leaves and hairless, mostly unbranched lower stems. The leaves have 8–20 oval leaflets, each up to 2½" long and 1" wide, with small, bristlelike points at the tips. Flowers are in branched clusters at the tops of the stems or on stalks arising from the junction of an upper leaf with the stem. Each flower is about 1" wide, with 5 pale yellow sepals, 5 yellow petals, and 10 brownish purple-tipped stamens, the lower 3 of which are larger than the others. The dangling, flattened fruit pods are up to 4" long and ½" wide.

Bloom Season: Mid–late summer.

Habitat/Range: Occasional in moist open areas along prairie streams, in open moist thickets, and shaded habitats; found in the southern tallgrass region north into northern Illinois and Iowa.

JOHN TAFT

BUFFALO CLOVER
Trifolium reflexum
Bean family (Fabaceae)

Description: Low, sprawling annuals with alternate compound leaves and stems up to 1' long. The leaves have long stalks, with 2 conspicuous, broad, pointed stipules at the base of each stalk. Each leaf is divided into 3 broadly oval leaflets typically ¾–1" long, with toothed edges. Flowers are in ball-like heads at the tops of the stems, with each head about 1" wide. Each narrow, pale yellow to creamy or slightly pinkish flower is about ½" long and has a calyx with 5 long, narrow lobes, a flaring upper petal, and 2 smaller side petals surrounding a keel-like lower lip.

Bloom Season: Late spring–midsummer.

Habitat/Range: Uncommon in dry to somewhat mesic prairies and open woodlands; scattered through the southern tallgrass region, from eastern Nebraska east and southward.

FRANK OBERLE

SPOTTED BEE BALM
Monarda punctata
Mint family (Lamiaceae)

Description: Although the true flowers of this plant are dull yellow with purple spots, people often see only the conspicuous pinkish purple bracts of the flower heads. Plants are about 3' tall, with finely hairy stems and toothed, opposite leaves on short stalks. The leaves are up to 3½" long and less than 1" wide. Flowers are in a vertical series of 2–5 clusters spaced along the top of the stem, with each cluster directly above a whorl of greenish and pinkish purple, leaflike bracts. Each tubular flower is about 1" long and has a calyx with tiny, triangular teeth and a dark-spotted, dull yellowish corolla with 2 widely spreading lips. There are 2 stamens under the upper lip of the corolla, and the lower corolla lip is 3-lobed.

Bloom Season: Summer–fall.

Habitat/Range: Occasional in open sandy soil in sand prairies, and in pastures and old fields in sandy regions; scattered and local through all but the northernmost tallgrass region.

140

FRANK OBERLE

FRANK OBERLE

YELLOW STAR GRASS
Hypoxis hirsuta
Lily family (Liliaceae)

Description: Small, hairy, plants seldom exceeding 1' tall, with bare flowering stems and grasslike basal leaves. The leaves have long hairs and are typically up to 8" long and ¼" wide. The flower stalks are usually shorter than the leaves and topped with an umbrella-like cluster of 2–12 individually stalked, yellow flowers. Each flower is about ½–1" wide, with 3 petal-like yellow sepals, 3 yellow petals, and 6 yellow stamens.

Bloom Season: Midspring–early summer; also in fall.

Habitat/Range: Common throughout the tallgrass region in prairies ranging from dry to moist, as well as in open savannas and woodlands.

FALSE GARLIC
Nothoscordum bivalve
Lily family (Liliaceae)

Description: Small, soft plants typically no more than 12" tall. The leaves are all basal, long and grasslike, and only about ⅛" wide. Flowers are on individual stalks up to 2" long, all arising from a common point at the top of the stem. There are 2 papery bracts where the flower stalks arise; otherwise the stem is bare. Each flower is usually a little less than 1" wide, with 6 pale yellow to off-white "petals" (actually 3 petals and 3 similar sepals) and 6 stamens surrounding a central ovary.

Bloom Season: Spring; also in fall.

Habitat/Range: Common in dry to mesic prairies and open woodlands, also occasional in wet prairies, in the southern tallgrass region from eastern Nebraska east through central Illinois into Ohio.

Comments: This plant resembles a wild onion, but the foliage has no onionlike odor.

G. YATSKIEVYCH

GROOVED YELLOW FLAX

Linum sulcatum
Flax family (Linaceae)

Description: Slender annuals to about 2½' tall, with erect, angular branches in the upper half. The lower leaves are sometimes opposite, while the upper leaves are alternate. The leaves are stalkless, narrow and pointed, up to 1" long and ⅛" wide, but smaller near the top of the stem. There are 2 small, dark, round glands where the leaf joins the stem. The individually stalked flowers are in an open cluster along the upper branches. Each flower is about ¾" wide, with 5 unequal, pointed, irregularly toothed sepals, 5 pale yellow petals that fall soon after opening, and 5 yellow stamens.

Bloom Season: Midspring–early fall.

Habitat/Range: Frequent in dry upland prairies, often on hill prairies or in sandy soils, through most of the tallgrass region east into Indiana.

Comments: A related species, Small Yellow Flax *(L. medium* variety *texanum),* occurs in similar sites; it is a perennial and lacks the dark glands at the base of the leaves. A blue-flowered species of flax native to Europe *(L. usitatissimum)* is cultivated for linseed oil and linen.

G. YATSKIEVYCH

TOOTHED EVENING PRIMROSE
Calylophus serrulatus
Evening Primrose family (Onagraceae)

Description: Slender plants to 1½' tall, with narrow, alternate, stalkless leaves. The leaves are usually toothed or wavy along the edges, hairy, and typically up to 2" long and ⅛" wide. There are sometimes clusters of smaller leaves arising where the main leaves join the stem. Flowers are stalkless and solitary at the bases of the main stem leaves. Each flower is about ⅝–1" wide, with a basal, 4-angled ovary, a long tube topped by 4 reflexed sepals, each with a raised rib on its back, 4 yellow petals with irregular edges, 8 stamens, and a 4-lobed stigma.

Bloom Season: Late spring–summer.

Habitat/Range: Occasional in well-drained open sites, including hill prairies, rocky or gravelly prairie slopes, and dry sandy prairies; scattered through the western tallgrass region east to northwestern Indiana.

143

FRANK OBERLE

FRANK OBERLE

SEEDBOX
Ludwigia alternifolia
Evening Primrose family (Onagraceae)

Description: Loosely bushy-branched plants to 4' tall, with alternate stalkless or short-stalked leaves to 4" long and less than 1" wide. The leaves taper to pointed tips and slender bases. By flowering time, plants often have reddish stems. Flowers are solitary on stalks less than ¼" long, arising from the junction of leaf bases with the stem. Each flower is about ¾" wide, with 4 reddish to green, triangular sepals, 4 small, yellow petals which fall shortly after flowering, and 4 stamens. The fruit is a squarish capsule with a tiny hole at the top.

Bloom Season: Summer.

Habitat/Range: Common in wet open places in prairies, along streams and shores, and in wet depressions, often in sandy or acidic soils; found through all but the northern tallgrass region, from Iowa and southern Ontario southward.

COMMON EVENING PRIMROSE
Oenothera biennis
Evening Primrose family (Onagraceae)

Description: Hairy biennial plants to 9' tall, with alternate leaves and often reddish-tinged stems. The leaves are hairy on both sides, with prominent raised veins on the undersides. Each leaf is up to 8" long and 2½" wide and weakly toothed to smooth-edged. Leaves are progressively smaller upward along the stem. Flowers are stalkless in elongate clusters along the upper stems, with a single flower at the base of each small leaflike bract. Each flower has a cylindrical ovary, a long tube at the top of which are 4 long, pointed, reflexed sepals, 4 spreading, rounded, pale yellow petals each up to 1" long, 8 yellow stamens, and a prominent style with a 4-lobed, cross-shaped stigma. The flowers spring open from bud to full bloom within minutes in the evening and smell like creosote, which attracts night-flying moths.

Bloom Season: Late spring–fall.

Habitat/Range: Abundant in waste areas and disturbed ground, including fields, overgrazed pastures, disturbed areas in prairies, and along streams throughout the tallgrass region. This may have been one of the few native weeds of our tallgrass prairies.

JOHN TAFT

FRANK OBERLE

MISSOURI EVENING PRIMROSE
Oenothera macrocarpa
Evening Primrose family (Onagraceae)

Description: Low, sprawling to erect plants with stems up to 15". The leaves are alternate, up to 5" long and 1" wide, covered with small, silky hairs, and have pointed tips and long, tapering bases. Each plant has 1 to a few flowers occurring singly where a leaf joins the stem. Each flower is composed of a small, greenish, ribbed ovary and a slender floral tube up to 4" long. At the top of the tube are 4 reflexed, narrow sepals each over 1" long, usually partially joined along their lengths, and 4 large, broad, bright yellow petals forming a flower up to 5" wide. There are 8 stamens and a style with a cross-shaped stigma. The fruits are 3–4" papery capsules with 4 broad wings.

Bloom Season: Midspring–midsummer; also rarely in fall.

Habitat/Range: Locally frequent over limestone in dry rocky prairies and glades, usually in areas of sparse vegetation; from southeastern Nebraska southward, and east through southern Missouri; formerly occurring at a single site in western Illinois.

Comments: The showy flowers open in the evening and wilt during the next day. They are pollinated by night-flying sphinx moths.

THREAD-LEAVED SUNDROPS
Oenothera linifolia
Evening Primrose family (Onagraceae)

Description: Erect-branching annuals averaging 1' tall, with many threadlike, alternate leaves. The main stem leaves are up to 1½" long and often have clusters of smaller leaves at their bases. Flowers are scattered alternately along the upper parts of the branches. Each flower has a small, hairy ovary, above which are 4 sepals that point outward or downward, and 4 yellow petals that form a flower less than ½" wide when fully open in early evening. Inside the flower are 8 stamens and a 4-lobed stigma.

Bloom Season: Midspring–midsummer.

Habitat/Range: Locally frequent in dry, sandy or rocky, and acidic sites, including prairies, pastures, and rocky barrens in the southern tallgrass region, from eastern Kansas to southern Illinois and southward.

FRANK OBERLE

PRAIRIE SUNDROPS
Oenothera pilosella
Evening Primrose family (Onagraceae)

Description: Alternate-leaved plants to 2½' tall, with softly hairy stems and leaves. The leaves are widest near the middle, up to 4" long and about 1" wide, with stalkless bases and pointed tips. The flowers occur singly at the junction of leaf bases and the stem. Each flower is about 2" wide, with a small, ribbed, green ovary and a long, slender tube ending in 4 narrow sepals, 4 broadly rounded yellow petals with irregular edges, 8 stamens, and a style with a cross-shaped stigma at the tip.

Bloom Season: Midspring–midsummer.

Habitat/Range: Occasional in mesic to wet prairies and wet swales in upland prairies, from eastern Missouri and Iowa eastward.

FRANK OBERLE

LARGE YELLOW LADY'S SLIPPER
Cypripedium parviflorum var. *pubescens*
Orchid family (Orchidaceae)

Description: Plants up to 2½' tall, with finely hairy stems and leaves. The pleated, parallel-veined leaves vary from narrow to broadly rounded and are up to 9" long by nearly 5" wide. The tips of the leaves are pointed, and the leaf bases clasp the stem. There are 1–2 flowers per stem, just above an erect, leaflike bract. Each flower has a prominent, inflated, cup-shaped, yellow petal, the "slipper," which can be nearly 2" long. On each side of this is a thin, pointed, twisted, strap-shaped petal to 2½" long. Two broad sepals arch above and below the slipper. The sepals and lateral petals are yellowish green to brown, sometimes with purplish brown spots and streaks.

Bloom Season: Midspring–early summer.

Habitat/Range: An uncommon plant usually occurring in woodlands and wetlands, but occasionally in prairies and even on some eastern hill prairies. Generally in the eastern and northern tallgrass region, although occurring infrequently through all but the western fringe of the region.

Comments: Small Yellow Lady's Slipper (var. *parviflorum),* has dark purple sepals and lateral petals, and a smaller slipper usually less than 1" long. It infrequently occurs in mesic prairies, wet sand prairies, and seepage areas in prairie wetlands.

147

DON KURZ

GRAY-GREEN WOOD SORREL
Oxalis dillenii
Wood Sorrel family (Oxalidaceae)

Description: The leaves of this plant are shaped like those of Violet Wood Sorrel, but are smaller, lighter green, and usually without purple undersides. Unlike Violet Wood Sorrel, this species has branched, leafy stems covered with small grayish hairs lying close against their surfaces. The plants grow up to 1' tall, but are typically half that height. The individually stalked flowers are in open clusters at the tips of branches arising from where the main leaf stalks join the stem. Each flower is ½–1" wide, with 5 pointed green sepals, 5 yellow petals, 10 stamens, and 5 styles. The fruits are erect, hairy pods up to 1" long.

Bloom Season: Spring–fall.

Habitat/Range: Common to abundant in a variety of habitats, especially in disturbed sites, throughout the tallgrass region. This plant regularly occurs in prairies, but often does not flower so is overlooked.

Comments: Wood Sorrel has been used as food by Native Americans and pioneers and is still used occasionally in salads. Oxalic acid gives the plant a distinctive, sour taste.

FRANK OBERLE

MORTON ARBORETUM

LANCE-LEAVED LOOSESTRIFE
Lysimachia lanceolata
Primrose family (Primulaceae)

Description: Plants to 2' tall, with very short side branches and narrow, opposite leaves. The lowest leaves on the stem are usually rounded and stalked, while the middle and upper leaves are narrow and taper evenly from the widest point to the base. There are long bristly hairs along the base of the leaf stalk. The stem leaves are up to 6" long and less than ¾" wide, often somewhat folded along the middle veins, and have pointed tips. Flowers dangle on long individual stalks, with each flower about ¾" wide and consisting of 5 narrow, pointed, green sepals and a nearly flat, 5-lobed, yellow corolla with the ragged lobes ending in finely pointed tips. The 5 yellow stamens protrude from the flower.

Bloom Season: Late spring–midsummer.

Habitat/Range: Frequent in dry to moist prairies, pastures, and open woodlands in much of the tallgrass region, west through Missouri and north into Wisconsin.

Comments: Fringed loosestrife *(L. ciliata)* is a related species, with leaves more than 1" wide, which usually grows in moist shaded areas, but occasionally grows in prairies.

NARROW-LEAVED LOOSESTRIFE
Lysimachia quadriflora
Primrose family (Primulaceae)

Description: Slender plants to 2' tall, usually unbranched in the lower half, with narrow, stalkless opposite leaves each up to 3" long and less than ¼" wide. The leaves have smooth edges that are slightly turned down, and there are often pairs of small leaves at the bases of the main stem leaves. The flowers are on long, slender, individual stalks arising at the junction of upper leaves with the stem. Each flower has a green calyx with 5 narrow, pointed lobes and a yellow corolla with 5 broad lobes and pointed tips. The corolla lobes are usually widest near the middle and often ragged along the outer edges.

Bloom Season: Mid–late summer.

Habitat/Range: Frequent in moist prairies and low seepage areas on upland prairies, also in fens; scattered through the tallgrass region except from Kansas southward.

FRANK OBERLE

FRANK OBERLE

MARSH MARIGOLD
Caltha palustris
Buttercup family (Ranunculaceae)

Description: Smooth, hairless plants with finely ridged, weak, hollow stems up to 2' long. The leaves are alternate, stalked, and broadly rounded, with heart-shaped bases and often with teeth along the edges. The largest leaves are up to 5" long and sometimes wider than long, with the upper stem leaves much smaller and often stalkless. The bright yellow flowers are up to 2" wide on individual stalks near the top of the plant. Each flower has 5–6, rarely up to 9, shiny, petal-like sepals surrounding numerous stamens. There are no true petals.

Bloom Season: Spring.

Habitat/Range: Common in wet, marshy sites, muddy seepage areas, fens, and along streams; often in shallow water, and usually growing where competition from other vegetation is minimal. Found through the northern tallgrass region, south to northwestern Missouri, central Illinois, and Indiana.

EARLY BUTTERCUP
Ranunculus fascicularis
Buttercup family (Ranunculaceae)

Description: Hairy plants less than 1' tall, with many long-stalked basal leaves and 1–3 smaller, stalkless leaves on the flowering stem. All of the leaves are divided into 3 narrow segments, with the segments further lobed and divided. Flowers are single at the tops of weak stalks that are longer than the leaves. Each flower is about 1" wide with 5 greenish yellow sepals and 5–10 larger, bright yellow petals surrounding numerous yellow stamens. The flowers develop into burlike clusters of flattened, rounded, seedlike fruits with pointed tips.

Bloom Season: Late winter–spring.

Habitat/Range: Frequent in dry prairies and savannas, especially in rocky, sandy, or clayey soils, through the tallgrass region northwest to southwestern Minnesota.

CLARK SCHAACK

FRANK OBERLE

PRAIRIE BUTTERCUP
Ranunculus rhomboideus
Buttercup family (Ranunculaceae)

Description: Plants less than 1' tall, with long, soft hairs on the leaves and stems. The long-stalked basal leaves are up to 2" long and about as wide, with coarse, rounded teeth or even small lobes. The stem leaves are usually stalkless and divided into 3 narrow lobes. Each lobe may be further lobed or toothed. There are usually several individually stalked flowers per plant. Each flower is about ¾" wide with 5 small, hairy sepals and 5 yellow petals surrounding many yellow stamens.

Bloom Season: Midspring–early summer.

Habitat/Range: Restricted to dry prairies and dry, open woodlands, usually in areas of sparse, low vegetation; found in the northwestern tallgrass region from northeastern Nebraska to northern Illinois and northward.

SWAMP AGRIMONY
Agrimonia parviflora
Rose family (Rosaceae)

Description: Stout, hairy plants to 5' tall, with alternate compound leaves. Each leaf is divided into as many as 23 saw-toothed leaflets arranged opposite each other along the main leaf axis, with a single leaflet at the tip. There are often smaller leaflets scattered between the main leaflets. Small yellow flowers are arranged alternately along the upper stems above the leaves. Each flower is about ¼" wide, with 5 yellow petals. The flowers develop into rounded, bristle-fringed, conical fruits that can cling to hairs and clothing.

Bloom Season: Midsummer–early fall.

Habitat/Range: Common in marshes, depressions in prairies, and along streams and shores through the southern tallgrass region, but becoming rare or absent north of a line from southeastern Nebraska to southern Michigan.

DON KURZ

PRAIRIE CINQUEFOIL
Potentilla arguta
Rose family (Rosaceae)

Description: Sturdy plants to 3' tall, with spreading hairs on the stems and leaves. The stems are unbranched below the flower clusters, with alternate compound leaves. The lower leaves are long-stalked, with the stalks and leaves becoming progressively smaller upward along the stem. Each leaf is composed of 3–11 toothed leaflets that are widest near the middle. Sometimes there are small, leaflike segments along the main axis of the leaf between the leaflets. The leaflets near the end of each leaf are usually the largest, ranging up to 3" long.

The individually stalked flowers are in a compact cluster at the tops of the stems, with each flower about ¾" wide. Each flower has 5 pointed, hairy, green sepals nearly as long as the 5 creamy white to pale yellow, rounded petals, surrounding 25 or more stamens and a cone-shaped center.

Bloom Season: Late spring–summer.

Habitat/Range: A typical plant of both dry and mesic prairies throughout the tallgrass region, but uncommon southward.

KEITH BOARD

COMMON CINQUEFOIL
Potentilla simplex
Rose family (Rosaceae)

Description: Sprawling or trailing plants with hairy stems up to 3' long that often root at their tips. The leaves are alternate and long-stalked, and each leaf has 5 leaflets arranged like the fingers of a hand. These leaflets are up to 3" long and have toothed edges, at least along the upper half of each leaflet. Flowers are on long individual stalks arising singly along the stem. Each flower is about ½" wide and has 5 pointed, green sepals alternating with 5 narrower green bracts, 5 bright yellow petals with broadly rounded or short-pointed tips, and 20 central stamens.

Bloom Season: Midspring–midsummer.

Habitat/Range: Very common and widely distributed in dry prairies, open woodlands, pastures, and old fields through most of the tallgrass region, but becoming scarce north and west of Iowa.

FRANK OBERLE

FRANK OBERLE

KITTEN TAILS
Besseya bullii
Snapdragon family (Scrophulariaceae)

Description: Small, unbranched plants to 15" tall, with hairy stems and leaves. The basal leaves are long-stalked, heart-shaped, up to 5" long, and have toothed edges. The single flower stalk has a series of small, stalkless, alternate leaves below the dense flower cluster, which is up to 6" long. Each ¼"-long flower is on a short stalk above a small leaflike bract, and consists of a 4-toothed, green calyx and a 2-lipped, pale yellow corolla with the upper lip longer than the calyx and the short lower lip usually divided into 3 irregular lobes. A style and 2 yellow stamens protrude from the flower.

Bloom Season: Late spring–early summer.

Habitat/Range: Rare and local in dry prairies, usually on open slopes in clay, gravel, or sand among sparse low vegetation; scattered in the central tallgrass region from Ohio to Minnesota, south to central Illinois.

DOWNY YELLOW PAINTED CUP
Castilleja sessiliflora
Snapdragon family (Scrophulariaceae)

Description: Partially parasitic, yellowish to gray-green plants less than 15" tall, with several hairy stems from a single base. The leaves are alternate, up to 2" long, and mostly divided near the middle of the leaf into 3 narrow segments, thus resembling bird's feet. The middle lobe may be divided again into smaller lobes. The leaves near the base of the plant are often long, narrow, and undivided. Flowers are long, tubular, and very thin, in a dense, leafy cluster at the top of the stems. Each flower has a slender tubular calyx about 1½" long and a curved, pale yellowish, 2-lipped corolla 1½–2¼" long, with the shorter lower lip divided at the tip into 3 segments.

Bloom Season: Midspring–early summer; also rarely in early fall.

Habitat/Range: Occasional in dry prairies, often on exposed hillsides and slopes; found in the northern tallgrass region from northern Illinois to eastern Kansas and northward.

FRANK OBERLE

WOOD BETONY
Pedicularis canadensis
Snapdragon family (Scrophulariaceae)

Description: Plants usually with several scattered flowering stems from a mat of basal leaves. The hairy stems are usually less than 18" tall, with a few stalked, alternate leaves. The leaves appear fernlike and crinkly surfaced and are divided along their lengths into numerous short, toothed lobes. Basal leaves are up to 6" long. Flowers are in a dense cluster at the top of the stem, with each flower directly above a small leaflike bract. Each flower is about 1" long and has a hairy, green calyx with a slanting mouth and a pale yellow, tubular corolla with 2 long lips. The longer upper lip of each flower has 2 downward-pointing teeth at the end, and the lower lip is usually wrinkled and lobed.

Bloom Season: Mid–late spring.

Habitat/Range: Frequent in dry to mesic prairies, open woodlands, and prairie hay meadows throughout the tallgrass region.

Comments: This plant is also called Lousewort, from the belief that it would cause lice if eaten by livestock. Wood Betony is partially parasitic, obtaining nutrients from the roots of other plants, which may account for its characteristic yellow-green color.

KENNETH DRITZ

LANCE-LEAVED GROUND CHERRY
Physalis virginiana
Nightshade family (Solanaceae)

Description: Branching plants to 1' tall, with hairy stems and stalked, alternate leaves. The leaves are up to 2½" long, nearly 1" wide, and smooth-edged to wavy or even slightly toothed. The flowers arise singly from the bases of the leaf stalks, with each flower on a slender, dangling stalk. The bell-shaped flowers are about ¾" wide, with a small, 5-toothed, green calyx, a 5-angled, pale yellow corolla with purple near the base, and 5 yellow stamens. Each fruit is enclosed in an inflated, papery husk that is the enlarged calyx.

Bloom Season: Late spring–summer.

Habitat/Range: Frequent throughout the tallgrass region in dry prairies, old fields, and pastures.

Comments: The plant was used medicinally by Native Americans, and Native Americans and pioneers used the ripe fruits as food, although the unripe fruits are poisonous. There are several other ground cherries in the region. A related plant, Horse Nettle *(Solanum carolinense)* is common in weedy pastures and very degraded prairies. It has spiny stems and leaves and white to pale-violet flowers.

KENNETH DRITZ

WHITE FLOWERS

FRANK OBERLE

This section includes flowers that are predominantly white. Since white flowers
grade into both pale pink flowers and pale
blue flowers, and off-white flowers may
appear yellowish, readers should check the
pink, blue, and yellow sections as well.

FRANK OBERLE

FRANK OBERLE

WINGED SUMAC
Rhus copallinum
Cashew family (Anacardiaceae)

Description: These colonial shrubs usually grow in extensive patches seldom exceeding 8' tall. The juice is milky white, and the brown twigs and leaf stalks are densely hairy. The alternate leaves are compound, with each leaf composed of up to 17 rounded, mostly untoothed leaflets with pointed tips. Each leaflet is up to 3½" long, with yellowish green undersides. The main axis of the leaf between the leaflets is usually fringed with an uneven band, or "wing," of leafy tissue. Flowers are in pyramidal clusters at the ends of branches; each small flower has 5 green sepals and 5 white petals. The small, round, bristly-hairy fruits are dark reddish.

Bloom Season: Late spring–summer.

Habitat/Range: Abundant in disturbed prairies, thickets, old fields, and pastures, in well-drained acid soils with full sunlight; found from southeastern Nebraska and southern Michigan south and eastward.

SMOOTH SUMAC
Rhus glabra
Cashew family (Anacardiaceae)

Description: Tall colonial shrubs with sticky, milky juice and alternate compound leaves that have whitish undersides. The young twigs and leaf stalks often have a bluish white cast. The leaves are divided into 11–25 narrow, toothed leaflets, each tapering to a narrow, pointed tip. Flowers are in branched, elongate clusters at the tops of the stem branches. Each small flower has 5 tiny, green sepals, 5 white petals, and 5 stamens. The small, round, red fruits are covered with short, thick, reddish hairs.

Bloom Season: Late spring–midsummer.

Habitat/Range: Common throughout the tallgrass region in dry, often rocky sites in disturbed prairies, thickets, old fields, and pastures, and along woodland edges.

Comments: This species rapidly invades degraded upland prairies, and can be a problem weed in the absence of fire. The blunt hairs on the fruits contain an acidic liquid, and a lemonade-like beverage can be made by steeping the ripe berries in cold water. Native Americans made a flour from Smooth Sumac seeds.

FRANK OBERLE

FRANK OBERLE

WATER HEMLOCK
Cicuta maculata
Parsley family (Apiaceae)

Description: Branching, thick-stemmed, hairless, biennial plants up to 6' tall, with stalked, alternate, compound leaves. The lower parts of the stems are hollow and often purple-spotted. Each leaf is divided into 3 to many narrow, sharply toothed leaflets which themselves may be lobed or divided. The leaflets are up to 5" long and 1½" wide. This is the only prairie plant in the Parsley family where the veins of the leaflets end at the notches rather than at the tips of the teeth. Abundant small flowers occur in umbrella-shaped clusters on stalks at the top of the plant, with the individual 5-petaled, white flowers less than ⅛" wide.

Bloom Season: Late spring–fall.

Habitat/Range: Common in wet sites throughout the tallgrass region, including wet prairies, marshes, along streams, and in moist marshy depressions of upland prairies.

Comments: All parts of this plant, especially the roots, are poisonous, and ingestion of a small fragment of the root can be fatal to humans.

RATTLESNAKE MASTER
Eryngium yuccifolium
Parsley family (Apiaceae)

Description: Stout, hairless plants to 4' tall, with a blue-green cast. The leaves resemble Yucca leaves and are long, strap-shaped, and less than 1½" wide, with small, needlelike teeth scattered along the edges. The basal leaves grow up to 2½' long, with the leaves progressively smaller upward along the stem. The flowers are in several individually stalked heads at the top of the plant, forming an open, flattened cluster of dense ball-like flower heads. These heads are covered with numerous tiny, white, 5-petaled flowers and pointed whitish bracts. Each flower has 2 protruding, threadlike styles.

Bloom Season: Summer.

Habitat/Range: Frequent in prairies and open, rocky savannas through most of the tallgrass region north and west to Iowa and southern Minnesota; becoming more local east of Illinois.

159

DON KURZ

KENNETH DRITZ

COWBANE
Oxypolis rigidior
Parsley family (Apiaceae)

Description: Smooth, hairless plants to 5' tall, with alternate compound leaves that are divided into 5–9 narrow leaflets. These leaflets may be smooth or irregularly toothed along the edges, and are up to 5" long and 1½" wide, although the upper leaflets are usually much narrower. The flowers are in flattened, umbrella-like clusters up to 6" wide at the tops of the stem branches, with each cluster having about 20 stalks radiating from the top of the stem. Each tiny flower has 5 white petals.

Bloom Season: Mid-late summer.

Habitat/Range: Common in marshes and wet prairies, and occasionally in seepage areas of mesic prairies, from Minnesota south and eastward.

Comments: Cowbane has smooth to coarsely and irregularly toothed leaflets, as opposed to the finely and regularly toothed leaflets of Water Parsnip.

WATER PARSNIP
Sium suave
Parsley family (Apiaceae)

Description: Smooth, hairless plants to 6' tall with stout, hollow lower stems. The large, alternate, compound leaves are divided into as many as 17 narrow leaflets each up to 4" long, with finely and regularly toothed edges. The leaflets are usually widest just above the rounded bases, and taper to pointed tips. Each leaf has a wide stipule sheathing the base of the leaf stalk. At the top of the branches, abundant small flowers are grouped in umbrella-like clusters 2½–3" wide, with a series of small papery-edged bracts at the base of each cluster. Each tiny flower is about ⅛" wide, with 5 protruding stamens alternating with 5 shorter, white petals.

Bloom Season: Summer.

Habitat/Range: Common in wet open areas, often in shallow standing water in wet prairies, marshes, wet depressions in upland prairies, and along slow streams; found through the tallgrass region south and west to southeastern Kansas and northern Arkansas.

FRANK OBERLE

PRAIRIE DOGBANE
Apocynum cannabinum
Dogbane family (Apocynaceae)

Description: Plants to 4' tall and branched in the upper half, with white, milky juice and often with reddish stems. The leaves are opposite, mostly broadest near the middle, and up to 6" long and 3" wide, with raised veins on the undersides. The leaves are short-stalked and rounded to tapering at the ends. Flowers occur in small branching clusters at the tips of the stem branches or on short side stalks. Each white flower is less than ⅛" wide, with 5 tiny, narrow, green sepals and a cuplike corolla with 5 small lobes. The fruits are paired, stiff, thin pods up to 8" long.

Bloom Season: Late spring–midsummer.

Habitat/Range: Common in open, well-drained sites, including prairies, roadsides, old fields, and pastures; found throughout the tallgrass region, but becoming rare southward.

Comments: Prairie Dogbane is also called Indian Hemp, because Native Americans used the fibers for rope and nets. This is a variable species, and plants with stalkless, often somewhat clasping leaves on the lower parts of the stems are sometimes separated as another species *(A. sibiricum).*

FRANK OBERLE

TALL GREEN MILKWEED
Asclepias hirtella
Milkweed family (Asclepiadaceae)

Description: Stout-stemmed plants to 3' tall, with white, milky sap, and narrow leaves up to 6" long and mostly less than ¾" wide. The leaves are mostly alternate along the stem, but are occasionally so crowded that they can appear opposite or even whorled. Several flower clusters occur along the stem on stalks up to 1½" long. Each cluster has up to 100 individually stalked flowers. Each flower is less than ½" long and pale greenish, with the 5 reflexed petals often white-edged or purple-spotted at the tips. The fruits are smooth, slender pods about 4" long and less than 1" thick.

Bloom Season: Late spring–summer.

Habitat/Range: Common in dry, often rocky or sandy prairies in the southwestern tallgrass region, north and east to southern Iowa and southern Wisconsin; becoming more local eastward through Ohio.

DON KURZ

FRANK OBERLE

NARROW-LEAVED MILKWEED
Asclepias stenophylla
Milkweed family (Asclepiadaceae)

Description: Slender-stemmed plants to 3' tall, with milky sap and many pairs of narrow, mostly opposite leaves. Each leaf is up to 8" long, but less than ½" wide. Several rounded flower heads occur along the upper half of the plant on very short stalks from where the leaves join the stem. Each cluster has up to 25 white flowers that are each less than ½" long. The flowers have 5 spreading to reflexed petals flanking 5 erect hoods and are sometimes tinged with green or yellow. The seed pods are smooth, less than ½" wide and up to 5" long.

Bloom Season: Early–midsummer.

Habitat/Range: Occasional in dry, sandy or rocky prairies, often associated with limestone, from Nebraska south and eastward into western Illinois.

WHORLED MILKWEED
Asclepias verticillata
Milkweed family (Asclepiadaceae)

Description: Milky-sapped plants usually less than 2' tall, with slender, usually unbranched stems and several soft, threadlike leaves arising from each point along the stem. The leaves are less than ⅛" wide and usually less than 3" long. There are small, stalked clusters with less than 20 flowers each near the top of the plant. Each individually stalked flower is less than ½" long, with 5 reflexed, greenish petals and 5 erect white hoods. The smooth, narrow seed pods are about 3" long and less than ½" thick.

Bloom Season: Late spring–summer.

Habitat/Range: Common throughout the tallgrass region in dry prairies and pastures, including disturbed or overgrazed areas.

Comments: This plant is poisonous to livestock, but is seldom consumed in sufficient quantities to cause problems. The milky sap can be hard to detect.

JESSIE M. HARRIS

FRANK OBERLE

YARROW
Achillea millefolium
Aster family (Asteraceae)

Description: Mostly unbranched, hairy plants typically 1½' tall, with alternate, aromatic, finely divided leaves that appear feathery and fernlike. The leaves are up to 6" long and 1" wide. Basal leaves are on stalks, while all but the lowest stem leaves are stalkless. Flower heads are in a flat, branching cluster at the top of the plant. Each head is less than ½" wide, with about 5 white, petal-like ray flowers surrounding a central disk with mostly 10–20 small, tubular, yellowish disk flowers.

Bloom Season: Late spring–fall.

Habitat/Range: Abundant and widespread in fields, pastures, disturbed sites, and along roadsides, as well as in prairies, especially prairies with a history of previous disturbance; found throughout the tallgrass region.

Comments: Yarrow is native to Eurasia as well as North America, and some of our populations are introduced weeds. The plant has antiseptic properties and was formerly used to pack wounds and for a variety of other medicinal purposes, including treatment of tooth and ear aches.

FIELD CAT'S FOOT
Antennaria neglecta
Aster family (Asteraceae)

Description: Mat-forming colonial plants with numerous clusters of small basal leaves. The leaves are up to 2" long and less than ¾" wide, with curving edges, pointed tips, narrow tapering bases, and a single prominent vein along the middle of the underside. The undersides of the leaves are covered with dense white hairs and appear bright white. Flower stalks are white-hairy and 8" or less tall, with small, narrow, alternate leaves. The flower heads are in a dense cluster at the top of the plant, with male and female flowers on separate plants. There are no petal-like ray flowers, so the heads appear as white disks less than ¼" wide. The fluffy fruiting heads on the female plants resemble miniature dandelion fruiting heads.

Bloom Season: Spring.

Habitat/Range: Common in dry prairie sites throughout the tallgrass region, although often present only as basal leaves under taller plants and hence overlooked.

Comments: This is one of a group of plants also called Pussy Toes. A species more common in open woodlands, *A. plantaginifolia* has broader leaves with 3 parallel veins along their length.

FRANK OBERLE

FRANK OBERLE

PALE INDIAN PLANTAIN
Arnoglossum atriplicifolium
Aster family (Asteraceae)

Description: Smooth plants with a whitish cast, typically 3–5' tall, but occasionally to 8', with stalked, alternate leaves that are white on the underside. The lowest leaves are the largest and can be up to 12" long and nearly as wide, with shallow lobes and large teeth along the edges, and a shape somewhat like Maple or Sycamore leaves. The upper leaves are progressively smaller or reduced to small bracts. Numerous cylindrical flower heads occur in an open, branching, somewhat flattened cluster at the tops of the stems. Each flower head is less than ¼" wide, with 5 long, narrow bracts surrounding 5 small, white to greenish white, tubular disk flowers.

Bloom Season: Summer–fall.

Habitat/Range: In the eastern tallgrass region, from Illinois eastward, this plant regularly occurs in mesic to dry prairies, as well as in open woodlands. Westward to eastern Nebraska, the plant generally occurs in open woodlands.

PRAIRIE INDIAN PLANTAIN
Arnoglossum plantagineum
Aster family (Asteraceae)

Description: The unmistakable basal leaves of these plants are smooth, thick, rubbery, and long-stalked. These leaves are up to 8" long and 4" wide, with several prominent parallel lengthwise veins. The angled stems are erect, hairless, and generally less than 4' tall, with scattered, small, alternate leaves. Stems are unbranched below, and usually branch abundantly at the top, forming a wide, flat-topped cluster of up to 100 flower heads. Each head is less than 1" tall, and surrounded by 5 light green sepal-like bracts, with elevated white ribs along the back of each bract. There are 5 small, tubular, white flowers with 5-lobed corollas in each disklike head.

Bloom Season: Late spring–midsummer.

Habitat/Range: Frequent in wet to mesic prairies and occasionally in drier prairies; found in the southern tallgrass region north to southern Minnesota and southern Ontario.

FRANK OBERLE

DON KURZ

WHITE SAGE
Artemisia ludoviciana
Aster family (Asteraceae)

Description: Narrow, aromatic, densely white-hairy plants to 3' tall, with branches only on the upper half of the stems. The leaves are stalkless, narrow, pointed, and up to 4" long and ¾" wide. The leaf edges may be smooth but sometimes have a few teeth or even lobes. The leaves are densely covered with hairs on their undersides and appear bright white, and range from green to white on the upper surface. Numerous small flower heads occur in narrow, elongate clusters at the tops of the branches. Each head is less than ⅛" wide, and contains several small, tubular, disk flowers.

Bloom Season: Summer–early fall.

Habitat/Range: Common on dry, often rocky, uplands in prairies, pastures, and old fields; found in the western tallgrass region east into Illinois, and occasionally introduced in disturbed areas eastward.

Comments: Native Americans used this plant for medicinal and ceremonial purposes and burned it to repel insects. Pioneers used it as an incense.

HEATH ASTER
Aster ericoides
Aster family (Asteraceae)

Description: Low, bushy-branched asters to 3' tall, with very leafy branches. The leaves are alternate, small, narrow, and pointed, with even the largest less than 3" long and less than ¼" wide. Most of the upper leaves are far smaller, with many less than 1" long and about ⅛" wide. The branches have numerous flower heads along their upper lengths, with each head on a short stalk. These stalks usually have small, narrow, leaflike bracts. Flower heads are about ½" wide, with up to 20 white, petal-like ray flowers surrounding a small yellow disk.

Bloom Season: Midsummer–fall.

Habitat/Range: Common in upland prairies and occasional in pastures and old fields; found throughout the tallgrass region, but becoming more rare in the southern portions.

Comments: This is usually a colonial plant with numerous stems growing together. The larger stem leaves often fall off before flowering, leaving a bushy-headed plant with abundant tiny leaves, white flowers, and a bare lower stem.

FRANK OBERLE

PANICLED ASTER
Aster lanceolatus
Aster family (Asteraceae)

Description: Highly variable plants, usually growing in dense colonies, with stems to 5' tall and at least slightly hairy near the top. The leaves are alternate, long, narrow, widest near the middle, and sometimes irregularly toothed along the edges, ranging up to 6" long and 1½" wide. The flower heads are in an open, leafy, conical cluster at the top of the plant. Each head is about 1" wide, with 25–40 white, petal-like ray flowers surrounding a yellow disk.

Bloom Season: Midsummer–fall.

Habitat/Range: Common throughout the tallgrass region in wet prairies, low wet depressions, and along streams.

ROBERT TATINA

HAIRY ASTER
Aster pilosus
Aster family (Asteraceae)

Description: Tall, spindly, bushy-branched asters with many thin, needlelike alternate leaves along the upper stems and flowering branches. The lower leaves are larger, up to 4" long, and usually wither before the plant flowers. The main stem leaves have a fringe of hairs along either edge near their bases. There are usually many flower heads scattered along the side branches and upper stems. Each small head is on a short stalk, which usually has several tiny sharp-tipped bracts. The heads are about ½" wide or slightly larger, with mostly 15–23 white, petal-like ray flowers surrounding a small, yellow disk typically with 20 or more disk flowers.

Bloom Season: Late summer–fall.

Habitat/Range: An abundant weed in disturbed open sites through much of the tallgrass region; rare north and west of Iowa.

Comments: This plant does not usually occur in high-quality prairies, but is frequently found in disturbed or overgrazed prairies and pastures, as well as along the edges of prairies and on roadsides with prairie associates. It is similar to Heath Aster, but much coarser and weedier. A close relative of Hairy Aster, Small-Headed Aster (*A. parviceps*) has shorter ray flowers and fewer than 13 disk flowers.

FRANK OBERLE

FLAT-TOP ASTER
Aster umbellatus
Aster family (Asteraceae)

Description: Plants to 5' tall, with mostly hairless stems. The leaves, widest near the middle and tapering to narrow bases and pointed tips, range up to 6½" long and are less than 1½" wide, with smooth, toothless edges. They are alternate along the stem, but sometimes so close together that they initially appear opposite. Flower heads are numerous on the ends of branches, in a nearly flat-topped crown at the tops of the stems. Each head is a little less than 1" wide, with 7–14 white, petal-like ray flowers surrounding a yellow disk.

Bloom Season: Midsummer–fall.

Habitat/Range: Frequent in moist to wet areas in both exposed and lightly shaded sites, including wet swales and low thickets in prairies; found through the eastern tallgrass region, west and south to west-central Illinois.

Comments: This species is replaced in the northwestern tallgrass region by a different variety *(A. umbellatus* variety *pubens),* which has hairy stems and slightly smaller heads with 4–7 petal-like ray flowers.

FRANK OBERLE

JOHN TAFT

FALSE ASTER
Boltonia asteroides
Aster family (Asteraceae)

Description: Bluish green, smooth, hairless plants to 7' tall, with ascending branches. The leaves are alternate, narrow, tapering to the bases, and up to 8" long and 1" wide, but mostly much smaller. The flowers are in a loose, open cluster at the top of the plant. Each flower head is about 1–1¾" wide, with up to 60 white, petal-like ray flowers surrounding a rounded yellow disk. The ray flowers are sometimes pale pink or blue.

Bloom Season: Midsummer–fall.

Habitat/Range: Common in wet areas, including wet, muddy prairies subject to flooding, stream banks, and low depressions; scattered through the tallgrass region.

FALSE BONESET
Brickellia eupatorioides
Aster family (Asteraceae)

Description: Plants up to 4' tall and at least somewhat hairy, with toothed or smooth, mostly alternate leaves up to 4" long and 1½" wide, but often much narrower. The narrowly cylindrical flower heads are in a rounded cluster at the tops of the branches, with each head up to ¾" tall. Several overlapping, narrow, sharp-pointed, green bracts occur at the base of each head, surrounding about 7–20 small, tubular, yellowish white disk flowers with protruding styles.

Bloom Season: Midsummer–fall.

Habitat/Range: Frequent in dry prairies throughout the tallgrass region, often in rocky or sandy soils and occasionally in moister sites, although more sporadically distributed eastward.

Comments: False Boneset is sometimes confused with Tall Boneset. False Boneset has mostly alternate, one-veined leaves, while Tall Boneset has opposite, 3-veined leaves.

MORTON ARBORETUM

DAISY FLEABANE
Erigeron strigosus
Aster family (Asteraceae)

Description: Slender, erect, annual or biennial plants to 2½' tall, with flowers resembling miniature daisies and stems with scattered hairs lying flat against the stem. The leaves are all less than 1" wide, with the stalked basal leaves in a circular cluster at the base of the stem, and the stem leaves alternate, narrow, and smooth-edged to slightly toothed. The flower heads are on individual branches in a spreading cluster, with each head up to 1" wide. The heads have a fringe of more than 40 white, threadlike ray flowers, each about ¼" long, surrounding a circle of densely packed, yellow disk flowers.

Bloom Season: Midspring–early fall.

Habitat/Range: Very common throughout the tallgrass region in mesic to dry prairies, old fields, pastures, and other sites.

Comments: Annual Fleabane *(E. annuus)* is a related species found in waste places and disturbed sites. It is coarser, with spreading hairs along the stem and often with wider, toothed leaves.

171

FRANK OBERLE

FRANK OBERLE

TALL BONESET
Eupatorium altissimum
Aster family (Asteraceae)

Description: Hairy plants usually unbranched below the flower heads, typically 3' but up to 6' tall, with widely spaced pairs of opposite leaves. The upper half of each leaf is usually toothed along the edges. Each leaf is up to 5" long and 1⅓" wide, with 3 prominent veins along its length. A narrow, flattish cluster of small flower heads tops the stems. Each flower head is about ⅛" wide, with a series of narrow, hairy, green, white-edged bracts surrounding 5 small, white, tubular disk flowers. Each flower has 2 protruding, threadlike, white style branches.

Bloom Season: Late summer–fall.

Habitat/Range: Common in dry upland prairies, pastures, old fields, and open woodlands from southwestern Minnesota and eastern Nebraska south and eastward; most abundant in sites with a history of disturbance, such as intensive grazing.

COMMON BONESET
Eupatorium perfoliatum
Aster family (Asteraceae)

Description: Plants with the stems and leaves covered with conspicuous spreading hairs. Each pair of long-tapering, toothed, opposite leaves is united across the stem, so that the stem appears to pierce the leaf pair. The leaves are up to 8" long, and the plants are usually 4' tall or less. The stems are unbranched except near the top, where numerous many-branched clusters of flower heads form a broad, shallow dome. Each flower head is about ¼" tall, with 9–23 small, white, tubular disk flowers but no ray flowers. Occasional plants will have the leaves in whorls of 3 rather than opposite.

Bloom Season: Midsummer–fall.

Habitat/Range: Common and widely distributed in open wet places throughout the tallgrass region, including wet prairies, marshes, along streams, and low depressions in upland prairies.

Comments: Based on the appearance of the fused pairs of leaves, people once believed that a potion made from this plant would help heal fractured bones. A bitter, vile-tasting tea made from this plant was used as folk medicine for a variety of ailments.

FRANK OBERLE

DON KURZ

LATE BONESET
Eupatorium serotinum
Aster family (Asteraceae)

Description: Opposite-branched plants to about 4' tall, with stalked, mostly opposite leaves that are coarsely toothed along their edges. The stems are evenly and finely hairy, at least in their upper halves. The leaves are typically 5" long by 2" wide, widest near their bases, and taper evenly to long, pointed tips. Flower heads occur in abundant, branched clusters near the top of the plant. Each head is about ⅛" wide, with several small bracts and about 13 small, tubular, white, 5-lobed disk corollas with protruding thread-like style branches.

Bloom Season: Late summer–fall.

Habitat/Range: Abundant in open, well-drained, disturbed areas, including pastures, fields, thickets, and overgrazed prairies; found through most of the tallgrass region, but uncommon to absent north and west of Iowa.

SNEEZEWORT ASTER
Oligoneuron album
Aster family (Asteraceae)

Description: Slender plants to 2½' tall, with the stems unbranched in the lower half. The narrow leaves are alternate and widely spaced along the stem, with the lower leaves up to 8" long and ½" wide, usually with 3 fine veins running along the length of the leaf. There are many flower heads in an open, flat-topped, branching cluster at the top of the plant. Each head is about ¾" wide, with up to 25 white, petal-like ray flowers surrounding a white to pale yellow disk.

Bloom Season: Midsummer–fall.

Habitat/Range: Occasional in dry prairies, especially hill prairies with calcium-rich gravels and limestones, in the southern and northwestern tallgrass region; local and scattered elsewhere.

173

FRANK OBERLE

FRANK OBERLE

OLD-FIELD BALSAM
Pseudognaphalium obtusifolium
Aster family (Asteraceae)

Description: Annual or biennial plants usually less than 2½' tall, with a whitish cast due to dense, woolly hairs on the stems and undersides of the leaves. Dried plants frequently have a strong maple fragrance. The leaves are untoothed, alternate, stalkless, up to 4" long and less than ½" wide, with green tops and white undersides. Flower heads are small and occur abundantly at the tops of the branches. Each head is about ¼" tall, with white, papery bracts surrounding a narrow head with numerous narrow, yellowish white disk flowers.

Bloom Season: Midsummer–fall.

Habitat/Range: Common in old fields, pastures, and degraded upland prairies, particularly in sandy or rocky soils; found through the southern tallgrass region north to Iowa and Nebraska and, rarely, northward.

Comments: Parts of this plant have been used in folk medicines for both people and livestock.

WILD QUININE
Parthenium integrifolium
Aster family (Asteraceae)

Description: Most parts of these plants are rough or covered with short, bristly hairs. The basal leaves are long-stalked, up to 9" long, widest near the middle, tapering at each end, and toothed along the edges. The stem leaves are alternate and progressively smaller upward along the stem, with the upper leaves often stalkless and even clasping the stem. Flower heads are in a nearly flat, branching cluster at the top of the plant. The individual flower heads are less than ⅓" wide, with 5 tiny, white, petal-like ray flowers, each less than ⅛" long, surrounding a thick head of sterile disk flowers.

Bloom Season: Late spring–summer.

Habitat/Range: Frequent in dry to mesic prairies in both loamy and sandy soils, as well as in open upland savannas and woodlands; found through the tallgrass region west to southeastern Kansas, but rarely in the northwestern part of the region.

Comments: A tea from Wild Quinine has been used to treat fevers. During World War I, when tropical supplies of quinine from the bark of the Cinchona tree were cut off, there was a brief commercial trade in Wild Quinine plants.

FRANK OBERLE

BILL SUMMERS

ROUGH WHITE LETTUCE

Prenanthes aspera
Aster family (Asteraceae)

Description: Plants typically unbranched and up to 6' tall, with hairy leaves and stems. The leaves are alternate, with the leaves on the lower stems stalked, but the upper and middle stem leaves smaller, stalkless, and often clasping the stem at their bases. The stem leaves are up to 4" long and 1¾" wide and may be coarsely toothed or have smooth edges. Flower heads are in leafy clusters along the upper parts of the stems. Each cylindrical head is up to ¾" tall, with 8 long, pointed, hairy, green bracts surrounding 10–14 creamy white flowers, each with a petal-like ray with 5 small teeth at the tip, and 2 protruding, threadlike style branches.

Bloom Season: Midsummer–fall.

Habitat/Range: Occasional in dry prairies and open savannas scattered through much of the tallgrass region, northwest to northeastern South Dakota; also in moister prairies in the western tallgrass region.

Comments: The bitter roots of this plant were once thought to be a cure for snakebite. Glaucous White Lettuce *(P. racemosa)* occurs in moist prairies; it has purple flowers and hairless lower and middle leaves and stems.

WILD SWEET POTATO

Ipomoea pandurata
Morning Glory family (Convolvulaceae)

Description: Trailing or twining vines with stems that can exceed 10' long. The leaves are alternate, stalked, and broadly heart-shaped, with pointed tips. They are smooth-edged and up to 6" long and nearly as wide, rarely with some small lobes near the base. One to a few flowers occur on long stalks at the bases of the leaf stalks. Each flower has 5 blunt, green sepals and a broadly funnel-like, 5-angled, white corolla with a red center. The flowers are about 2½–3" wide when fully open.

Bloom Season: Late spring–summer.

Habitat/Range: Occasional in dry, open thickets, fencerows, pastures, and dry disturbed areas in prairies from southeastern Nebraska to Ontario and southward, but occurring as a prairie plant mostly in the western tallgrass region.

Comments: The large roots, which may weigh more than 20 pounds, were cooked and eaten by Native Americans.

FRANK OBERLE

LOW BINDWEED
Calystegia spithamaea
Morning Glory family (Convolvulaceae)

Description: Small plants with finely hairy stems and alternate leaves, with most of the plant erect, but the parts of the stem above the flowers often nodding or trailing. The leaves are short-stalked, up to 3½" long and 2" wide, and bluntly arrowhead-shaped, with shallow, heart-shaped bases. The white, bell-shaped flowers are about 2" long and occur individually on long stalks arising from the junction of a lower leaf with the stem. There are usually only 1–3 flowers per plant. Each flower has 5 sepals hidden by 2 large, green bracts at the flower base, and a 5-lobed white corolla.

Bloom Season: Late spring–midsummer.

Habitat/Range: Uncommon and sporadically distributed in mesic to dry prairies and open timbered uplands in the eastern tallgrass region, west to western Missouri; often in clayey soils.

FRANK OBERLE

PALE DOGWOOD
Cornus amomum
Dogwood family (Cornaceae)

Description: Bushy shrubs 3–6' tall, occasionally taller, with stalked opposite leaves and hairy twigs. Each leaf is up to 4" long and 1½" wide and tapers to a pointed tip. The leaves are notably paler on their undersides than on their smooth tops, with tiny hairs pressed against the underside (best seen with a magnifying glass). Flowers are in shallowly rounded clusters at the tips of the upper branches. Each flower is about ¼" wide and has 4 pointed, green sepals, 4 narrow white petals, and 4 protruding stamens. The clusters of deep blue, berrylike fruits are striking.

Bloom Season: Midspring–midsummer.

Habitat/Range: Frequent in open moist places, including banks of streams, low depressions in prairies, open wet thickets, and marshy areas; found in the southern tallgrass region north to southern Minnesota.

Comments: Three other dogwoods also occur regularly in prairies. Rough-Leaved Dogwood *(C. drummondii)* occurs in dry upland thickets and has leaves that are rough-hairy on the top sides. Gray Dogwood *(C. racemosa)* has smooth, hairless twigs. Red Osier Dogwood *(C. sericea)* occurs in marshy areas; it has bright red stems and white pith in the center of the twigs, as opposed to the brown pith of Pale Dogwood. All 3 species have white to grayish fruits.

KENNETH DRITZ

PRAIRIE DODDER
Cuscuta pentagona
Dodder family (Cuscutaceae)

Description: Unlike green plants, which produce their food using sunlight, Dodders are parasitic flowering plants that get their nutrients from other flowering plants. Prairie Dodder has stringy orange stems that twine around and over other plants and become attached to the stems of suitable host plants. There are no apparent leaves. The flowers are in dense clusters scattered along the stems. Each flower is less than ¼" wide and has a whitish calyx with 5 rounded lobes and 5 spreading, narrow, white corolla lobes with pointed tips.

Bloom Season: Summer–early fall.

Habitat/Range: Occasional in upland prairies and fields throughout the tallgrass region.

Comments: Prairie Dodder uses several prairie plants for hosts, especially plants in the Aster family (Asteraceae). Several other species of Dodder occur in prairies, particularly in wet prairies. Others occur in waste areas or are even crop pests. All are difficult to identify.

FRANK OBERLE

HOGWORT
Croton capitatus
Spurge family (Euphorbiaceae)

Description: Annuals typically less than 18" tall, with dense white to rusty hairs on the stems and leaves. Under magnification, the hairs can been seen to be starlike, with many radiating branches. The leaves are stalked, untoothed, and up to 4" long and less than 1" wide, with rounded bases. The tiny flowers are in dense clusters, with separate male and female flowers. Female flowers lack petals, while the male flowers have 5 petals, but each petal is only 0.04" long! There are 3 seeds in each fruit capsule.

Bloom Season: Midsummer–fall.

Habitat/Range: Common and weedy in dry pastures, grazed prairies, and other disturbed areas, especially in regions with limestone or well drained, calcium-rich soil. Found through the southern tallgrass region from southeastern Nebraska through central Illinois, and sporadically north and eastward, where many of the populations are recent introductions.

Comments: Prairie Tea *(C. monanthogynus),* a smaller, less densely white-hairy species with smaller leaves and only a single seed per fruit, occurs in similar habitats but is not as weedy.

179

FRANK OBERLE

FRANK OBERLE

FLOWERING SPURGE
Euphorbia corollata
Spurge family (Euphorbiaceae)

Description: Slender, erect plants with a pale bluish or yellowish green cast and white, milky sap. The smooth-edged, narrow leaves are usually alternate below and opposite or in whorls of 3 near the flower branches. The plants vary from smooth to hairy and from unbranched to much-branched. The flower clusters are many-headed and much-branched, with each flower head about ⅓" wide, with 5 rounded, white, petal-like structures. The center of the head contains several, tiny, yellowish, male flowers and a single female flower. Sometimes the leaves fall before flowering, creating tall bare stalks crowned with white flower heads. The fruit is a round, 3-lobed ball on a tiny stalk above the petal-like structures.

Bloom Season: Midspring–fall.

Habitat/Range: Widely distributed in dry to moist prairies in soils ranging from pure sand to rich loam, also in pastures, old fields, and other disturbed sites. Found throughout the tallgrass region, but rare to absent north of Iowa and southeastern Nebraska.

SNOW-ON-THE-MOUNTAIN
Euphorbia marginata
Spurge family (Euphorbiaceae)

Description: Annuals with finely hairy stems to 3' tall. The leaves are alternate and up to 4" long and 2½" wide, with pointed tips and rounded, stalkless bases. Near the top of the stem is a whorl of leaves under 3–5 leafy branches which are themselves branched. Leaves on these flower branches are often opposite or densely clustered and have broad, white bands along the edges. The numerous flower heads are far smaller and less showy than the leaves. Each head is less than ½" wide, with 5 white petal-like structures surrounding a single female and several tiny male flowers. The edges of the upper leaves are occasionally light pinkish instead of white.

Bloom Season: Summer–fall.

Habitat/Range: Occasional in dry prairies, upland fields, and pastures in the westernmost tallgrass region, east to southwestern Minnesota and northwestern Missouri, but absent from the northern prairies.

Comments: This plant is cultivated throughout the Midwest for its attractive foliage, and may escape and spread. The milky juice is a skin irritant to some people. Cattle avoid eating it, and the plant can become abundant in heavily grazed sites.

FRANK OBERLE

CANADIAN MILK VETCH
Astragalus canadensis
Bean family (Fabaceae)

Description: Smooth, stout-stemmed plants to 5' tall, with alternate compound leaves. Each leaf is composed of 13–31 oblong leaflets, each about 1½ by ⅜". The flowers are in elongate clusters at the ends of long stalks, with many flowers per cluster. Each creamy white flower is about ¾" long and has a small, hairy calyx with 5 narrow teeth and a corolla with a hood-like upper petal over 2 smaller side petals flanking a lower lip.

The fruits are rounded, beanlike pods less than 1" long, with pointed tips.

Bloom Season: Summer.

Habitat/Range: Occasional throughout the tallgrass region in moist thickets, low areas in prairies, along streams, and along prairie/woodland edges.

FRANK OBERLE

WHITE WILD INDIGO
Baptisia alba variety *macrophylla*
Bean family (Fabaceae)

Description: Smooth, hairless, bushy plants to 6' tall, often with a yellowish green cast and a thin, whitish coating on the stem and leaves. The leaves are alternate, on stalks up to ½" long, and divided into 3 leaflets. The leaflets are 1–3" long, broadest above the middle, and taper to wedge-shaped bases with rounded tips. The leaves are typically concentrated around the middle of the plant. Above the leafy portion of the plant are long, erect stems bearing scattered, individually stalked, white flowers each up to 1" long. Each flower has a 4-lobed calyx, an erect, fanlike upper petal, and 2 smaller side petals flanking a keel-like lower lip. The fruits are fat, pointed, hairless, black seed pods less than 2" long.

Bloom Season: Late spring–midsummer.

Habitat/Range: Widely distributed in moist to dry prairies through most of the tallgrass region, north and west to southeastern Minnesota and northwestern Iowa.

Comments: This deep-rooted plant can persist long after its prairie associates have been destroyed by clearing or overgrazing and is frequently seen in weedy fields and along roadsides. Although poisonous to livestock if consumed in quantity, the plant was used medicinally by Native Americans and European settlers.

FRANK OBERLE

SESSILE-LEAVED TICK TREFOIL
Desmodium sessilifolium
Bean family (Fabaceae)

Description: Stems mostly 3–4' tall, hairy and usually unbranched below the flowers,, with widely spaced, alternate, compound leaves. Each leaf is stalkless or a very short stalk, with 3 long, narrow leaflets; the middle leaflet is on a stalk longer than the main leaf stalk. The leaflets are typically 1½–4" long and usually less than ½" wide. Flowers are on slender individual stalks on erect branches at the top of the plant. Each white to pinkish flower is less than ¼" long, with an erect, spreading upper petal and 2 smaller side petals flanking a protruding lower lip. The fruits are 2- to 4-segmented, flattened pods, with each segment about ¼" long.

Bloom Season: Late spring–summer.

Habitat/Range: Common in upland prairies and savannas, especially in sandy soils, through the southern tallgrass region north to Michigan and northern Illinois.

DON KURZ

WHITE PRAIRIE CLOVER
Dalea candida
Bean family (Fabaceae)

Description: Smooth, delicate plants generally less than 2½' tall. The dull-green leaves are alternate along the stem, with each leaf composed of 5–9 narrow, elongate leaflets up to 1½" long and less than ¼" wide. The flowers are in 1–3" long, dense cylindrical spikes at the tops of the stems. Flowers at the base of the spike bloom first, and flowering proceeds upward resulting in a narrow wreath of white fringing a green column. Each flower is about ¼" long, with a small, green calyx, one large petal, 4 smaller petals, and 5 protruding stamens.

Bloom Season: Late spring–summer.

Habitat/Range: Found in high-quality dry to mesic prairies throughout the tallgrass region.

Comments: A variant with trailing stems and smaller leaflets occurs in the western part of the tallgrass region (variety *oligophylla*). White Prairie Clover is drought-resistant, with roots that penetrate up to 5' into the soil, but is sensitive to overgrazing. Native Americans brewed a tea from the leaves and used the raw roots as food.

FRANK OBERLE

FRANK OBERLE

ILLINOIS BUNDLE FLOWER
Desmanthus illinoensis
Bean family (Fabaceae)

Description: Plants with tough, slender, grooved stems averaging about 3' tall, but occasionally exceeding 5' in fertile sites. The alternate leaves are doubly compound. Each leaf has branches that are themselves divided into numerous leaflets, creating a fernlike appearance. These leaflets are each less than ¼" long. The tiny, white flowers are in spherical heads at the ends of stalks arising from the points where the leaves join the stem. The 5 yellow-tipped stamens are longer than the 5 small, white petals, creating an attractive starburst effect. The flower develops into a round cluster of curved, brown, waferlike pods.

Bloom Season: Early–midsummer.

Habitat/Range: Common and somewhat weedy in disturbed prairies, pastures, sandy thickets, and along prairie edges; found in the western and central tallgrass region, becoming rare and local eastward.

Comments: This is an important food plant for livestock and wildlife, and is also used in revegetation plantings and prairie restoration.

ROUND-HEADED BUSH CLOVER
Lespedeza capitata
Bean family (Fabaceae)

Description: Plants to 6' tall, with slender stems and alternate compound leaves each composed of 3 narrow leaflets. The leaflets are frequently covered with silky hairs lying flat against the leaf surface, giving the foliage a distinctive silvery appearance. Flowers occur in dense, rounded heads, with leaflike bracts at the base of each head. Individual flowers are less than ½" long and creamy white, usually with a purplish spot at the base. Each flower has a flaring upper petal and two side petals flanking a lower lip. As the single-seeded fruits develop, the heads turn a distinctive tawny brown, making the plants an attractive winter feature on the prairies.

Bloom Season: Midsummer–fall.

Habitat/Range: A typical plant of dry, well-drained, or sandy prairies in all but the northern portions of the tallgrass region, becoming uncommon north and west of Iowa.

Comments: The rare Prairie Bush Clover *(L. leptostachya)* can have creamy white flowers, but has open flower clusters and much narrower leaflets.

FRANK OBERLE

FRANK OBERLE

AMERICAN BUGLEWEED
Lycopus americanus
Mint family (Lamiaceae)

Description: Square-stemmed plants to 2' tall. The leaves are opposite, up to 3½" long, with at least the lower leaves deeply cut into coarse, rounded lobes or teeth, and tapering to their bases. The upper leaves are usually coarsely toothed but unlobed. This plant does not have the aromatic foliage typical of many mints. Flowers are in dense heads surrounding the stem at the bases of the leaves. Each flower is less than ¼" long, with a tiny 5-toothed calyx, a 4-lobed white corolla, and 2 stamens.

Bloom Season: Early summer–fall.

Habitat/Range: Common in wet, marshy areas in depressions, along streams, bordering ponds, and in wet prairies; found throughout the tallgrass region, but less common at the southern edge.

Comments: This plant is also called Common Water Horehound.

SLENDER MOUNTAIN MINT
Pycnanthemum tenuifolium
Mint family (Lamiaceae)

Description: Plants to 3' tall, with hairless, square stems and abundant pairs of narrow, opposite leaves. There are typically many short branches with smaller leaves arising from where the larger leaves join the main stem branches. The largest leaves are up to 2" long and less than ¼" wide. Flowers are in a dense, slightly rounded cluster of heads at the top of the plant, with several pointed, leaflike bracts under each head. A head contains numerous flowers, each with a white to pale lavender, 2-lipped corolla about ⅛" wide, often with small purple spots.

Bloom Season: Late spring–summer.

Habitat/Range: Locally frequent in dry prairies, pastures, and old fields with prairie vegetation; found from eastern Nebraska and eastern Minnesota south and eastward.

JESSIE M. HARRIS

HAIRY MOUNTAIN MINT
Pycnanthemum verticillatum variety *pilosum*
Mint family (Lamiaceae)

Description: Square-stemmed plants to 4' tall, with spreading hairs and a strong minty fragrance. The leaves are abundant, opposite, and up to 3" long and ¾" wide, with rounded, nearly stalkless bases, mostly toothless edges, and pointed tips. There are often small, leafy branches arising from where the main leaves join the stem. Flowers are in dense heads, with several heads clustered together near the top of a branch. Each flower is less than ¼" long, with a tiny, densely hairy, 5-toothed, green calyx and a tubular corolla with a 3-lobed lower lip and a single upper lip. The corolla is white to pale lavender, with small purple spots.

Bloom Season: Midsummer–early fall.

Habitat/Range: Occasional in dry to moist prairies, open prairie thickets, seepage areas, and open woodlands; found in the southern tallgrass region from southeastern Nebraska through southern Ontario to Ohio, becoming uncommon at the southern edge of the region.

Comments: The leaves of this and other Mountain Mints have been used to make tea. Common Mountain Mint *(P. virginianum)* occurs in moist prairies and has stems that are hairy only along the edges.

FRANK OBERLE

PRAIRIE TROUT LILY
Erythronium mesochoreum
Lily family (Liliaceae)

Description: Soft, hairless plants with a pair of basal leaves flanking a taller bare stalk with a single nodding flower at the top. The leaves feel somewhat waxy and are typically 3–6" long and up to 1¼" wide, broadest near the middle, with pointed tips and sheathing bases. The leaves are strongly folded along their lengths. Flowers are up to 2" wide, with 6 spreading, pointed, petal-like segments that are often purplish on the back, 6 protruding yellow stamens, and a protruding white style. The fruits are green 3-lobed capsules that usually lie on the ground.

Bloom Season: Early–midspring.

Habitat/Range: Common in dry to mesic prairies and occasional in open, sunny woodlands; found in the southern tallgrass region from eastern Nebraska east into Illinois.

Comments: White Trout Lily *(E. albidum)* is a closely related woodland species that sometimes occurs in prairies. It has flat to slightly folded leaves that are mottled with purple, petals and sepals bent strongly backward, and fruiting capsules held nearly erect. Both plants are also called White Dog-Tooth Violet.

FRANK OBERLE

STARRY FALSE SOLOMON'S SEAL

Maianthemum stellatum
Lily family (Liliaceae)

Description: Unbranched plants with slightly zigzag stems typically 1' tall or less, and alternate, stalkless leaves with pointed tips and clasping bases. The leaves are typically up to 5" long and 1¾" wide, with finely hairy undersides and several parallel veins along their lengths. The edges of the leaves are usually folded or curled upward. Flowers are on short individual stalks in a small cluster at the top of the stem. Each starlike white flower is about ⅓" wide, with 6 petal-like segments and 6 yellow stamens. The fruits are small berries about ¼" in diameter.

Bloom Season: Mid–late spring.

Habitat/Range: Locally frequent in open sandy prairies and savannas, in a variety of moisture conditions, through the northern two-thirds of the tallgrass region.

FRANK OBERLE

ROBERT TATINA

BUNCHFLOWER
Melanthium virginicum
Lily family (Liliaceae)

Description: Stout plants to 5' tall, with long, grasslike, alternate leaves and finely hairy upper stems and branches. The lower leaves are up to 20" long and less than 1" wide, with the upper leaves similar but much shorter. Flowers occur along the upper branches in dense, elongate clusters up to 18" tall. Each individually stalked flower is ½–1" wide, with 6 creamy white, spoon-shaped "petals" (actually 3 petals and 3 sepals), each with 2 small glands on the inside just above their narrowed bases. There are 6 stamens and a 3-lobed central ovary with 3 styles.

Bloom Season: Late spring–midsummer.

Habitat/Range: Occasional in mesic to wet prairies and wet savannas in the southern part of the tallgrass region, from southern Iowa and eastern Kansas eastward.

WHITE CAMASS
Zigadenus elegans
Lily family (Liliaceae)

Description: Pale, stout-stemmed plants to 2½' tall, with grasslike leaves that are up to 15" long and less than ½" wide. The individually stalked flowers are alternate along the upper stem, with a small leaflike bract at the base of each flower stalk. Each flower is ½–¾" wide and composed of 6 identical, white, petal-like segments with tapering bases. Each of these segments has a greenish, 2-lobed gland at the base. There are 6 prominent stamens, and a central ovary with 3 short styles.

Bloom Season: Early–midsummer.

Habitat/Range: Occasional in prairies, often in rocky areas, in the northwestern tallgrass region from Minnesota and northern Iowa westward.

Comments: This plant is poisonous to humans and livestock and is sometimes called Death Camass.

FRANK OBERLE

WHITE LADY'S SLIPPER
Cypripedium candidum
Orchid family (Orchidaceae)

Description: Finely hairy plants generally less than 1' tall, with 3 or 4 leaves that gracefully arch or ascend upward and away from the stem. The leaves are up to 6" long and 2" wide and are delicately pleated lengthwise. There is usually a single flower at the top of the stem, above an erect, leaflike bract. The main feature of the flower is the white "slipper," actually a modified petal, which is less than 1" long and usually marked with purple streaks and spots. Arching above and below the flower are 2 narrow, pale greenish sepals. Two twisted, greenish petals slant downward along the sides of the slipper. These sepals and side petals are usually streaked purplish brown.

Bloom Season: Midspring–early summer.

Habitat/Range: Rare and local in seepage areas in moist prairies and fens, usually occurring in calcium-rich sites; scattered through the northern half of the tallgrass region, but eliminated from many places where it formerly grew.

FRANK OBERLE

WESTERN PRAIRIE FRINGED ORCHID
Platanthera praeclara
Orchid family (Orchidaceae)

Description: Stout, erect orchids growing up to 2½' tall, with smooth, hairless stems and leaves. The leaves are alternate and up to 10" long, with their bases strongly clasping the stem and their tips tapering to long points. The flowers are in clusters along the tops of the stems, often with more than 20 flowers per plant. Each flower has 3 rounded, whitish sepals about ½" long, 2 rounded, creamy white upper petals that are usually slightly larger than the sepals, and a distinctive, creamy white lower petal, called a lip, which can be over 1" long and wide, and is divided into 3 narrow lobes, each of which is fringed with long, narrow segments. The flowers have a downward-pointing, tubelike spur which can be over 2" long.

Bloom Season: Early–midsummer.

Habitat/Range: Very rare in moist to mesic prairies, as well as in somewhat wetter sites; found through the western tallgrass region west of the Mississippi River.

Comments: A closely related species, Eastern Prairie Fringed Orchid *(P. leucophaea),* is a rare plant of the eastern tallgrass region, also found in a few sites west of the Mississippi River. The 2 Prairie Fringed Orchids appear very similar, except for some internal details of the flower structure, but the western species has slightly larger flowers. These orchids were once widespread, but the wholesale loss of intact prairie systems has placed their future in jeopardy. Both are federally listed as threatened.

FRANK OBERLE

SPRING LADIES' TRESSES

Spiranthes vernalis
Orchid family (Orchidaceae)

Description: The tallest of our Ladies' Tresses, sometimes growing to 3' tall, with the upper half of the stem finely hairy and with 2–3 grasslike leaves at the base. The flowers are in a dense spike climbing the twisted upper stem like the steps on a spiral staircase. There is a small, pointed, green bract about ½" long below the flower. Each white flower appears tubular, with 3 sepals and 3 petals. The lowest petal is larger than the sepals and other petals, with a central yellow spot. The flowers are about ⅓" long.

Bloom Season: Late spring–summer.

Habitat/Range: Uncommon in mesic or slightly drier prairies in the southern tallgrass region, north to southern Illinois and northern Missouri, and sporadically north to southeastern South Dakota. Also found in old fields in the eastern part of the region.

DON KURZ

NODDING LADIES' TRESSES
Spiranthes cernua
Orchid family (Orchidaceae)

Description: Small plants usually less than 8" tall, with finely hairy upper stems. The leaves are hairless, strap-shaped, and up to 7" long, with pointed tips. There are fewer than 6 leaves per plant, all near the base of the stem. The flowers are white, tubelike, and stalkless in a spiraled arrangement on the upper part of the stem, with a small, pointed, green bract under each flower. The flowers are less than ½" long, with 3 white sepals and 3 white petals, the lowest of which is larger and sometimes yellow within.

Bloom Season: Midsummer–fall.

Habitat/Range: Frequent in a variety of moist to well-drained sites, including prairies, pastures, and old fields. Often in acidic soils, but sometimes in neutral and alkaline soils as well; found throughout the tallgrass region.

Comments: A similar species, Prairie Ladies' Tresses *(S. magnicamporum)*, occurs in the tallgrass region from northwestern Indiana westward. It is characterized by extremely fragrant flowers, spreading lateral sepals, and a strong preference for limestone and calcium rich, basic to neutral soils. It also tends to grow in drier sites than those of Nodding Ladies' Tresses.

DON KURZ

SENECA SNAKEROOT
Polygala senega
Milkwort family (Polygalaceae)

Description: Plants to 18" tall, usually with several unbranched stems from a single base. The leaves are alternate, up to 3" long and over 1" wide, and taper to narrowed bases and pointed tips. The lowest leaves on the stem are usually very small. Flowers are in a small cluster at the top of the stem, with each flower about ¼" wide and consisting of 3 small, greenish sepals, 2 larger, white, petal-like inner sepals, and 3 small, fringed, white petals.

Bloom Season: Midspring–early summer.

Habitat/Range: Occasional in dry to mesic prairies and open woodlands, often in calcium-rich soils; scattered throughout the tallgrass region.

Comments: Seneca Snakeroot was used by Native Americans to treat snakebite, and the plants are known to contain medicinally active chemicals.

FRANK OBERLE

MORTON ARBORETUM

MEADOW ANEMONE
Anemone canadensis
Buttercup family (Ranunculaceae)

Description: Hairy-stemmed plants to about 2' tall, with long-stalked basal leaves each deeply divided into 3 narrow segments which are themselves toothed and sometimes lobed. The stem has a single whorl of leaves similar to the basal leaves, but without stalks. Above these leaves are 1 or more stalks with whorls of smaller leaves. There is a single white flower at the top of each stalk; this flower is ¾–1¾" wide, with 5 white, petal-like sepals and numerous yellow stamens. The seed head is a spiny cluster of flattened seedlike fruits with long tips.

Bloom Season: Late spring–summer.

Habitat/Range: Locally frequent in moist prairies, prairie swales, and along streams and shores in the northern tallgrass region from eastern Kansas to east-central

Indiana northward; uncommon southward.

Comments: The roots and leaves were used by Native Americans to make medicine for treating wounds.

CAROLINA ANEMONE
Anemone caroliniana
Buttercup family (Ranunculaceae)

Description: Plants typically less than 8" tall, with numerous, long-stalked, deeply cut, basal leaves arising from a small, tuberous underground stem. The leaves, with blades to 2" long, are divided into 3 main divisions, which are themselves toothed and divided into pointed segments. The hairy, flowering stems are bare except for a single whorl of 3 stalkless leaves. There is a single flower at the top of each stem, with about 10–20 petal-like sepals, each up to about ¾" long, and numerous yellow stamens. Both the color and number of sepals are variable, and white, pink, and pale blue flowers occur. The flattened, seedlike fruits are in a short, oval head.

Bloom Season: Early–midspring.

Habitat/Range: Infrequent in dry, often gravelly prairies through the western tallgrass region, becoming rare from Illinois eastward.

THIMBLEWEED
Anemone cylindrica
Buttercup family (Ranunculaceae)

Description: Hairy-stemmed plants about 2' tall or occasionally taller. There are both basal leaves and one or more whorls of leaves on the flowering stems. All the main leaves are stalked and deeply divided, typically into 5 main segments, with the segments toothed and lobed. Each of the main leaf segments tapers to a wedge-shaped base. There are usually several tall flower stalks above the main whorl of leaves, with a single flower at the top of each. The flowers have about 5 white, petal-like sepals, each about ½" long. The fruits develop on a dense cylinder up to 1½" tall in the center of the flower, from which the plant gets its common name.

Bloom Season: Late spring–midsummer.

Habitat/Range: Frequent in dry and well-drained prairies and sandy areas through the northern tallgrass region, from northeastern Kansas to northern Indiana and northward.

Comments: A similar species, Tall Anemone *(A. virginiana)* occurs in fields and open woodlands, and occasionally in prairies in the east. It is distinguished by the short, oval fruiting head, as contrasted with the elongate cylindrical head of Thimbleweed. Thimbleweed has more than 3 leaves in the main whorl of stem leaves, while Tall Anemone has only 1–3 leaves in the main whorl.

CLARK SCHAACK

197

FRANK OBERLE

PURPLE MEADOW RUE
Thalictrum dasycarpum
Buttercup family (Ranunculaceae)

Description: Plants usually 3–5' tall, with alternate compound leaves. Each leaf is multi-compound, that is, each leaf is divided into 3 segments, with the segments divided once or twice more into 3 parts. The leaflets are typically 1–2" long and almost fork-shaped in general outline, with rounded bases, nearly parallel sides, and usually with 3 pointed lobes at the tips. The individually stalked flowers are in branching clusters at the tops of the stems, with the male and female flowers usually on separate plants. Both flower types are about ⅓" wide and have 4–5 white to pale purplish, petal-like sepals. The male flowers have many threadlike stamens, while the female flowers have a small, burlike head of ovaries, each with a tiny, fuzzy stigma.

Bloom Season: Late spring–early summer.

Habitat/Range: Frequent throughout the tallgrass region in moist prairies, damp thickets, wet meadows, and occasionally in low portions of mesic prairies.

Comments: This plant was used medicinally and in rituals by Native Americans. A closely related species, Waxy Meadow Rue *(T. revolutum),* occurs in similar habitats, as well as in slightly drier sites, from Missouri and Illinois eastward. The leaves of Waxy Meadow Rue smell bad when crushed and are distinctly hairy with gland-tipped hairs on their undersides. The leaves of Purple Meadow Rue are odorless and the undersides are smooth to finely hairy with pointed hairs.

FRANK OBERLE

NEW JERSEY TEA
Ceanothus americanus
Buckthorn family (Rhamnaceae)

Description: Branching, slender-stemmed shrubs up to 3' tall, often appearing to be non-woody. The leaves are alternate, toothed along the edges, and up to 4" long and 2" wide, with curved edges, pointed tips, and softly hairy undersides. Small white flowers occur in dense rounded clusters at the ends of long stalks arising where the upper leaves join the stem. Each flower is about ⅛" wide and has a calyx with 5 triangular lobes that are folded inward, 5 folded petals with threadlike bases, 5 tiny erect stamens, and a small 3-lobed style protruding from the center of the flower.

Bloom Season: Late spring–fall.

Habitat/Range: Common in dry to mesic prairies, rocky slopes, and open upland woods; found throughout the tallgrass region, but rare and sporadic at the northern edge.

Comments: New Jersey Tea was used extensively for medicinal purposes by Native Americans. It has also been used as a tea substitute and to tan hides. A related species that also occurs in prairies, Prairie Redroot *(C. herbaceus)*, has narrower leaves with straighter edges and flatter flower clusters mostly at the ends of leafy branches of the current year's growth. Prairie Redroot occurs through much of the tallgrass region, except the extreme north; it is uncommon east of Nebraska and Kansas.

FRANK OBERLE

WILD STRAWBERRY
Fragaria virginiana
Rose family (Rosaceae)

Description: Low, spreading, colony-forming plants with stalked leaves. The leaves are each divided into 3 rounded leaflets with toothed edges and wedge-shaped bases. The individually stalked flowers are in small clusters, with each flower up to 1" wide and consisting of 5 green sepals alternating with 5 small, leaflike bracts, 5 white petals, and more than 15 yellow stamens.

The fruit is a small and delicious version of the familiar cultivated strawberry.

Bloom Season: Spring; also in fall.

Habitat/Range: Common in moist to well-drained sites in prairies, pastures, open woodlands, and old fields throughout the tallgrass region.

KENNETH DRITZ

COMMON DEWBERRY
Rubus flagellaris
Rose family (Rosaceae)

Description: Plants with long, creeping, woody stems with many sharp spines; the stems sometimes root at the tips. There are usually several short, erect branches along the main stem. The leaves are alternate and compound, with each leaf divided into 3 toothed leaflets that are widest below the middle. Some leaflets also have a lobe near the base. The flowers are individually stalked in groups of 1–5 at the tips of the branches. Each flower is about 1" wide, with 5 small, hairy, green sepals and 5 white petals surrounding many stamens. The fruit resembles a blackberry, although it has fewer and larger round segments.

Bloom Season: Spring–early summer.

Habitat/Range: Common in well-drained sites, including prairies, pastures, old fields, and open thickets through most of the tallgrass region, but becoming scarce north and west of Iowa.

Comments: The fruits are edible and tasty. The genus *Rubus* includes several species of blackberries and raspberries that occur in prairie thickets, open woodlands, and along prairie edges. Of these, Common Blackberry *(R. allegheniensis)* is one of the most common. Unlike Dewberry, Common Blackberry has tall, erect to arching stems.

FRANK OBERLE

AMERICAN BURNET
Sanguisorba canadensis
Rose family (Rosaceae)

Description: Plants to 5' tall and usually unbranched, with alternate compound leaves. The leaves are divided into 7–15 individually stalked leaflets, with each leaflet up to 3" long, widest near the middle, and evenly toothed along the edges. The leaves and stalks are progressively smaller upward along the stem. Flowers are in dense, feathery, cylindrical clusters at the tops of the stem, well above the leaves. Each flower is about ¼" wide, with 4 white, petal-like sepals and 4 protruding stamens about ½" long. There are no petals.

Bloom Season: Mid–late summer.

Habitat/Range: Rare in moist to mesic prairies from central Illinois north and eastward; also in marshy areas north and east of the tallgrass region.

DON KURZ

BUTTONBUSH
Cephalanthus occidentalis
Madder family (Rubiaceae)

Description: Shrubs 3' tall or more, with spreading branches and stalked leaves that are usually opposite but occasionally in whorls of 3. Each leaf is shiny on its top surface, widest near the middle, up to 6" long and nearly 3" wide, and tapers to a pointed tip. Flowers occur in dense, stalked, ball-like heads arising at the bases of the leaf stalks. Each tiny flower has a minute, green, 4-lobed calyx and a tubular, white corolla less than ⅓" long with 4 slightly spreading lobes. There are 4 small stamens and a protruding, threadlike style in the corolla tube. The fruits occur in ball-shaped clusters more than 1" in diameter.

Bloom Season: Late spring–summer.

Habitat/Range: Common in wet open areas, including wet prairies, thickets, and along streams, as well as in marshes; found through most of the tallgrass region, north and west to northwestern Iowa.

FRANK OBERLE

FRANK OBERLE

NORTHERN BEDSTRAW
Galium boreale
Madder family (Rubiaceae)

Description: Plants to 3' tall, with whorls of 4 long, narrow leaves spreading at right angles from each point along the stem. The leaves are up to 2" long and less than ¼" wide, and broadest near the base, with 3 lengthwise veins–the middle vein is the most prominent. There are often smaller leaves arising from where the main leaves join the stem. The small, white flowers are abundant in a branching cluster of rounded heads at the top of the plant, usually with the branches occurring in threes. Each flower is ⅛–¼" wide, with a 4-lobed white corolla.

Bloom Season: Late spring–summer.

Habitat/Range: Frequent in moist, mesic, and even dry prairies and pastures in the northern tallgrass region, from southeastern South Dakota and Iowa eastward.

Comments: A related plant, Wild Madder *(G. obtusum)*, occurs in wet prairies and wet depressions in upland prairies through most of the tallgrass region. It is low and sprawling, and the flowers are in scattered clusters, in contrast to the erect stems of Northern Bedstraw, which has flower clusters at the tops of the stems. Stiff Bedstraw *(G. tinctorium)* occurs in wet prairies and marshy areas; it has flowers with 3 corolla lobes.

FALSE TOADFLAX
Comandra umbellata
Sandalwood family (Santalaceae)

Description: Yellowish green plants to about 1' tall or occasionally taller, with alternate leaves. The leaves are up to 1½" long, stalkless or on very short stalks, tapering to their bases, and rounded or slightly pointed at the tips. Flowers are numerous in flattened to rounded clusters, with each flower less than ¼" long, and consisting of 5 (rarely 4) white petal-like sepals united at their bases into a very short tube. The flowers develop into rounded, single-seeded fruits about ¼" in diameter; these turn from green to brown as they ripen.

Bloom Season: Midspring–early summer.

Habitat/Range: Frequent in dry prairies, sandy sites, and open oak savannas throughout the tallgrass region.

Comments: False Toadflax has a shallow horizontal root and is partially parasitic on a number of other flowering plants. The fruits were eaten by Native Americans and are said to have a sweet taste.

FRANK OBERLE

FRANK OBERLE

FOXGLOVE BEARD TONGUE
Penstemon digitalis
Snapdragon family (Scrophulariaceae)

Description: Smooth, shiny plants to 4' tall, with opposite leaves that are widest near their clasping or heart-shaped bases and taper to pointed tips. The leaves are usually toothed along their curved edges, and up to 6" long and 2½" wide, with fewer and smaller leaves on the upper stems. Flowers are on spreading, branched stalks usually arising in pairs or clusters near the tops of the stem branches, with a pair of small leaves below each cluster. The white, tubular flowers are ¾–1¼" long and often hairy on the outside. The end of the corolla flares into 5 petal-like lobes with thin, purplish lines inside the throat. The seeds heads produce a sharp odor.

Bloom Season: Late spring–midsummer.

Habitat/Range: Frequent in moist to mesic sites in prairies, wet thickets, and along streams and swales; found through the tallgrass region north and west to southeastern South Dakota.

TUBE BEARD TONGUE
Penstemon tubaeflorus
Snapdragon family (Scrophulariaceae)

Description: Smooth-stemmed plants to 3' tall, with narrow, opposite, mostly smooth-edged leaves. The stem leaves are up to 5" long and mostly less than 1" wide, with broadly rounded bases and pointed tips. Flowers are numerous in a narrow, elongate, branching series of clusters at the tops of the stem branches. Each tubular, white flower is up to 1" long, with sticky hairs inside, and flares to a 2-lobed upper lip and a 3-lobed lower lip.

Bloom Season: Midspring–midsummer.

Habitat/Range: Frequent in dry to mesic prairies from southeastern Nebraska to southern Indiana and southward; also reported from Wisconsin and occasionally introduced elsewhere.

FRANK OBERLE

FRANK OBERLE

CULVER'S ROOT
Veronicastrum virginicum
Snapdragon family (Scrophulariaceae)

Description: Stems to about 5' tall, usually with a few upright branches in the upper half. The leaves are in whorls of 3-8 at wide intervals along the stem. Each leaf is up to 6" long and 1" wide, sharply toothed along the edges, widest near the middle, and tapers to a pointed tip and short stalk. Flowers are in dense clusters of tapering, candlelike spikes at the tops of branches. Each flower has 4-5 small, pointed, green sepals and a tubular, 4-lobed, white (rarely pale pinkish) corolla about ¼" long, with a protruding threadlike style and 2 protruding stamens with yellow to brownish red tips.

Bloom Season: Summer.

Habitat/Range: Occasional throughout the tallgrass region in mesic prairies, open savannas, and moist swales in upland prairies.

Comments: The roots contain a number of powerful chemicals and have been used in folk medicine and to induce vomiting.

COMMON VALERIAN
Valeriana edulis variety *ciliata*
Valerian family (Valerianaceae)

Description: Thick-stemmed plants up to 4' tall, with widely separated pairs of flat-stalked, opposite, dark green leaves. These stem leaves are thick, fringed with tiny hairs along the edges, and divided into many narrow lobes arranged like the rays of a feather. The basal leaves are up to 12" long and undivided. Flowers are in clusters of dense heads at the top of the plant. Each flower is about ⅛" wide, with a small, 5-lobed, creamy white corolla. Some flowers have 3 stamens protruding from the corolla. The calyx is tiny during flowering, but later expands into 10 feathery threads at the top of the fruit.

Bloom Season: Midspring–midsummer.

Habitat/Range: Occasional in mesic and moist prairies in the northeastern part of the tallgrass region, from northeastern Iowa north and east; also found in the western states.

Comments: The plants smell much like unwashed socks, but the carrotlike roots were extensively eaten as cooked vegetables by Native Americans and pioneers. Common Valerian was also cultivated for food in the eastern states.

GREEN FLOWERS

FRANK OBERLE

This section includes broad-leaved plants with inconspicuous flowers, as well as large flowers that are green or have a greenish cast. Since green flowers grade into white flowers, readers looking for green flowers should check the white section as well.

KENNETH DRITZ

KENNETH DRITZ

SAND MILKWEED
Asclepias amplexicaulis
Milkweed family (Asclepiadaceae)

Description: Plants with smooth, erect to sprawling, unbranched stems about 3' tall, with up to 5 pairs of stalkless opposite leaves and white milky sap. These leaves are up to 6" long and broadly oval, with wavy edges and heart-shaped or flattened bases. There is usually a single long-stalked flower head well above the leaves, with a rounded cluster of greenish purple flowers each on a stalk up to 2" long. Each flower is up to ¾" long, with the reflexed greenish purple petals flanking 5 cuplike, yellow to pink or purple structures called hoods. The slender seed pods are up to 5" long, with downward-angled stalks.

Bloom Season: Midspring–early summer.

Habitat/Range: In dry, usually sandy areas, often in sites with sparse vegetation and a history of disturbance, through most of the southern tallgrass region, north and west to eastern Nebraska and southeastern Minnesota.

WOOLLY MILKWEED
Asclepias lanuginosa
Milkweed family (Asclepiadaceae)

Description: Low, hairy plants typically less than 1' tall, with milky sap and narrow, alternate leaves up to 3" long. There is a single domed cluster of flowers at the top of the stem, with each individually stalked, green flower less than ½" long. The 5 narrow, reflexed, pale greenish petals are sometimes purple-tinged on the back, and flank 5 erect, pale green hoods. The seed pods are smooth, hairy, about 4" long, and seldom more than ½" thick.

Bloom Season: Late spring–midsummer.

Habitat/Range: Rare in high-quality, well-drained rocky prairies in the western tallgrass region from western Minnesota south to east-central Kansas; also rare in hill prairies in northern Illinois and southern Wisconsin.

FRANK OBERLE

MEAD'S MILKWEED
Asclepias meadii
Milkweed family (Asclepiadaceae)

Description: Slender plants with white, milky sap, usually with a single stem less than 2' tall. The leaves are opposite, stalkless, smooth, broad at the bases, and taper to pointed tips. A single, stalked flower cluster at the top of the plant produces less than 20 individually stalked white to pale greenish flowers, each less than ½" long. The flowers are somewhat nodding, with 5 reflexed petals flanking 5 yellowish green to purplish, cuplike hoods. The seed pods are very slender, up to 4" long and less than ½" thick.

Bloom Season: Late spring–early summer.

Habitat/Range: Rare and local in dry prairies in eastern Kansas and southwestern Missouri, becoming extremely rare in Illinois and southern Iowa; formerly in northwestern Indiana.

Comment: This is one of the rarest plants of the tallgrass prairie, and is a federally listed threatened species. Mead's Milkweeds can only produce seeds when pollen from one plant reaches a different individual. Recent research suggests that some populations of Mead's Milkweed may be genetically identical, and thus incapable of pollination within the group. This raises concern about the future of many populations and demonstrates the need for protecting multiple prairies in a region.

FRANK OBERLE

FRANK OBERLE

GREEN MILKWEED
Asclepias viridiflora
Milkweed family (Asclepiadaceae)

Description: Plants usually less than 2' tall, with milky sap and leaves that range from narrow to broadly oval. The thick leaves are usually opposite but may be alternate, stalkless or on stalks less than ¼" long, and usually have wavy edges. Rounded flower clusters arise from where the leaves join the stem in the upper part of the plant, with each cluster on a stalk less than 1" long and the entire flower cluster shorter than the leaf immediately below it. There are usually more than 25 individually stalked flowers per cluster, with each flower about ½" long and consisting of 5 reflexed, greenish petals and 5 erect pale hoods. The smooth, narrow seed pods are up to 6" long and less than 1" thick.

Bloom Season: Late spring–midsummer.

Habitat/Range: Occasional in dry or sandy prairies throughout the tallgrass region; seldom abundant at any single locality, but typically occurring as widely scattered individuals.

SPIDER MILKWEED
Asclepias viridis
Milkweed family (Asclepiadaceae)

Description: Large, somewhat sprawling plants to 2' tall with thick stems, milky sap, and mostly alternate, stalked leaves. The leaves are up to 5" long by 2½" wide. Flowers occur in one to a few loose clusters near the tops of the stems, with less than 35 flowers per cluster. These individually stalked flowers are larger than other milkweed flowers, sometimes reaching 1" across. The 5 green petals spread upward, whereas in all other milkweeds they are reflexed. In a starlike array within each flower are 5 prominent purple structures called hoods. The seed pods are up to 5" long and less than 1" thick, usually without pointed projections on the surface.

Bloom Season: Late spring–midsummer.

Habitat/Range: Common in well-drained or rocky prairies, often associated with limestone, through the southern tallgrass region, north to southeastern Nebraska and southern Illinois, becoming sporadic and uncommon eastward.

KENNETH DRITZ

WESTERN RAGWEED
Ambrosia psilostachya
Aster family (Asteraceae)

Description: Ragweeds are notorious for the hay fever caused by their irritating airborne pollen. Most ragweeds in the Midwest are annuals, but Western Ragweed is a colony-forming perennial from shallow, horizontally creeping roots. The plants are usually hairy and can grow to 3' tall, but are typically less than 1' tall, with the leaves deeply divided into many narrow lobes. Lower leaves are opposite, but the upper leaves are often alternate. The tiny, drab flowers point downward and are inconspicuous. Ragweeds produce separate male and female flowers on the same plant. The male flowers are in a narrow, elongate cluster at the tops of the branches, while the female flowers are in small clusters at the bases of the upper leaves.

Bloom Season: Midsummer–fall.

Habitat/Range: Common in dry, often sandy prairies in the western tallgrass region, becoming abundant in overgrazed areas. Native from western Illinois westward, and occasional as an introduced weed eastward.

Comments: This species is similar to the ubiquitous Common Ragweed *(A. artemisiifolia),* which occurs in degraded prairies. Common Ragweed is an annual from a shallow taproot, with thinner leaves that are often doubly divided—some of the lobes are further divided into lobes.

FRANK OBERLE

BUR OAK
Quercus macrocarpa
Beech family (Fagaceae)

Description: Bur Oaks can grow as magnificent canopy trees or as scattered low shrubs in prairie landscapes. They are characterized by thick, deeply furrowed bark and lobed, alternate leaves that have pale undersides because of a dense covering of fine, starlike hairs. Each leaf is up to 10" long and typically has 3–7 pairs of bluntly rounded lobes, with an irregularly scalloped, larger lobe at the tip. The tiny flowers are seldom noticed, with separate male and female flowers on the same plant. The male flowers occur along dangling filaments, and the female flowers occur singly or in small clusters, with each flower adjacent to a bract. The fruits are large acorns nearly 2" long, each with a large, bristly-fringed cup of overlapping scales. The cup typically covers more than half of the nut.

Bloom Season: Early–midspring.

Habitat/Range: Common in moist to dry sites, often forming open savannas or groves in prairie landscapes and regularly growing in prairie vegetation throughout the tallgrass region.

Comments: Although trees are not thought of as major components of tallgrass prairies, Bur Oak is *the* prairie tree. Bur Oaks are superbly adapted to prairie life and are tolerant of extremes of climate, drought resistant, and incredibly resistant to fire because of the protection provided by their thick, corky outer bark. Many of the famous "oak openings" referred to by early prairie travellers were open groves of bur oak. Dwarf Chinkapin Oak *(Q. prinoides)* is another oak regularly found on prairies from western parts of Iowa and Missouri westward. It usually grows as a coarse shrub and has leaves with small, regular lobes or scallops along their edges.

FRANK OBERLE

SMOOTH SOLOMON'S SEAL
Polygonatum biflorum variety *commutatum*
Lily family (Liliaceae)

Description: Smooth, hairless plants with gracefully arching stems to about 3' tall. Alternate leaves are arranged ladderlike along the stems. The leaves are stalkless and somewhat clasping at the base, up to 7" long and 3" wide, and have smooth edges and pale undersides. There are up to 20 fine, parallel veins running the length of the leaf. Flowers occur in several widely spaced, small, branched clusters dangling along the lower side of the stem. Each greenish white flower is about ¾" long, with a narrow tubular flower ending in 6 short lobes. The fruits are dark blue berries about ⅝" in diameter.

Bloom Season: Midspring–early summer.

Habitat/Range: Typically a woodland plant, but occasional in moist thickets and streambanks in prairie regions, as well as in moist prairies; found throughout the tallgrass region, but occurring in prairie areas mostly in the eastern half of the region.

Comments: The roots were used as medicine and food by Native Americans and pioneers, and were ground into flour or eaten boiled.

FRANK OBERLE

RAGGED FRINGED ORCHID

Platanthera lacera
Orchid family (Orchidaceae)

Description: Delicate plants with single, unbranched stems to about 2' tall, with up to 4 narrow, alternate leaves on the lower part of the stem. The lowest leaf can be up to 6" long, but the upper leaves are much smaller. Flowers are in a loose cluster at the top of the plant, with each flower less than ½" wide and located directly above a small, pointed, green bract. The flowers have 3 rounded green sepals, 2 similar but narrower pale green petals, and a large pale green lower petal that is divided into 3 segments, each of which is finely fringed and divided.

Un-der the flower is a long, downward-pointing, tubular spur. The flowers are usually slightly more than ½" long, not including the spur.

Bloom Season: Late spring–midsummer.

Habitat/Range: Occasional in prairies ranging from moist to dry, usually in acidic soils, from northeastern Oklahoma to western Illinois and Wisconsin, and eastward.

Comments: This orchid varies greatly in abundance from year to year.

MORTON ARBORETUM

PRAIRIE WILLOW
Salix humilis
Willow family (Salicaceae)

Description: Low, branched shrubs with yellowish brown to brown, usually hairy, twigs. The plants are usually less than 4' tall in prairies, but occasionally up to 8' in thickets. The thick, stalked leaves are alternate, widest above the middle, usually no larger than 4" long and ¾" wide, and have downturned, smooth or somewhat wavy edges, pointed tips, and hairy undersides. The flowers bloom before the leaves appear, with male and female flowers on separate plants. The flowers are in dense, elongate clusters, called catkins, along the twigs. The densely hairy catkins resemble miniature Pussy Willows. Each catkin contains many flowers, with each male flower consisting of 2 stamens and a basal gland, and each female flower composed of a single ovary and a basal gland.

Bloom Season: Early spring–midsummer.

Habitat/Range: Frequent throughout the tallgrass region in dry to mesic prairies and open woodlands, especially in sandy or rocky soil.

Comments: There are several other species of willow in the tallgrass region, but Prairie Willow is the only one that regularly occurs on dry upland prairie sites. The pliable twigs of willows have been used in baskets, and a tonic from the bark of willows was used to treat fevers and other ailments. Willow bark was the original source of aspirin.

FRANK OBERLE, INSET BY CAROL GRACIE

PRAIRIE ALUM ROOT
Heuchera richardsonii
Saxifrage family (Saxifragaceae)

Description: Hairy plants with leafless flowering stems to 2½' tall, arising from a dense cluster of long-stalked basal leaves. These leaves are up to 3½" wide and about as long, with shallowly lobed and toothed edges and heart-shaped bases. The small flowers are in an elongate cluster at the top of the usually solitary flowering stem. Each flower is less than ½" long, with a greenish calyx flaring to small yellow to purplish lobes, 5 small green to purplish petals, and 5 slightly protruding stamens with orange tips.

Bloom Season: Midspring–summer.

Habitat/Range: Frequent in dry to mesic prairies in all but the extreme southern tallgrass region, east to Indiana.

Comments: In previous centuries a powder from the roots of this plant was used to control bleeding.

GRASSES, SEDGES, AND RUSHES

FRANK OBERLE

Grasses and sedges are among the most common plants in tallgrass prairies. This section includes examples of typical grasses, sedges, and rushes. Although these are flowering plants just like the more showy prairie wildflowers, they have tiny, wind-pollinated flowers, which typically lack well-developed petals and sepals.

KENNETH DRITZ—MORTON ARBORETUM

PRAIRIE SEDGE
Carex bicknellii
Sedge family (Cyperaceae)

Description: Grasslike plants growing in tufts or bunches, with unbranched, triangular stems. The leaves are long, less than ¼" wide, and taper to thin, pointed tips. The flowers occur in dense heads clustered near the top of the stem. The male flowers are in a cluster of overlapping, pale brown scales at the base of each head. Each female flower is associated with a pointed, pale brown scale with a green vein along its middle. The fruits are flattened, papery ovals, each with a finely 2-pointed beak at the tip.

Bloom Season: Midspring–early summer.

Habitat/Range: Frequent in upland and wet prairies throughout the tallgrass region, but becoming uncommon southward.

Comments: There are more than 60 other species of *Carex* that occur in tallgrass prairies, and many are difficult to tell apart. These sedges are important components of prairie vegetation, but are often mistaken for grasses. Most sedges in the genus *Carex* have triangular stems, as opposed to the round stems of grasses, although some other sedges also have round stems.

KENNETH DRITZ

MEAD'S SEDGE
Carex meadii
Sedge family (Cyperaceae)

Description: Small sedges usually less than 1' tall, often occurring as solitary stems rather than in bunches. The leaves and triangular stems are a distinctive, pale bluish green. The grasslike leaves occur mostly near the base of the plant, are less than ⅓" wide, and are often somewhat folded along their lengths. The inconspicuous male flowers are in a stalked, clublike head above the rest of the plant, with each flower hidden by a small scale. The female flowers are also in stalked heads, with each flower directly above a small, greenish scale with purple-brown edges. The fruits are about ⅛" long and consist of tapering, 3-sided seeds in a thin, green husk.

Bloom Season: Spring.

Habitat/Range: Common in upland prairies and pastures, but seldom abundant in any one spot, and usually overlooked; found through most of the tallgrass region, but uncommon eastward.

KENNETH DRITZ

TORREY'S RUSH
Juncus torreyi
Rush family (Juncaceae)

Description: Stout, round-stemmed plants with long, narrow leaves that at first glance resemble grass leaves. The leaves are rounded, hollow, and divided internally by cross-partitions at regular intervals. These can be easily felt by running the leaf between the thumbnail and forefinger while applying gentle pressure. There are usually 2–5 leaves on the stem. The flowers are in stalked, round heads at the top of the plant. Each head is about ½" wide and contains up to 100 flowers. Each flower has 3 brownish, narrow, pointed sepals and 3 similar petals. The tiny seeds develop in a brown, pointed capsule slightly longer than the sepals.

Bloom Season: Summer–fall.

Habitat/Range: Frequent throughout the tallgrass region in moist open areas (especially in alkaline or neutral waters), prairies, swales, and low pastures.

Comments: Many other species of rushes (*Juncus*) occur in tallgrass prairies; although they are difficult to distinguish, all have round stems, and many have hollow leaves with internal cross-partitions.

FRANK OBERLE

BIG BLUESTEM
Andropogon gerardii
Grass family (Poaceae)

Description: This grass grows in tufted bunches or turfs, with the flowering stalks averaging 3–6' tall but occasionally growing up to 9'. Portions of the stout, round stems are frequently bluish or purplish. The leaves are up to 2' long and less than ½" wide, with a small, scalelike collar (ligule) where the leaf blade joins the stem. The leaves are rolled into a tube in the buds, and unroll as they emerge. Flowers are at the tops of tall stalks, usually in 3 dense, elongate clusters from a common point. The flowering stems may produce several erect side branches, each with its cluster of flowers. The individual clusters are 2–4" long, and each hairy seed has a long,

twisted, bristle-like awn. The leaves turn a handsome reddish bronze after frost.

Bloom Season: Summer.

Habitat/Range: A major ground cover throughout the tallgrass region in a variety of prairies ranging from dry to wet– most common and often dominant in mesic sites.

Comments: Big Bluestem can form extensive turfs and is a major forage and hay grass throughout the region. This plant was used by Native Americans to treat digestive problems. The arrangement of the flower heads gives rise to another common name, Turkey-Foot Grass.

FRANK OBERLE

SIDE-OATS GRAMA
Bouteloua curtipendula
Grass family (Poaceae)

Description: A relatively low grass to nearly 3' tall, growing in small clumps or as solitary stems. The leaves are up to 12" long and less than ¼" wide, with long, pointed tips. There are usually widely spaced, long, pale hairs along the edges of the leaves just above the stem. Flower clusters are in 2 rows mostly along one side of the upper stem. Although the flower parts are inconspicuous, in full bloom the bright reddish orange stamens protrude and are delicately showy.

Bloom Season: Summer.

Habitat/Range: Common throughout the tallgrass region on dry hillsides and in well-drained prairies, often associated with limestone or calcium-rich soil.

ROBERT TATINA

HAIRY GRAMA
Bouteloua hirsuta
Grass family (Poaceae)

Description: A low, delicate, tufted grass mostly less than 10" tall. The leaves are mostly near the base of the plant and are less than ⅛" wide and up to 5" long, with hairy blades and a tuft of hairs at the base of the leaf blade. The flowers are in 1–3 comblike, one-sided clusters along the top of the stem. The main axis of the cluster projects beyond the "comb" as a short, stiff bristle.

Bloom Season: Midsummer–fall.

Habitat/Range: Local in upland sand prairies and on dry hill prairies in Wisconsin, northern Illinois, and northwestern Missouri, becoming more frequent in Iowa and westward.

Comments: Blue Grama *(B. gracilis)* is a similar species common to locally abundant in dry prairies from western Minnesota and Iowa westward. It can be distinguished by the lack of a well-developed bristle at the end of the main axis of the flower cluster and mostly smooth to slightly hairy leaves.

223

TIM BURKE—MORTON ARBORETUM

KENNETH DRITZ

PRAIRIE BROME
Bromus kalmii
Grass family (Poaceae)

Description: Delicate grasses growing singly or in small clumps, with stems to 3' tall. The leaves are widely spaced along the stem, with each leaf up to 10" long and ⅓" wide. The flower heads are on a series of gracefully dangling, slender stalks at the top of the plant, with each head up to 1" long and consisting of a series of finely hairy, overlapping, bractlike structures with slender, pointed tips.

Bloom Season: Early–midsummer.

Habitat/Range: Occasional and scattered in moist to mesic prairies in the northern tallgrass region, south to central parts of Illinois and Indiana.

Comments: Several other species of Brome *(Bromus)* are introduced weeds in the region, but lack the delicately elegant stature of Prairie Brome.

CANADA WILD RYE
Elymus canadensis
Grass family (Poaceae)

Description: Stout grasses growing in bunches up to 3–5' tall. The leaves are flat or curled inward near their tips, about ⅜–¾" wide, and up to 15" long. These leaves clasp the stem at their bases, and taper to long, pointed tips. The flowers occur above the leaves in an elongate, nodding, 4–10" long cluster at the top of the stem. The long, stiff, bristlelike awns of the flowers are up to 2" long and often curved outward.

Bloom Season: Late spring–early fall.

Habitat/Range: Common through most of the tallgrass region in moist to moderately dry prairies, thickets, fields, and along stream banks, usually in areas with a history of previous disturbance.

Comments: Native Americans are reported to have used the seeds as food.

FRANK OBERLE

K. YATSKIEVYCH

PORCUPINE GRASS
Heterostipa spartea
Grass family (Poaceae)

Description: Plants growing in small tufts, with unbranched stems to 4' tall. The leaves are long, slender, and usually somewhat rolled lengthwise, growing up to 2½' long and seldom more than ⅛" wide. Typically there are hairs on the upper surfaces of the leaves. The flowers are in narrow, gracefully arching clusters, with each flower having 2 unequal, pale, papery, pointed bracts, each over 1" long, enclosing a single seed. The seeds are narrow and less than 1" long, with sharp-pointed, furry bases, and a twisted, curving, bristlelike awn 5–8" long.

Bloom Season: Late spring–early summer.

Habitat/Range: Common in dry upland prairies in the northern tallgrass region, and occasionally southward to southern Missouri and southern Illinois.

Comments: Because of the needle-sharp fruit tip and long awn, this and related grasses are also called Needle-and-Thread. The awn twists in response to changing moisture conditions, drilling the seed into the soil. The sharp-pointed seeds can injure livestock.

JUNE GRASS
Koeleria macrantha
Grass family (Poaceae)

Description: Low, bunching grasses to 2' tall, with most of the leaves in a basal clump. The leaves are less than ⅛" wide and up to 1' long. The stems are finely hairy and hollow near the base. Flowers are arranged in a pale green, short-branching, narrow, cylindrical cluster at the top of the stem. The flowers have several overlapping, scalelike parts, without awns or bristles.

Bloom Season: Midspring–midsummer.

Habitat/Range: Common in dry upland prairies and open upland savannas throughout the tallgrass region, and becoming a dominant grass in some northern prairies.

KENNETH DRITZ

SCRIBNER'S PANIC GRASS
Panicum oligosanthes variety *scribnerianum*
Grass family (Poaceae)

Description: Stout-stemmed, usually somewhat hairy, low grasses to 2' tall, but usually smaller, with broad, short leaves up to 5" long and ½" wide, and widest in the lower half. The tiny ball-like flowers are numerous in a pyramidal, branching cluster of small individual stalks at the top of the stem. Each flower is hairy and about ⅛" wide.

Bloom Season: Midspring–early fall.

Habitat/Range: Common throughout the tallgrass region in a variety of exposed, well-drained sites, including prairies, old fields, and pastures.

Comments: More than 20 species of panic grass (*Panicum*) occur in tallgrass prairies, but most have much smaller flowers and fruits. Another large-fruited species found in the southern half of the region, Velvety Panic Grass *(P. scoparium),* is a robust, sturdy plant with conspicuous dense, spreading hairs on the stems. It grows in moist areas in prairies.

FRANK OBERLE

FRANK OBERLE

SWITCH GRASS
Panicum virgatum
Grass family (Poaceae)

Description: Flowering stems often in large bunches, growing to 6' tall, but typically 4' or less. The leaves are up to 18" long and ¾" wide, usually with a zone of dense hairs on the upper surface of the leaf near where it joins the stem. The tops of the stems have a large cluster of many slender branches bearing the tiny, budlike flowers. These branches spread widely away from the main stem, with scattered individual flowers near the tips of the branches. Each flower appears to have 3 small, pointed, overlapping bracts.

Bloom Season: Summer–early fall.

Habitat/Range: Common and characteristic throughout the tallgrass region in prairies ranging from wet to mesic, and occasional in drier sites, particularly over limestone.

LITTLE BLUESTEM
Schizachyrium scoparium
Grass family (Poaceae)

Description: A bunched grass, growing in dense clusters, with the flowering stems up to 4' tall. The leaves are folded lengthwise in bud, unfolding as they emerge, and are up to 12" long and less than ¼" wide, turning bronzed orange after frost. The stems are usually hairy and strongly flattened near the base. Flowers are scattered along the upper parts of nearly vertical side stalks, with long hairs creating a feathery appearance. There is a single, white-hairy, elongate flower cluster at the tip of each stalk. The seeds have bristlelike awns.

Bloom Season: Midsummer–fall.

Habitat/Range: One of the most characteristic tallgrass prairie grasses throughout the tallgrass region, occurring as a major ground cover in prairies ranging from extremely dry to mesic, on both acid and alkaline soils.

Comments: A related species, Broom Sedge *(Andropogon virginicus)*, is a more weedy plant of sterile sites in old fields and pastures, as well as occasionally in prairies. In Broom Sedge, the flattened stem bases are usually large, wide, and shiny, and there is more than one flower cluster at the end of each stalk.

FRANK OBERLE

INDIAN GRASS
Sorghastrum nutans
Grass family (Poaceae)

Description: Flowering stems to 7' tall, with plants occurring as dense tufts or single stems mixed with other grasses, especially Big Bluestem. The leaves are up to 2' long, long-tapering, and rarely more than ½" wide. Each leaf has a distinctive pair of toothlike, erect, narrow, pointed lobes at the point where the leaf blade joins the stem—these lobes are usually reddish to yellowish. The flower heads are narrow, elongate, and initially chestnut brown, later fading to grayish brown. The hairy seeds have twisted bristle tips about ½" long. Although the individual flowers are inconspicuous, the pollen is produced on protruding yellow stamens.

Bloom Season: Midsummer–early fall.

Habitat/Range: Common in mesic to dry prairies as well as pastures, fields, and open savannas throughout the tallgrass region.

FRANK OBERLE

FRANK OBERLE

PRAIRIE CORD GRASS
Spartina pectinata
Grass family (Poaceae)

Description: Stout-stemmed grasses to 10' tall, with leaves up to 4' long and about ½" wide, tapering to long, bristlelike tips. The edges of the leaves are sharply roughened. Each stem is topped by an elongate cluster of up to 32 side branches, with each side branch 1½–6" long, and consisting of numerous straw-colored flowers in a comblike arrangement. Each flower has 4 overlapping, scalelike bracts, the outer 2 of which have short, bristlelike awns.

Bloom Season: Midsummer–early fall.

Habitat/Range: Abundant and often forming dense stands in wet prairies and prairie marshes, also occurring in wet depressions and along shores and streams in upland prairies. Occasional as scattered plants in the moister zones of mesic prairies; found throughout the tallgrass region.

Comments: This grass is also called Slough Grass or Ripgut, the latter from the sharp-edged leaves. It has been used for thatching and fuel.

PRAIRIE DROPSEED
Sporobolus heterolepis
Grass family (Poaceae)

Description: A distinctive grass characterized by dense tufts of long, very narrow leaves which are usually somewhat rolled lengthwise. The leaves are up to 20" long and less than ⅛" wide. Flowering stalks emerge from these tufts and are usually less than 2½' tall, although occasionally taller. The pinkish brown to blackish flowers are in an open, elongate, branching cluster at the tops of the stems, with each flower on an individual stalk. The flower heads have a pungent, waxy aroma, and produce small, ball-like seeds.

Bloom Season: Midsummer–early fall.

Habitat/Range: A common and characteristic species of mesic prairies, but also occurring on drier sites, including hill prairies and rocky prairie slopes; found through most of the tallgrass region, although sometimes locally scarce.

Comments: Native Americans made flour from the seeds of Prairie Dropseed.

229

FRANK OBERLE

GAMA GRASS
Tripsacum dactyloides
Grass family (Poaceae)

Description: Stout, bunched grasses typically 4–5' tall or sometimes taller, with thick stems that are somewhat flattened toward the base. The leaves are dark green, up to 2½' long and about 1" wide, with a prominent light-colored rib along the middle. The flowers are in 1–3 cylindrical spikes at the tops of the stems, with the upper flowers all male with prominent orange stamens, and the lower flowers female with purple stigmas. The female flowers develop into a chain of irregularly cylindrical, hardened fruits, each about the size of a corn kernel and usually containing a single round seed.

Bloom Season: Late spring–fall.

Habitat/Range: Occasional but sporadic in wet to mesic prairies, open wetlands, and sometimes in drier sites, from southeast Nebraska east and southward.

WEEDS

Over the past centuries, more than 1,000 species of non-
native plants have been deliberately or accidentally established
in the tallgrass region. Some of these have become common
weeds in prairie landscapes, and a few are aggressive invaders
with the potential to degrade prairies and suppress prairie
plantings and restorations. Most of the worst problem weeds
are native to Europe and Asia. Some common, conspicuous,
and invasive prairie weeds are depicted in this section. Several
of these have been legally designated as noxious weeds in
various states in the region.

FRANK OBERLE

FRANK OBERLE

MUSK THISTLE
Carduus nutans
Aster family (Asteraceae)

Tall biennial thistles with spiny wings along the stems, spiny alternate leaves, and large nodding purple heads with spiny bracts at the base; locally abundant in disturbed or overgrazed uplands, and sometimes a problem in prairie plantings, since the rosettes of first year leaves cover the ground, suppressing other plants and impeding fire. Other thistles in the tallgrass region, both native and exotic, have hairy leaves and/or spineless stems.

CANADA THISTLE
Cirsium arvense
Aster family (Asteraceae)

Narrow-leaved thistles to 4' tall, with spineless stems, alternate spiny leaves, and abundant pale pink flower heads each less than 1" wide, with spineless bracts at their bases; an abundant weed in disturbed areas throughout the northern half of the tallgrass region, and often a problem in degraded prairies and prairie plantings. Unlike other thistles in the region, male and female flowers are on separate plants.

ROBERT TATINA

FRANK OBERLE

CROWN VETCH
Coronilla varia
Bean family (Fabaceae)

Sprawling dense mats with smooth angular green stems and alternate leaves each divided feather-like into numerous leaflets each less than 1" long, with stalked round heads of pink flowers. An aggressive and destructive weed of disturbed soils in open areas, often planted in the mistaken belief that it will control erosion when in fact it actually increases erosion. This plant can be a major problem in some prairie restorations, and is difficult to eradicate.

QUEEN ANNE'S LACE, WILD CARROT
Daucus carota
Parsley family (Apiaceae)

Spindly biennials with hairy, ribbed stems and widely spaced alternate leaves each divided into many narrow segments; many tiny white 5-petaled flowers occur in a circular cluster at the tops of the stems, usually with a single purple flower at the center of each cluster. An abundant weed of old fields, roadsides, and pastures that can become pervasive in degraded, unburned, or overgrazed prairies.

JESSIE M. HARRIS

G. YATSKIEVYCH

CUT-LEAVED TEASEL
Dipsacus laciniatus
Teasel family (Dpisacaceae)

Coarse biennials to 6' tall, with prickly stems, wrinkled, spineless opposite leaves with long narrow lobes along the edges, and large short-cylindrical heads with dense needle-like bracts and tiny, closely packed, white 4-lobed flowers; a rapidly increasing weed in the tallgrass region, becoming established in degraded prairies that do not receive regular fires, particularly in the eastern half of the region. The first year leaves form large flat rosettes that suppress other plants and inhibit fire. Common Teasel (*D. sylvestris*) is a similar weed with purplish flowers and unlobed leaves.

LEAFY SPURGE
Euphorbia esula
Spurge family (Euphorbiaceae)

Stems about 2' tall, with smooth narrow alternate leaves and topped with a branched array of paired, yellow round bracts, with each pair of bracts surrounding a small cluster of inconspicuous greenish flowers; widely established in pastures, fields and prairies through the western and northern parts of the tallgrass region, where it is very difficult to control.

FRANK OBERLE

FRANK OBERLE

SERICEA LESPEDEZA, SILKY BUSH CLOVER

Lespedeza cuneata
Bean family (Fabaceae)

Narrow erect stems to about 3' tall, with abundant, usually upright, alternate leaves each divided into 3 narrow leaflets with squarrish tips; whitish flowers each with the fan-like upper petal marked with purple at the center occur singly at the bases of the upper leaf stalks. An abundant aggressive weed in the southern and western portions of the region, where it has completely taken over and destroyed some prairie pastures, forming nearly pure stands. This plant is very difficult to control and is a major threat to prairie systems.

OX-EYE DAISY

Leucanthemum vulgare
Aster family (Asteraceae)

Small clumps of erect stems to 2' tall, with widely spaced alternate leaves that have coarse teeth or small lobes along the margins; flattish flower head at the top of the stems each look a single 2" wide flower, with a yellow button-like center and many white petal-like ray flowers—a common field and roadside weed occurring in unburned prairies and prairie hay meadows.

ROBERT TATINA

JESSIE M. HARRIS

BIRD'S FOOT TREFOIL
Lotus corniculatus
Bean family (Fabaceae)

Sprawling clover-like plants with alternate leaves each divided into 5 narrow leaf-like segments and stalked rounded clusters of golden yellow flowers each about ½" long; common in pastures, fields, and along roadsides throughout the tallgrass region and sometimes overseeded into prairie pastures. Once established, this species can be difficult to eliminate.

WHITE SWEET CLOVER
Melilotus albus
Bean family (Fabaceae)

Spindly biennials to 7' tall with upwards-angled branches and widely spaced alternate leaves each divided into 3 rounded leaflets with irregular margins; flowers occur in numerous narrow upright clusters, with each flower up to ⅜" long. Abundant in dry disturbed soils throughout the tallgrass region, increasing with severe over-grazing or other disturbance. A similar species, Yellow Sweet Clover (*M. officinalis*) has yellow flowers and is also abundant throughout the region.

FRANK OBERLE

CAROL GRACIE

WILD PARSNIP
Pastinaca sativa
Parsley family (Apiaceae)

Biennials to 5' tall, with stout, smooth angular stems and alternate leaves each divided feather-like into many toothed segments each up to 4" long; the stems are topped with flattened circular clusters of tiny 5-petaled yellow flowers on spoke-like branches. Common in disturbed open areas, especially in somewhat moist soils, and often forming large colonies. Contact with the sap can cause a sunlight-induced rash.

RED CLOVER
Trifolium pratense
Bean family (Fabaceae)

Low soft plants in open clumps, with widely spaced alternate leaves each divided into 3 rounded leaflets which usually have a pale green marking on their lower half, with dense rounded heads of pinkish red tubular flowers; commonly planted as a forage and cover crop, and widely escaping into disturbed areas, pastures, fields, and roadsides, where it can be quite persistent. A related species, White Clover *(T. repens)* is smaller and has white to pinkish flowers.

WOODY WEEDS

Although tallgrass prairies are dominated by grasses and other flowering perennials that die back to the ground each year, several native woody plants also occur in prairies, for example Prairie Willow and Indigo Bush. Some of these native shrubs, including Smooth Sumac and Winged Sumac, can aggressively increase in disturbed or poorly managed prairies. Even more of a problem are several exotic woody plants, such as the six shown here. These plants are native in Asia, except for Black Locust, which is from the southern United States. All of these species can spread rapidly into unburned prairie remnants, overgrazed prairies, and in poorly prepared or managed prairie plantings. If uncontrolled, they can form dense stands that shade out and suppress native plants. **Japanese Honeysuckle** is a trailing or high climbing vine with opposite oval leaves that have broad bases and occasionally have lobes along the edges. The showy flowers are initially white, becoming yellow with age, and emit a potent sweet fragrance. **Amur Honeysuckle** is a tall multi-stemmed shrub with grayish twigs, opposite, smooth-edged leaves, and pairs of small white to yellowish flowers that produce bright red berries. Once established, this plant can rapidly shade out all competition and become the dominant vegetation. Another tall shrub that is a similar problem, especially in more open areas, is **Autumn Olive,** with alternate, wavy-edged leaves that are covered with silvery scales on the lower surface. Abundant small clusters of creamy 4-petaled flowers produce small, edible, orange-red berry-like fruits.

Japanese Honeysuckle

JESSIE M. HARRIS

Amur Honeysuckle

JOHN TAFT

Autumn Olive

CAROL GRACIE

Common Buckthorn is a special problem is rich shaded soils, but also invades degraded prairies. This tall shrub has numerous short, sharp-tipped branches and mostly opposite finely toothed leaves with prominent raised veins beneath. Small clusters of 4-5 petaled greenish flowers produce black berry-like fruits about ¼" broad.

Black Locust can grow either as a shrub or tree, forming large suckering stands that resprout even after repeated cutting or spraying. This species has alternate compound leaves, each with nine or more rounded leaflets, pairs of short sharp spines along the stems, and drooping clusters of fragrant, creamy white flowers, each with the fan-like upper petal marked with yellow. **Multiflora Rose** is a sprawling shrub with arching stems that have sharp hooked thorns and alternate compound leaves each divided into numerous rounded leaflets with toothed margins. Stalked, white to pinkish flowers about 1" broad occur in clusters at the tips of upper branches. This shrub can invade pastures, unburned prairies, and old fields, making them nearly impenetrable to people.

Common Buckthorn

Black Locust

Multiflora Rose

239

WEEDY GRASSES

Tallgrass prairies are characterized by several prominent native grasses, but other grasses originally native to Europe and Asia have become established in the region and can invade and degrade prairies and prairie restorations. This problem is particularly severe in overgrazed, unburned, or otherwise improperly managed prairies. All four weedy perennial grasses illustrated here are widely planted in the region, and are also aggressive weeds. **Smooth Brome** is a tall grass with broad, hairless leaves and clusters of stalked, elongate nodding to erect heads each more than ½" long. It is common in pastures and along roadsides through all but the southern part of the region. **Tall Fescue** forms dense low mats of shiny green leaves to ½" wide, with a prominent pale yellowish zone at the base of the leaf. In late spring, plants produce a tall pale green open cluster of branched heads. Tall Fescue is the most common grass of any kind in the southern half of the tallgrass region, and is widely planted for pasture and hay. It invades prairies and can create major problems when prairie plantings are installed in areas with fescue. Many populations of Tall Fescue contain a fungus that makes the plant more competitive, but can be toxic to grazing animals. Despite its name, local populations of **Kentucky Bluegrass** are originally from Eurasia. This delicate narrow-leaved grass has spread widely through the region as a planted forage and lawn grass and as a weed. The leaves end in distinctive tips that are shaped like the bow of a boat, and the stems are topped with sprays of small heads clustered towards the ends of fine flexible branches. Although inconspicuous and often overlooked, Kentucky Bluegrass is one of the most common invasive weeds in prairies. **Reed Canary Grass** is a stout tall grass with broad, relatively short leaves and lobed clusters of heads that are often tinged with purplish. This is an abundant aggressive weed in wet areas throughout the region, often forming nearly pure stands.

FRANK OBERLE

Tall Fescue

FRANK OBERLE

Reed Canary Grass

GLOSSARY

Alternate—placed singly along a stem or axis, one after another, usually each successive item on a different side from the previous; often used in reference to the arrangement of leaves on a stem (*see* Opposite).

Angular—having angles or sharp corners; generally used in reference to stems, as contrasted with round stems.

Annual—a plant completing its life cycle, from seed germination to production of new seeds, within a year and then dying.

Awn—a slender, stiff bristle or fiber attached at its base to another part, such as a leaf tip.

Basal—at the base or bottom of; generally used in reference to leaves.

Biennial—a plant that completes its life cycle in two years, and normally not producing flowers during the first year.

Bract—reduced or modified leaf, often associated with flowers.

Bristle—a stiff hair, usually erect or curving away from its attachment point.

Bulb—underground plant part derived from a short, usually rounded, shoot that is covered with scales or leaves.

Capsule—a dry fruit that releases seeds through splits or holes.

Calyx—the outer set of flower parts, composed of the sepals, which may be separate or joined together; usually green.

Clasping—Surrounding or partially wrapping around a stem or branch.

Cluster—any grouping or close arrangement of individual flowers that is not dense and continuous.

Compound Leaf—a leaf that is divided into two to many leaflets, each of which may look like a complete leaf, but which lacks buds. Compound leaves may have leaflets arranged along an axis like the rays of a feather or radiating from a common point like the fingers on a hand (*see* illustration p. 21).

Corolla—the set of flower parts interior to the calyx and surrounding the stamens, composed of the petals, which may be free or united; often brightly colored.

Disk Flower—small, tubular flowers in the central portion of the flower head of many plants in the Aster family (Asteraceae) (*see* illustration p. 25).

Disturbed—referring to habitats that have been impacted by actions or processes associated with European settlement environment, such as ditching, grading, or long intervals of high-intensity grazing.

Draw—a small, elongate depression with gentle side slopes in an upland landscape, resembling a miniature valley or ravine.

Erect—upright, standing vertically or directly perpendicular from a surface.

Escape—referring to plants that have been cultivated in an area, and spread from there into the wild.

Family—a group of plants having biologically similar features, including flower anatomy, fruit type, etc.

Fen—a specialized wetland permanently supplied with mineralized groundwater.

Flower Head—as used in this guide, a dense and continuous group of flowers, without obvious branches or space between them; used especially in reference to the Aster family (Asteraceae).

Genus—a group of closely related species, such as the genus *Viola,* encompassing the violets (*see* Specific Epithet).

Gland—a bump, projection, or round protuberance, usually colored differently than the object on which it occurs, and often sticky or producing sticky or oily secretions.

Hood—curving or folded, petal-like structures interior to the petals and exterior to the stamens in milkweed flowers; since most milkweeds have reflexed petals, the hoods are typically the most prominent feature of the flowers.

Hooded—arching over and partially concealing or shielding.

Horn—a small, round or flattened projection from the hoods of milkweed flowers.

Host—as used here, a plant from which a parasitic plant derives nourishment.

Keel—a sharp lengthwise fold or ridge, referring particularly to the two fused petals forming the lower lip in many flowers of the bean family (Fabaceae).

Leaflet—a distinct, leaflike segment of a compound leaf.

Ligule—A protruding, often scalelike, structure at the base of the leaf blade in many grasses and some sedges.

Lobe—a segment of an incompletely divided plant part, typically rounded; often used in reference to leaves.

Mesic—referring to a habitat that is well-drained but generally moist through most of the growing season.

Opposite—paired directly across from one another along a stem or axis (*see* Alternate).

Ovary—the portion of the flower where the seeds develop, usually a swollen area below the style (if present) and stigma.

Parallel—side by side, approximately the same distance apart for the entire length; often used in reference to veins or edges of leaves.

Perennial—a plant that normally lives for three or more years.

Petal—component parts of the corolla, often the most brightly colored and visible parts of the flower.

Pistil—the seed-producing, or female, unit of a flower, consisting of the ovary, style (if present), and stigma; a flower may have one to several separate pistils.

Pod—a dry fruit that splits open along the edges.

Pollen—tiny, often powdery male reproductive cells formed in the stamens and typically necessary for seed production.

Prickle—a small, sharp, spinelike outgrowth from the outer surface.

Ray Flower—flower in the Aster family (Asteraceae) with a single, strap-shaped corolla, resembling one flower petal; ray flowers may surround the disk flowers in a flower head, or in some species such as Dandelions, the flower heads may be composed entirely of ray flowers (*see* illustration p. 22).

Resinous—containing or covered with sticky to semi-solid, clearish sap or gum.

Rosette—a dense cluster of basal leaves from a common underground part, often in a flattened, circular arrangement.

Sap—the juice within a plant.

Savanna—in the Midwest, referring to open woodlands with well-developed grass cover, usually with the shrub layer poorly developed.

Sedge—a large group of grasslike plants, many of which grow in wetlands; there are several hundred different sedges in the tallgrass region.

Seepage—referring to an area supplied with small volumes of subsurface water.

Sepal—component part of the calyx; typically green but sometimes enlarged and brightly colored.

Simple Leaf—a leaf that has a single leaflike blade, although this may be lobed or divided.

Specific Epithet—the second portion of a scientific name, identifying a particular species; for instance in Lead Plant, *Amorpha canescens,* the specific epithet is *"canescens".*

Spike—an elongate, unbranched cluster of stalkless or nearly stalkless flowers.

Spine—a thin, stiff, sharp-pointed projection.

Spreading—extending outward from; at right angles to; widely radiating.

Stalk—as used here, the stem supporting the leaf, flower, or flower cluster.

Stalkless—lacking a stalk; a stalkless leaf is attached directly to the stem at the leaf base.

Stamen—the male unit of a flower, which produces the pollen; typically consisting of a long filament with a pollen-producing tip.

Standard—the usually erect, spreading upper petal in many flowers of the Bean family (Fabaceae).

Sterile—in flowers, referring to inability to produce seeds; in habitats, referring to poor nutrient and mineral availability in the soil.

Stigma—portion of the pistil receptive to pollination; usually at the top of the style, and often appearing fuzzy or sticky.

Stipule—bract or leafy structure occurring in pairs at the base of the leaf stalk.

Style—the portion of the pistil between the ovary and the stigma; typically a slender stalk.

Subspecies—a group of plants within a species that has consistent, repeating, genetic and structural distinctions.

Succulent—thickened and fleshy or juicy.

Swale—a depression or shallow hollow in the land, typically moist.

Taproot—a stout, main root extending downward.

Tendril—a slender, coiled or twisted filament with which climbing plants attach to their support.

Toothed—bearing teeth, or sharply angled projections, along the edge.

Tuber—thick, creeping underground stems; sometimes also used for thickened portions of roots.

Tubular—narrow, cylindrical, and tubelike.

Variety—a group of plants within a species that has a distinct range, habitat, or structure.

Veins—bundles of small tubes that carry water, minerals, and nutrients.

Whorl—three or more parts attached at the same point along a stem or axis and often surrounding the stem.

Winged—having thin bands of leaflike tissue attached edgewise along the length.

Wings—the two side petals flanking the keel in many flowers of the Bean family (Fabaceae).

TALLGRASS PRAIRIE DIRECTORY

This directory provides a sample of high-quality tallgrass prairies across the region that are open to public visitation. Additional information can be obtained from the listed web sites or by calling the phone numbers listed for each site.

The Nature Conservancy is an international non-profit conservation organization dedicated to protecting the diversity of life on earth by conserving the lands and waters they need to survive. The Conservancy is a leader in tallgrass prairie conservation and restoration throughout the region. The Conservancy works with partners and private landowners to implement conservation that meets the needs both of natural systems and people. You can learn more about The Nature Conservancy at www.nature.org

ARKANSAS

Baker Prairie

70 acres of tallgrass prairie on flinty soil in the Ozarks with grasshopper sparrows and rare plants. Interpretive brochure and maps are available. In the town of Harrison along Goblin Drive. Owner: The Nature Conservancy (501-663-6699; www.nature.org/arkansas) and Arkansas Natural Heritage Commission (501-324-9619; www.naturalheritage.org).

ILLINOIS

Goose Lake Prairie Nature Preserve

1,537 acres including dry-mesic, wet-mesic, and wet prairie, and prairie potholes. Interpretive center and trails. Southeast of Morris, north of Lorenzo Road, on Jugtown Road. Owner: Illinois Department of Natural Resources (815-942-2899; www.dnr.state.il.us).

Illinois State Beach Park

829 acres of wet to dry sand prairie and dune habitat on Lake Michigan. Interpretive center and trails. From Zion, take Sheridan Road south about 1 mile to Wadsworth Road and go east to the Park; prairie is in the southern part of park. Owner: Illinois Department of Natural Resources (708-662-4211; www.dnr.state.il.us).

Indian Boundary Prairies

A 252-acre cluster of four prairies that are among the finest black soil prairies in the Midwest. In Markham; take Whipple Avenue north from 159th St. Owners: The Nature Conservancy (312-580-2100; www.nature.org/illinois), The Natural Land Institute (815-964-6666; www.naturalland.org), and Northeastern Illinois University.

Iroquois County State Wildlife Area

1,700 acres of wet to dry prairie, savanna and marsh. Northeast of Beaverville in southern and eastern parts of conservation area. Part of the Kankakee Sands project (see Indiana sites). Owner: Illinois Department of Natural Resources (815-435-2218; www.dnr.state.il.us).

Midewin National Tallgrass Prairie

15,000 acre restoration project, with upland plovers, Henslow's sparrows, bob-o-links, and rare dolomite prairie. Visitor center, trails, brochures, and on-site native nursery. North of Wilmington, east of route 53. Owner: U.S.D.A. Forest Service (815-423-6370; www.fs.fed.us/mntp).

Nachusa Grasslands

Nearly 2,000acres of native prairie and restoration projects, with endangered upland sandpipers, loggerhead shrikes, and many rare grassland animals such as badgers and short-eared owls. From Rochelle, take highway 251 north to Flagg Road.

Turn west onto Flagg Road and continue approximately 16 miles west to Lowden Road. Turn south onto Lowden Rd. and continue past Stone Barn Road. The preserve ison the right. Owner: The Nature Conservancy (815-456-2340; www.nature.org/illinois).

Reavis Hill Nature Preserve

Some of the best loess hill prairie in Illinois, among woodlands in a rugged 417 acre preserve. Located 5.5 miles south of Easton, 8 miles east of Kilbourne, south of County Highway 5. Owner: Illinois Department of Natural Resources (309-543-3262; www.dnr.state.il.us).

Searls Park Prairie

42 acres of wet to mesic prairie in the southeast corner of the park. Parking and trails. Northwest edge of Rockford on Central Avenue. Owner: Rockford Park District (815) 987-8800; www.rockford parks.org).

INDIANA

Beaver Lake Prairie Nature Preserve

640-acre mixture of dry loose sand, wet depressions, and sterile flats. Go 3 miles north of Enos on highway 41, then east 1 mile, and north 1 mile. Permission to enter must be obtained from the Property Manager at LaSalle State Fish and Wildlife Area. Owner: Indiana Department of Natural Resources (219-992-3019; www.in.gov/dnr/).

Conrad Station Savanna/Conrad Savanna Nature Preserve

More than 800 acres of oak savanna and sand prairie on the northern edge of the Kankakee Sands restoration (see below). Go 9 miles north of Enos on highway 41 to county road 700N, then ½ mile east to parking lot. Owners: The Nature Conservancy (317-951-8818; www.natyure.org/indiana) and Indiana Department of Natural Resources (317-232-4052; www.in.gov/dnr/).

Efroymson Restoration at Kankakee Sands

8,500 acres of natural areas and associated prairie restoration. Most of the 7,000 acre restoration lies along highway 41, 3 miles north of Enos, with the project office west of the highway, 4.5 miles north of Enos. The restoration supports spectacular migrations and rare grassland birds. Owner: The Nature Conservancy (219-285-2184; www.nature.org/indiana).

Hoosier Prairie Nature Preserve

439 acres of black oak savannas, mesic sand prairie openings, wet prairies, sedge meadows and marshes with high levels of wildflower diversity. There is a 1-mile trail through the prairie. From Interstate 80/94 at the highway 41/Indianapolis Boulevard exit, go south 3.5 miles to Main St., then turn east toward Griffith. Parking lot is on right just past Kennedy Avenue. Owner: Indiana Department of Natural Resources (317-232-4052; www.in.gov/dnr/).

Spinn Prairie Nature Preserve

29-acre tallgrass prairie containing both mesic prairie and oak openings. From intersection of highways 421 and 24 in Reynolds, go north on 421 for 2 miles. Turn right and go 0.2 mile to a "T", then turn right. The prairie is on the right. Owner: The Nature Conservancy. Contact: TNC (317) 951-8818; www.nature.org/indiana).

IOWA

Anderson Prairie

200 acres of prairie habitats ranging from low wet swales and marshes to dry gravelly hilltops along the West Fork of the Des Moines River. From Estherville, take highway 9 west for 2.5 miles to 360th Avenue, then go north for 1.5 miles to preserve entrance on the east side of the road. Owner: Iowa Department of Natural Resources (515-281-3891; www.iowadnr.com/preserves).

Broken Kettle Grasslands

3,047 acres of rugged prairie at the northern end of the Loess Hills. From Sioux City, take highway 12 north to Butcher Road and turn east for 1 mile; the road runs through the preserve. Owner: The Nature Conservancy (515-244-5044; www.nature.org/iowa). Adjacent to Five Ridge Prairie (see below).

Cayler Prairie

160 acres ranging from dry to wet prairie and marsh. 40 species of butterfly are found on the prairie. From the junction of highways 86 and 9 west of Spirit Lake, take highway 9 west for 3.5 miles. Turn south on gravel road for 2.5 miles. The preserve is on the east side of the road. Owner: Iowa Department of Natural Resources (515-281-3891; www.iowadnr.com/preserves/).

Five Ridge Prairie

790 acres of dry prairie and woodland on steep wind-blown loess deposits. From Sioux City, take highway 12 north to county road K18. Turn northeast on K18 and go approximately 3 miles north, until you are 0.3 miles south of county road C43. Turn west onto gravel road to preserve entrance. Owner: Plymouth County Conservation Board (712-947-4270; www.co.plymouth.ia.us/locations). Adjacent to Broken Kettle Grasslands (see above).

Freda Haffner Kettlehole

110 acres of dry-mesic prairie, wetland, and hayfield. The two kettleholes on the preserve were formed when gravelly deposits settled around a large, isolated block of ice that broke off during a

glacial advance about 14,000 years ago. Go west on highway 86 from intersection with highway. 71 north of Milford. Continue west on gravel where county road 32 turns north. Preserve is 2 miles west of highway 86 on north side of road. Owner: The Nature Conservancy (515-244-5044; www.nature.org/iowa)

Hayden Prairie

240 acres of mesic to wet prairie community; the largest black soil prairie in Iowa. From the intersection of highways 9 and 63 in Howard County, take highway 9 about 4 miles west, then north onto county road V26. Continue north for 4.5 miles to the preserve. Owner: Iowa Department of Natural Resources (515-281-3891; www.iowadnr.com/preserves/).

Kalsow Prairie

160 acres ranging from mesic prairie to wet prairie and pothole wetlands. Near the center of the buried Manson Crater, formed by meteor impact in pre-glacial times. From highway 7 and county road N65 in Manson, take N65 north for 4 miles. Turn west 1 mile to prairie. Owner: Iowa Department of Natural Resources (515-281-3891; www.iowadnr.com/preserves/).

Neal Smith National Wildlife Refuge (formerly Walnut Creek National Wildlife Refuge)

The first national Wildlife Refuge dedicated to grassland restoration, this 5,600 acre site has extensive ongoing prairie restoration, trails, bison, and a Prairie Learning Center. From Des Moines, take highway 163 east to exit 18, then follow signs along the 4.5 mile entrance road to the Prairie Learning Center. Owner: U.S. Fish and Wildlife Service(515-994-3400; www.fws.gov/midwest/nealsmith/).

Rolling Thunder Prairie

123 acres of tallgrass prairie on a gently rolling landscape. From U.S. 69 and County Road G76 in Medora, in southern Warren County, take CR G76 west 3 miles to County Road R57. Turn north for 1 mile to the preserve on the west side of the road. Owner: Warren County Conservation Board (515-961-6169).

KANSAS

Chase County State Fishing Lake

More than 300 acres of high quality tallgrass prairie in the heart of the Flint Hills, located 3 miles due west of Cottonwood Falls. Owner: Kansas Department of Wildlife and Parks (620-767-5900; www.kdwp.state.ks.us/parks).

Flint Hills Scenic Byway

47 miles drive through spectacular prairie scenery in the last intact tallgrass prairie landscape on earth. Along highway 177 between Council Grove and Cassoday Owner: All off-road land except Tallgrass Prairie National Preserve (see below) is privately owned and closed to the public.

Konza Prairie

8,616 acres of tallgrass prairie including a nature trail. Managed by Kansas State University(785-587-0441; www.ksu.edu/konza). From exit 307 on Interstate 70, go 4 miles north on McDowell Creek Road, then follow signs. Owner: The Nature Conservancy (785-233-4440; www.nature.org.kansas).

Tallgrass Prairie National Preserve

Nearly 11,000 acres of Flint Hills tallgrass prairie ranchland. A small tract at the core of the site is owned by the National Park Service and contains an historic ranch with a visitor center providing educational materials and programs linking the cultural and natural history of the region. Located 2 miles north of Strong City on west side of highway 177. Owners: National Park Trust (202-548-0500; www.parktrust.org/zbar) and the National Park Service (620-273-8494; www.nps.gov/tapr).

MINNESOTA

Agassiz Dunes Scientific and Natural Area

1,024 acres in a large dune field associated with Glacial Lake Agassiz. From Fertile, go south on highway 32 to Sand Hill River, continue 0.5 miles and turn right onto a gravel road. Go 0.5 miles and turn left onto a dirt road leading to a parking area. Owner: The Nature Conservancy (218-498-2679; www.nature.org/minnesota).

Blazing Star Scientific and Natural Area

160 acres dominated by porcupine grass and numerous wildflowers, with a diversity of butterflies. Animals at the site include white-tailed jack rabbit, greater prairie chicken, marbled godwit, Baird's sparrow, chestnut-collared longspur, and Sprague's pipit. From Felton, drive 4.3 miles east on County Road 34. Turn right onto an improved township line road and go south 1 mile to prairie. Owner: The Nature Conservancy (218-498-2679; www.nature.org/minnesota).

Bluestem Prairie Scientific and Natural Area

4,400 acres within the range of the greater prairie chicken. Habitat for more than 300 native wild-flowers, including 54 native prairie grasses. From Glyndon, go east on highway 10 for 3 miles. Turn right onto highway9 and go 1.5 miles. Turn left onto a gravel road that transects the preserve, and park on north side of road. Owner: The Nature Conservancy (218-498-2679; www.nature.org/minnesota).

Ordway Prairie

581 acres including an oak grove and aspen thickets. From Brooten, drive east on highway 8 for about 7 miles. Turn left onto highway 104 and travel south 3 miles to the northwest corner of the preserve. Owner: The Nature Conservancy (218-575-3032; www.nature.org/minnesota).

Pembina Trail Scientific and Natural Area and Pankratz Memorial Prairie

Pembina—2,331 acres; Pankratz—920 acres. Both preserves contain tallgrass prairie and a natural community known as aspen parkland. Together they provide habitat for more than 60 species of birds. To reach Pembina, go east on county road 45 in Harold from the intersection at highway 102 for about 6.3 miles. The preserve is on the right and marked with signs. To reach Pankratz from here, continue west on county road 45. Turn right and head north on county road 46 to the preserve signs. Owners: The Nature Conservancy (218-498-2679; www.nature.org/minnesota) and Minnesota Department of Natural Resources (651-297-2357; www.dnr.state.mn.us/snas).

Richard and Mathilde Elliott Scientific and Natural Area

497 acres of mesic and wet tallgrass prairie in the heart of the greater prairie chicken range, with 120 species of prairie wildflowers, 19 butterflies, and other prairie wildlife. From Lawndale, go north 2.5 miles on highway 52 to county road 188. Turn right and go 1 mile to the preserve. Signs are posted. Owner: The Nature Conservancy (218-498-2679; www.nature.org/minnesota).

MISSOURI

Diamond Grove Preserve

840 acres of prairie on cherty soils in southwest Missouri with a rich display of spring wildflowers. Located 4 miles west of Diamond Grove on highway V, then 1.5 miles north on unpaved county road. Owner: Missouri Department of Conservation (417-895-6880; www.conservation.state.mo.us) .

Dunn Ranch

A 3,680 acre site that is part of the Grand River Grasslands, a large-scale grassland restoration project in northwestern Missouri and southeastern Iowa. Expansive rolling uplands with remnant prairie and active restoration, large population of prairie chickens and other grasslands birds. Parking lot 6.5 miles west of Eagleville on north side of highway M. Owner: The Nature Conservancy (660-867-3866; www.nature.org/missouri).

Golden Prairie

320 acres of high quality acidic prairie, 3 miles west of Golden City on highway 126, then south 2 miles and turn left. Prairie chickens and diverse wildflowers, Owner: Missouri Prairie Foundation (417-537-4412; www.moprairie.org).

Niawathe Prairie

320 acres of diverse prairie with showy wildflower displays in spring and early summer. Located 8 miles north of Lockwood, 3.25 miles east of Sylvania. Owner: Missouri Department of Conservation (417-895-6880; www.conservation.mo.state.us) and The Nature Conservancy (314-968-1105; www.nature.org/missouri).

Osage Prairie

1,467 acres containing diverse flora and fauna, including prairie chickens. 6 miles south of Nevada on highway 71, 0.5 mile west and 0.5 mile south on gravel road. Owner: Missouri Department of Conservation (660-885-6981; www.conservation.mo.state.us).

Paint Brush Prairie

313 acres of upland prairie over soils formed from cherty limestone and shale, with showy displays of spring wildflowers. In Pettis County, 9 miles south of Sedalia on east side of highway 65. Owner: Missouri Department of Conservation (573-751-4115; www.conservation.state.mo.us).

Prairie State Park

Nearly 4,000 acres of rolling upland prairie , with prairie chickens, northern harriers, coyotes, and herds of bison and elk. Trails, guidebook, and nature center on site. 3 miles west of Liberal on highways, then 1 mile south on gravel road. Owner: Missouri Department of Natural Resources (417-843-6711; www.mostateparks.com/prairie).

Taberville Prairie

1,680 acres with more than 400 species of wildflowers and a permanent flock of prairie chickens. Go 0.5 mile east of Appleton City on highway 52, then 2 miles south on highway A and 7 miles south on highway H. Owner: Missouri Department of Conservation (417-876-5226; www.conservation.state.mo.us).

Tucker Prairie

146 acres of flat, upland hardpan prairie over silt loam soils derived from loess. More than 225 species of wildflowers, including some unusual and rare species. Located 2.5 miles west of junction of Interstate 70 and highway 54, on south side of Interstate. Owner: University of Missouri (314-882-7541).

Wah-Kon-Tah Prairie

4,200 acres of upland prairie with three permanent springs and several wet draws. Large expanses of prairie on rolling terrain provide spectacular vistas of Missouri's grassland landscape. Regal fritillary butterflies and diverse wildflowers,can be found here, 2.5 miles northeast of El Dorado Springs along highway 82. Owners: The Nature Conservancy (417-876-2340; www.nature.org/missouri) and Missouri Department of Conservation (417-876-5226; www.conservation.state.mo.us).

NEBRASKA

Burchard Lake Wildlife Management Area

560 acres of tallgrass prairie with prairie chicken booming grounds. 3 miles east and 1 mile north of Burchard in Pawnee County. Owner: Nebraska Game and Parks Commission (402-471-0641; www.ngpc.state.ne.us/).

Cuming City Cemetery Prairie

11 acres of tallgrass prairie in an historic cemetery, with a variety of wildflowers. Take highway 75 north of Omaha through Blair. Go 3.5 miles north of Blair, just past the airport/golf course. Turn west on the county road that crosses highway 75. The prairie is on the south side of the road, approximately 0.1 mile from the intersection. Owner: Dana College (1-800-444-DANA; www.dana.edu).

Homestead National Monument of America

More than 100 acres of restored tallgrass prairie including 260 native tallgrass prairie species. Visitor center and self-guided trails through prairie. Approximately 40 miles south of Lincoln. Take highway 77 south from Interstate 80; at Beatrice turn west and take highway 4 for 4.5 miles to park entrance. Owner: National Park Service (402) 223-3514; www.nps.gov/home/home.htm).

Rock Creek Station

Over 500 acres of tallgrass prairie and wooded ravines at the western edge of the tallgrass range, with an interpretive center and visible Oregon Trail wagon wheel ruts. From Endicott, go 2.75 miles north, then 1 mile east. Owner: Nebraska Game and Parks Commission (402-471-0641; www.ngpc.state.ne.us/).

Twin Lakes Wildlife Management Area

More than 1,000 acres of native prairie rangeland. From Pleasant Dale interchange on Interstate 80, go north 1 mile. Owner: Nebraska Game and Parks Commission (402-471-0641; www.ngpc.state .ne.us/).

NORTH DAKOTA

Brown Ranch

1,531 acres including several types of tallgrass prairie natural communities, surrounded on two sides by Sheyenne National Grasslands (see below). From McLeod, go west and south on winding gravel road for 2.5 miles to first four way intersection, then west for two miles and turn north for 0.1 miles to house and office on right. Owner: The Nature Conservancy (701-439-0841; www.nature.org/northdakota).

Kraft Slough

1,310 acres of tallgrass prairie with some of North Dakota's rare animals including swamp sparrow, and rare plants including dwarf spikerush and small yellow lady's slipper. Located 4 miles south and 2 miles east of Crete. Owner: Bureau of Reclamation (701-250-4326; http://137.77.133.1/gp/dkao/).

McHenry School Prairie

130 acres of tallgrass prairie, home to Sprague's pipit, one of North Dakota's rare birds. Located 6 miles north and 4 miles east of Towner. Owner: North Dakota State Land Department (701-328-2800; www.land.state.nd.us/). Additional information from North Dakota Natural Heritage Program (701-328-5379; www.natureserve.org/nhp/us/nd/).224-4892.

Sheyenne National Grasslands

70,180 acres of sandhills tallgrass prairie, oak savanna, and hardwood timbers. Site of numerous state rare plants and one of the world's largest populations of the federally threatened western prairie fringed orchid. A 25-mile portion of the North Country National Scenic Trail crosses through the grasslands. Southeastern North Dakota, east of Lisbon. Owner: U.S. Forest Service (701-683-4342; www.fs.fed.us/r1/dakotaprairie/sheyenne.htm).

OHIO

Bigelow Cemetery Preserve

0.5-acre state nature preserve with some of Ohio's last tallgrass prairie. Royal catchfly blooms here. Located 8 miles west of Plain City, off highway161, 1 mile south on Rosedale Road. Owner: Pike Township Trustees. Contact: Ohio Department of Natural Resources Division of Natural Areas and Preserves (614-265-6463; www.ohiodnr.com/dnap).

Huffman Prairie

109 acres of black soil tallgrass prairie representing one of the largest remaining prairies in the eastern tallgrass, with Royal Catchfly, sedge wrens, and Henslow's sparrows. The Wright brothers

made many practice flights here in the early 1900s. Take Interstate 675 south to Dayton-Yellow Springs Roadexit and turn left into Fairborn, go to highway 444 and turn right. Follow 444 to Gate 8c and enter base to obtain visitor permit. Owner: Department of Defense—Wright-Patterson Air Force Base (937-257-1110; www.wpafb.af.mil); managed in cooperation with The Nature Conservancy (614-717-2770; www.nature.org/ohio).

Smith Cemetery Prairie

0.6 acres of original prairie sod supporting relics of the original prairie grasses and wildflowers, especially big bluestem. Take highway 161 west from Plain City andturn south on Kramer/Chapel Road, then go west on Boyd Road. The preserve is on the north side. Owner: Darby Township Trustees. Contact: Ohio Department of Natural Resources, Division of Natural Areas and Preserves (614-265-6463; www.ohiodnr.com/dnap).

OKLAHOMA

Tallgrass Prairie Preserve

39,000 acres of tallgrass prairie where fire and bison are being used to recreate a functioning tallgrass prairie ecosystem. The preserve includes self-guided nature trails, a 50-mile scenic drive on gravel roads, and free-ranging cattle and bison. From Pawhuska,go north on Osage Avenue and follow signs to the preserve. Owner: The Nature Conservancy (918-287-4803; www.nature.org/oklahoma).

SOUTH DAKOTA

Jacobsen Fen

160 acres of tallgrass prairie with ten small fens - specialized wetlands permanently supplied with ground water. Nesting site for sharp-tailed grouse. From Clear Creek, go 1 mile north on highway 15, then turn east at rodeo sign and go 3 miles to sign at top of hill. Owner: The Nature conservancy (605-874-8517; www.nature.org/southdakota).

Makoce Washte

Named with the native words for "beautiful earth", this diverse 40 acre site has an early spring display of Pasque Flowers. From the intersection of Interstate 29 and highway 42 in Sioux Falls, go west on 42 for 9.5 miles, then north on a gravel road for 0.5 miles to the preserve on the east side of the road. Owner: The Nature Conservancy (605-874-8517; www.nature.org/southdakota).

Sioux Prairie

200 acres of tallgrass prairie with several seasonal ponds and abundant grassland bird populations. Located 3.5 miles north of junction of highways 34 and 77, on east side of road. Owner: The Nature Conservancy (605-874-8517; www.nature.org/southdakota).

WISCONSIN

Avoca Prairie-Savanna

Wisconsin's largest prairie, with 1,885 acres dominated by big bluestem, prairie cord grass, Indian grass, and sedges. Habitat for northern harriers and short-eared owls. From Avoca, take highway 133 east 1.5 miles andturn north on Hay Lane Road. Follow road beyond Marsh Creek 0.3 mile to parking lot. Owner: Wisconsin Department of Natural Resources (608-266-7012; www.dnr.state .wi.us).

Black Earth Rettenmund Prairie

16 acres of dry-mesic prairie. From Black Earth, travel west on county road KP (off highway 78) for 1 mile. Then go south on county road F for 0.25 mile to Fesenfeld Road and turn right. Park along road, keeping at least 4 feet from the edge of road. Owner: The Nature Conservancy (608-251-8140; www.nature.org/wisconsin). Managed by: The Prairie Enthusiasts (www.theprairieenthusiasts.org).

Chiwaukee Prairie

580 acres of the richest known prairie in Wisconsin, with more than 400 native wildflowers, a variety of wildlife including kit fox, and more than 76 bird species. From the junction of highways 165 and 32 south of Kenosha, go south on 32 1 mile, then east on 116th St. 0.7 miles. Turn right onto 1st Court for 0.3 miles, then west on 121st St. for 1 block. Turn right onto Second Avenue to 119th St. and a parking lot. Owners: The Nature Conservancy (608-251-8140; www.nature.org/wisconsin), University of Wisconsin—Parkside, and Wisconsin Department of Natural Resources (608-266-7012; www.dnr.state.wi.us).

Kettle Moraine Fen and Low Prairie

250 acres of fen and wet , wet-mesic and dry-mesic prairies, southern sedge meadow, and oak openings. Butterflies, amphibians, and reptiles are abundant. From Eagle, go north 2.25 miles on highway 67 to gated access road. Follow lane 0.5 mile west to the site. Owner: Wisconsin Department of Natural Resources (608-266-7012; www.dnr.state.wi.us).

Muralt Bluff Prairie

62 acres of dry and dry-mesic prairie on a sweeping sandstone ridge. Home to rare plants such as kittentails. From Albany, go south two miles on highway 59, then north and west 1.8 miles on highway F to a parking lot south of the road. Owner: Green County; contact Wisconsin Department of Natural Resources (608-266-7012; www.dnr.state.wi.us).

Rush Creek

2,265 acres of outstanding dry prairie and oak woodland on a steep 400 foot tall bluff. Characteristic plants include side-oats grama, silky aster, and wood betony. From Ferryville, go north 4 miles on highway 35 to parking area on east side of road. Owner: Wisconsin Department of Natural Resources (608-266-7012; www.dnr.state.wi.us).

SELECTED FURTHER READING

Listed below are additional readings that provide information about tallgrass prairies, prairie plants, and prairie restoration. A visit to a local or university library should reveal many additional works that are useful for learning about tallgrass prairies.

Farney, Dennis. 1980. "The Tallgrass Prairie: Can It Be Saved?" *National Geographic,* January 1980: 37-61. [good introductory account of tallgrass prairie]

Farrar, Jon. 1990. *Wildflowers of Nebraska and the Great Plains.* Nebraskaland Magazine, Lincoln NE. [good popular-level guide to Great Plains wildflowers, including the northwestern tallgrass region]

Freeman, Craig, and Eileen Schofield. 1991. *Roadside Wildflowers of the Southern Great Plains.* University Press of Kansas, Lawrence. [popular-level wildflower guide focused on Kansas wildflowers, with good habitat descriptions and a wealth of useful details about plant identification; covers many plants in the southwestern tallgrass region]

Great Plains Flora Association. 1986. *Flora of the Great Plains.* University Press of Kansas, Lawrence, KS. [technical manual for the identification of plants in the Great Plains, including the western tallgrass region]

Kilde, Rebecca. 2000. *Going Native – A Prairie Restoration Handbook for Minnesota Landowners.* Minnesota Department of Natural Resources, St. Paul. [good introductory account of all aspects of prairie restoration and plantings]

Kindscher, Kelly. 1987. *Edible Wild Plants of the Prairie.* University Press of Kansas, Lawrence, KS. [discussion of many edible plants and their preparation, use, and history]

Kurtz, Carl. 2001. *A Practical Guide to Prairie Reconstruction.* University of Iowa Press, Iowa City. [the best overall introduction to prairie restoration, with lots of practical advice from an experienced restorationist]

Madson, John. 1982. *Where the Sky Began.* Houghton Mifflin Co., Boston, MA. [popular-level discussion of the prairie world]

Madson, John. 1993. *Tallgrass Prairie.* The Nature Conservancy/Falcon Press, Helena, MT. [spectacular photographic primer of the tallgrass prairie environment]

Packard, Stephen and Cornelia Mutel, editors. 1997. *The Tallgrass Restoration Handbook.* Island Press, Washington, D.C. [Comprehensive account of ecological restoration in the tallgrass region, including practical suggestions and lists of tallgrass prairie plants by state]

Pauly, Wayne. 1988. *How to Manage Small Prairie Fires.* Dane County Park Commission, Madison, WI. [practical introduction to fire management for small-scale applications with minimal equipment]

Pyne, Stephen. 1982. *Fire in America.* Princeton University Press, Princeton, NJ. [excellent discussion of fire and vegetation, including the prairie environment and an insightful examination of the role of Native American fire practices in shaping the North American landscape]

Rock, Harold. 1981. *Prairie Propagation Handbook.* Milwaukee County Parks, Franklin, WI. [good general summary of all facets of prairie restoration and prairie plantings]

Steyermark, Julian. 1963. *Flora of Missouri.* Iowa State University Press, Ames, IA. [technical keys and general habitat information for a majority of tallgrass plants; especially useful for the southern tallgrass region]

Swink, Floyd and Gerould Wilhelm. 1994. *Plants of the Chicago Region.* Indiana Academy of Science, Indianapolis, IN. [excellent identification keys and detailed habitat profiles for a majority of tallgrass plants]

Transeau, Edgar. 1935. *The Prairie Peninsula.* Ecology 16: 423-437. [classic account of the eastern tallgrass prairies and an analysis of their climate and environment]

Wasowski, Sally. 2002. *Gardening with Prairie Plants.* University of Minnesota Press, Minneapolis. [ecologically oriented approach to horticulture and landscaping with prairie plants]

Weaver, J. E. 1954. *North American Prairie.* Johnsen Publishing Co., Lincoln, NE. [classic study of prairies and the dynamics of their plant life]

INDEX

ABOUT THE AUTHOR

Doug Ladd is Director of Conservation Science for the Missouri Chapter of The Nature Conservancy and has spent more than 30 years working with midwestern prairies and their flora. He has a M.S. in botany from Southern Illinois University and is a research associate at the Morton Arboretum and the Missouri Botanical Garden. A native of Vermont, he also wrote the Falcon Guide *North Woods Wildflowers*. Ladd resides in Webster Groves, Missouri, with his wife Deborah and daughter, Melica.

ABOUT THE PHOTOGRAPHER

Frank Oberle, the premier photographer for this book, first became interested in prairie-scapes while photographing the Falcon Press book *Missouri On My Mind*. He photographed numerous prairies for *Tallgrass Prairie,* another Falcon Press/Conservancy book. An accomplished photographer of wildlife and nature, his photographs have appeared in many national magazines, books and calendars. He and his wife live in Northern Missouri on their 400-acre prairie where raising prairie wildflowers and grasses is their passion. Frank continues to photograph prairies and all of God's splendid creation.